"Fantastic! This is a perfect study that  deep expertise in New Testament studies an h to popular culture. The films Rindge has sel ned analysis, both in terms of the aesthetics ar .... compellingly, his own perspectives on American culture generally and the mythic realities of the American dream."

—**Gary Laderman**, Goodrich C. White Professor of American
Religious History and Cultures, Emory University

"Rindge is both sensitive and insightful in his film analysis, and the discussion of these movies as parables takes the analysis to a whole new level of sophistication. This book will be a very useful addition to both American Studies and 'religion and film' classes, as well as classes in New Testament parables."

—**Robert K. Johnston**, Professor of Theology and Culture,
Fuller Theological Seminary

"My gratitude to Matthew Rindge for recognizing and brilliantly dissecting the quest for salvation that supports the surface sound and fury of my novel and David Fincher's film."

—**Chuck Palahniuk**, author of *Fight Club*

PROFANE PARABLES
Film and the American Dream

Matthew S. Rindge

BAYLOR UNIVERSITY PRESS

Cover Design by the author. *Cover Layout* by *the*BookDesigners.
Cover image: Courtesy of Shutterstock

The Library of Congress has catalogued the hardcover edition as follows:

Library of Congress Cataloging-in-Publication Data

Rindge, Matthew S., author.
 Profane parables : film and the American dream / Matthew S. Rindge.
 191 pages cm
 Includes bibliographical references and index.
 ISBN 978-1-4813-0429-0 (hardback : alk. paper)
1. Motion pictures—Religious aspects—Christianity. 2. Motion pictures—United States. 3. American Dream—Religious aspects—Christianity. 4. Fight club (Motion picture) 5. American beauty (Motion picture) 6. About Schmidt (Motion picture) I. Title.
 PN1995.5.R56 2016
 791.43'682—dc23
                              2015026592

The ISBN for the 2017 paperback edition is 978-1-60258-994-0.

Printed in the United States of America on acid-free paper.

"Ce n'est rien de mourir; c'est affreux de ne pas vivre."
-Victor Hugo, *Les Misérables*

For Shannon, Andrew, and Sophia.
May we live before we die.

CONTENTS

ACKNOWLEDGMENTS

My love affair with film began in 1978, when my dad took a five-year-old boy to see a rerelease of *Pinocchio* in southern California. It was my first time in a theater; I was transfixed and instantly hooked. Disney was my gateway drug. I thank my dad, my original dealer, for providing the first hit.

Many people have shaped my understanding of Religion/Theology and Film, and deepened my love for the subject. I am indebted to Robert Johnston, Craig Detweiler, and Gary Laderman for encouraging my interest in this field, and my work on this specific project. As a student at Fuller Theological Seminary, I learned invaluable lessons from Rob, and I continue to do so from his writing. His influence is evident throughout these pages. Working as a teaching assistant with Craig was a delight, and instructive about how to teach well. This book's initial shape emerged in a seminar I took with Gary in the Graduate Division of Religion at Emory University. Coteaching with him allowed me to explore some of these initial ideas with students.

Since 2009 I have taught a "Bible and Film" course every semester at Gonzaga University. A segment of this course addresses cinematic critiques of the American Dream, and considerable material in this book had its origins in different iterations of this course. I thank Gonzaga Religious Studies department colleagues for supporting my creation of this course, and its ongoing development. I am grateful to be able to teach material I know and love. Conversations about cinema with colleagues Ron Large, Patrick McCormick, and Kevin McCruden are fun and informative. Students in this course offer insights that have helped sharpen this book.

When I first shared my vision for *Profane Parables* with editors Carey Newman and Nicole Murphy in Atlanta, they expressed genuine interest and enthusiasm in the project. Carey has since then been an indefatigable and careful editor, closely reading my insomnia cures, and encouraging me to transform them into compelling prose. Readers owe him a debt, for the book is much improved as a result of his involvement. I thank Carey and the many other Baylor University Press staff for enabling my vision to materialize in concrete form. I thank Jordan Rowan Fannin, who was especially helpful with permissions issues, and Cade Jarrell, whose copyediting of the entire manuscript was meticulous and thoughtful.

Readers of various chapters have been more than generous with constructive feedback. I thank Adele Reinhartz, Richard Walsh, Kent Brintnall, Robert Johnston, Michael Kates, and Shannon Rindge for their insights, questions, and critiques. The anonymous external reviewers of the manuscript provided supportive and helpful suggestions.

The Bible and Film section in the Society of Biblical Literature has been an academic home of sorts for me during the last several years. Jeffrey Staley and Richard Walsh warmly welcomed me into this coterie and extended collegial hospitality. Rhonda Burnette-Bletsch and Lloyd Baugh have encouraged my academic work. Robert Seesengood, Laura Copier, and Caroline Vander Stichele have offered insightful feedback, and I have learned much from their own work. I have presented some of this material at SBL annual meetings in San Francisco (2011), Chicago (2012), and Baltimore (2013). Deans Elisabeth Mermann-Jozwiak and Patrick Burke invited me to present some of these ideas at the Gonzaga-in-Florence *Capacity for Renaissance* conference in Firenze, Italia (2014). I thank John Carroll for inviting me to write an article on Luke's parables for *Interpretation*, and discuss the same subject in a Gospel of Luke section at the SBL annual meeting in San Diego (2014). Material from that article and address has been adopted for use here.

A few people were kind enough to grant me permission to include their fine work in this project. I thank Alexander Payne for letting me use so much dialogue from his film *About Schmidt*; Steve Pope for letting me use a political cartoon from the late Mike Ritter; and Robert M. Johnston for allowing me to use his translation of two rabbinic parables.

Many churches and other organizations have invited me to share some of the ideas in this book. I thank Central Presbyterian Church (Atlanta, Georgia), St. Joseph Parish (both in Colbert, Washington and Otis Orchards, Washington), and in Spokane, Washington: First Presbyterian Church, *Spiritus* (the Episcopalian diocesan center for spirituality), and Jewish Family Services.

Much of this book was written in three superb coffee shops in Spokane. I thank the owners and baristas at Revel 77, Indaba, and Coeur for providing hospitable service, stellar coffee, and patiently tolerating this pesky author. Manito Tap House, another writing site, offers exceptional beer and gracious service. I finished editing the book during a seven week stay in Firenze, Italia, and I remain grateful for the warmth and kindness of this city's residents.

Shannon, Andrew, and Sophia enrich my life in countless ways. Their presence is a recurring and luxurious grace. I count myself lucky—and am grateful—to be in their family. With deep love, I dedicate this book to them. We have been gifted by cinematic artists with occasional sacred encounters. I wish these would continue forever. Jorge Luis Borges once "imagined that Paradise will be a kind of library."* If he is right, and we ever find such a place, I hope it offers film screenings as well as books.

* Jorge Luis Borges, "Blindness," in *Seven Nights* (trans. Eliot Weinberger; New York: New Directions Books, 1984), 110.

INTRODUCTION

In the posteverything world it turns out humans can't kick the story
habit. Homer gets the last laugh.

—Glen Duncan[1]

We are lonesome animals. We spend our lives trying to be less lonesome. One of our ancient methods is to tell a story begging the listener
to say—and to feel—"Yes, that's the way it is, or at least that's the way I
feel it. You're not as alone as you thought."

—John Steinbeck[2]

Until your artists have conceived you in your unique and supreme form
you can never conceive yourselves, and have not, in fact, existed.

—William Carlos Williams[3]

This may seem like a strange book. For it draws together three subjects often treated separately. Readers may be tempted to think that this is a book about America, or Religion, or Film. And they would be right. This book is all the above, and it aims to enhance and enrich our understanding of each subject.

Although the mixture of Religion and Film may appear somewhat odd, this association has a lengthy history.[4] Early film critics thought about film in *religious* terms. In 1924 Jean Epstein christened film "profane revelation," and he described cinema as "polytheistic and theogonic."[5] Antonin Artaud wrote in 1927 of cinema's ability to produce a trance-like state in viewers, making them conducive to revelations.[6] A few decades later André Bazin asserted that the dramatic form of film was capable of being "specifically religious—or better still, specifically theological; a phenomenology of salvation and grace."[7] In the last couple decades, interest in Religion/Theology and Film has exploded, its burgeoning development evident in a torrent of books, articles, and university/seminary courses.[8]

A common religious category applied to films has been "parable." As early as 1911, Pastor Herbert A. Jump likened cinema to Jesus' parables.[9] Considering films as parables has persisted—both within the church and academia.[10] Unfortunately, the understanding of parable typically applied to films has been myopic, bland, and antiseptic. For the prevailing tendency is to think of parables—like Aesop's fables—as quaint stories that convey a moral lesson or spiritual truth.

Perceiving Jesus' parables in this manner is to misunderstand them. His parables do not defend morals; they devastate them. Jesus' parables are narratives of *dis*orientation, stories of subversion, in which conventional and cherished worldviews are demolished. Appreciating the disorienting effect of Jesus' parables is far more helpful and fruitful for understanding films that—like Jesus' parables—subvert established wisdom. This book explores three such parabolic films: *Fight Club* (d. Fincher, 1999), *American Beauty* (d. Mendes, 1999), and *About Schmidt* (d. Payne, 2002).

Understanding these three cinematic parables requires attending to the common target of their subversion: the American Dream. In light of this broader cultural context, these films function as parables, not in the traditional (and misinformed) sense of providing morals or lessons, but as cinematic narratives that dismantle orthodox myths. This book therefore begins by examining the object of these films' critique: the American Dream and its status as a sacred ethos of American religion.

One chapter will cover each film, and my goal is to treat each film on its own terms and in its own voice. This is but one way in which this book differs from some other studies of religion/theology and film. The reductionist tendency to impose foreign meanings onto films is all too common. Films need not be baptized into a certain religious (or any other) worldview. Doing so is to commit a sacrilege of reducing or conforming art to a preordained standard not of its own making.[11] This book aims to allow the films' potential meanings to emerge organically from the films themselves. Each film is covered separately for this reason—in order to avoid collapsing the films into a harmony that flattens and diminishes their unique voices.

These films do share certain themes, however, and chief among them is an indictment of the American Dream as spiritually anemic and religiously impotent.[12] The three films castigate the American Dream as bankrupt in its ability to enhance meaningful living. Each film also offers specific counterproposals for where a person might find meaning. This existential interest can be understood as fundamentally religious, especially given the notion of religion as "ultimate concern."[13] Religion, in this sense, is that to which people devote their primary psychic and material energies, and from which they derive fundamental meaning.

Fight Club, American Beauty, and *About Schmidt* each offer a dismal appraisal and blistering critique of a prevailing cultural "ultimate concern," the American Dream. The main character in each film suffers from what the Czechoslovakian philosopher Vítězslav Gardavský identified as the principal threat of our (post)modern world: "The terrible threat is that we might die before we really do die, before death has become a natural necessity. The real horror lies in just such a premature death, a death after which we go on living for many years."[14] Each film identifies the American Dream as the primary source of this psychic death, and depicts the main character's development as a spiritual or religious journey toward meaningful living. Each film suggests that spiritual or religious vitality requires rejecting America's culture of denying death, and turning instead to face death and confront mortality.

In other respects, this book differs from many works on religion/theology and film. It is, for example, not a book on the Bible *in* Film (concerned with identifying parallels between films and biblical texts, or how films utilize biblical texts). It is closer to a book on the Bible *and* Film, for it places two of the three films into a kind of dialogue with biblical texts.[15] *Fight Club* is illuminated by biblical laments and Ecclesiastes; *About Schmidt* and Jesus' parable of the Rich Fool have some noteworthy similarities. The book's primary focus is not, however, in such comparisons. *Fight Club,* for example, shares certain elements with biblical laments, but even more significant is how the film functions as a cinematic lament.

In addition to illuminating their unique voice, this book highlights the religious function of these films, arguing that they perform as parables that disorient viewers by subverting conventional wisdom. The idea that film can operate religiously is not new.[16] What is distinctive about this book is its attention to a *specific* religious function of films, as parables of subversion that provoke rather than comfort, and disrupt rather than stabilize.[17]

This book treats films—like biblical texts—as sacred texts in their own right.[18] Biblical texts are not privileged over films as more significant or authoritative. On the contrary, as the main objects of inquiry, films take primacy and precedence. For this reason Jesus' parables are examined in the final chapter. Their subversive edge reinforces the parabolic nature and function of *Fight Club*, *American Beauty*, and *About Schmidt*.

One final pragmatic note: I recommend watching each of the three films prior to reading their respective chapters. Doing so will increase understanding of these films, and make it easier to evaluate and draw conclusions about my analysis. Perhaps such viewing may even provide experiences of profane revelation.

THE AMERICAN DREAM

The Sacred Ethos of American Religion

Modern myths are even less understood of the people than *ancient myths,* eaten up with *myths* though we may be.

—Balzac[1]

When you put all your eggs in one basket you must clutch that basket for dear life.

—Ernest Becker[2]

A "love of life" that seeks to exclude or refuse death is not, in fact, a love of life at all, but the worship of an idealistic myth whose inevitable effect will be devaluing life in its real and tragic fullness.

—Alexander Irwin[3]

We're half awake in a fake empire.

—The National[4]

The dominant religion in America is America itself. The religion of Americanism is more firmly embedded in the national psyche than Judaism, Christianity, or any other "official" religion. Adherents of diverse religious persuasions perceive this American *civil* religion to be compatible with their own religious commitment. For Americans find the chief concern of America's deity appealing: the blessing, protection, and prospering of America.[5] This largely unconscious syncretism enables Americanism to thrive, even when such dual allegiances constitute idolatry.[6]

A telling shift in presidential inaugural speeches reveals an increasing tendency to deify America. Whereas early presidential inaugurals focused on modesty, American exceptionalism, and the Constitution, inaugurals since FDR have increasingly praised America itself, accenting "immodesty" about limitless America and "American universalism."[7] Since FDR, "God is still invoked, but America's real faith is *faith in America* . . . The American way is God's way."[8] Since President Wilson, "America is the secular proxy for the Kingdom of God."[9] One historian concludes that this worship of America "amounts to something that prophets in Judaism, Christianity, and Islam would have summarized in a simple term: idolatry of the nation."[10] In the religion of Americanism, however, idolatry is the elevation of anything above the perceived good of the nation.[11] Criticism of America is the most offensive blasphemy.

America's status as a religion is evident if we consider the following religious ingredients or markers:

	Judaism	Christianity	Islam
Sacred Text	Tanakh	Bible	Qur'an
Sacred Symbol	Star of David	Cross	Crescent Moon
Sacred Rituals	Circumcision, Bar/ Bat Mitzvah, Mikvah Immersion	Baptism, Eucharist	Salat, Hajj, Zakat, Sawm, Shadadah
Sacred Hymns	The Shemah	Amazing Grace	Recitation of the Qur'an
Sacred Days	Passover, Channukah, Yom Kippur	Christmas, Easter	Eid al-Fitr, Eid al-Adha
Myth of Origins	Genesis 1–3	Genesis 1–3	Qur'anic versions of Genesis 1–3
Sacred Values	Love God and Neighbor	Love God and Neighbor	Submission, Belief, Righteous Action

Each of the above seven elements are also key components in the religion of America.[12]

SACRED TEXT

The Constitution and Declaration of Independence are America's sacred texts.[13] Their hallowed status is evident not so much in their content (the Declaration of Independence has four specific references to God or a divine being), but in their function as holy objects. Of chief concern at Supreme Court nomination hearings is the specific interpretive method a future justice will apply to the Constitution. *Do you interpret the text literally? Can it speak to issues it does not explicitly mention?* Jewish and Christian communities debate these same questions regarding biblical interpretation. Elected American officials swear to defend the Constitution. Undergirding America's current gun debate is—for many—a sincere belief that bearing arms is a divinely mandated right because of its presence in the inviolable Bill of Rights. Jon McNaughton's 2009 painting "One Nation Under God" epitomizes the consecration of the Constitution. He depicts the risen Jesus holding a copy of the Constitution, as though Jesus himself authored the document.[14]

SACRED SYMBOL

The U.S. flag is America's chief sacred symbol. Numerous efforts have been made to protect the flag's sanctified status; its use in advertising has been banned since 1907 when two businessmen placed the flag on beer bottles (*Halter v. Nebraska*). Flag burning debates are contentious and ongoing. In 1989 the U.S. Supreme Court (*Texas v. Johnson*) ruled that the First Amendment protected a man who was convicted under a Texas law for burning a flag. Congress responded by passing the Flag Protection Act, which was subsequently overturned (*US vs. Eichman*). In 1990 over thirty state legislatures considered passing "Beat up a Flagburner" bills which would have reduced the penalty for assault to a minimal fine ($5–$25) if the victim had burned a flag.[15] Such bills would have granted greater value to the flag than to the person who harmed it.[16] In 1995 the U.S. Senate rejected adding the Flag Protection Amendment to the Constitution. In 2002 forty-seven states outlawed the desecration of the U.S. flag. In 2006 the Senate was one vote short of passing a constitutional amendment banning flag desecration. Fueling these clashes between Congress and the Supreme Court are conflicting commitments to disparate sacred elements of Americanism, Congress favoring the sacred symbol (the flag), the

Supreme Court preferring the sacred text (Bill of Rights). The political cartoon below recognizes this conflict, and the ironic idolatry of flag worship.

1.1 "American Idolatry" by Mike Ritter. Used with permission.

The flag's susceptibility to desecration signals its sacrosanct status. Mistreating it is regarded as profane, even in unexpected places. On April 13, 1996, NBC's Saturday Night Live, a program not known as a bastion of conservatism, ejected musical guest Rage Against the Machine before their second set because they had two U.S. flags draped upside down on their amplifiers during their opening performance.[17]

After the 9/11 attacks, the flag was imbued with renewed reverence. In a 2008 Democratic primary debate between Barack Obama and Hilary Clinton, ABC moderators Charles Gibson and George Stephanopoulos spent three minutes and thirty-four seconds asking then-Senator Obama why he so seldom wore a flag pin on his lapel.[18] Gibson's preface to his question made clear the issue's gravity: "Senator Obama, I want to do one more question that goes to the *basic issue of electability.*"[19] A woman then asked Obama if he "believe[d] in the American flag." Gibson reiterated the issue's importance before letting

Obama answer: "It comes up again and again when we talk to voters . . . it is all over the Internet . . . it could give you *a major vulnerability* if you're the candidate in November."[20]

SACRED RITUALS

The flag's consecrated status is inculcated through the ritual of the Pledge of Allegiance. Written in 1892 by Francis Bellamy, a Christian socialist, the original version of the Pledge read:

> I pledge allegiance to my Flag
> And to the republic for which it stands
> One Nation indivisible,
> With Liberty and Justice for all.

In 1954, during the politically charged "Red Scare" and amidst anxiety over the spread of "godless" Communism, Congress modified the phrase to "One nation *under God*."[21] This addition of "under God"—and its acceptance—reflects a syncretic coalescence of monotheistic faiths with Americanism.

A more overt conflict in the conjoining of these dual faiths is the use of "*allegiance*," a word from the Old (Anglo-Norman) French term *liege*, a lord or sovereign to whom one owed and rendered service. Pledging allegiance to someone other than Adonai or Jesus seems irreconcilable with the Jewish-Christian ban on idolatry. This shifting—or amalgamation—of allegiances reinforces the power of Americanism to enlist the devotion of Americans across a broad spectrum of religions.[22]

SACRED HYMNS

Facilitating the veneration of the flag is America's sacred hymn, "The Star-Spangled Banner." Penned by Francis Scott Key in 1814, the song commemorates the U.S. victory in the War of 1812. In 1931 Congress declared the song the national anthem. The most explicit religious language in the song appears in the fourth (unsung) stanza:

> Oh! thus be it ever, when freemen shall stand
> Between their loved home and the war's desolation!
> Blest with victory and peace, may the heav'n rescued land
> Praise the Power that hath made and preserved us a nation.
> Then conquer we must, when our cause it is just,

> And this be our motto: "In God is our trust."
> And the star-spangled banner in triumph shall wave
> O'er the land of the free and the home of the brave!

These lyrics inscribe central elements of Americanism: that God has blessed and protected America, and that, when the cause is "just," military victory is a mandated divine duty.

Singing the national anthem is a consecrated rite, usually enacted in the realm of sports, yet another hallowed arena of Americanism.[23] According to the U.S. Code, when this song plays and the flag is displayed people should stand and place their right hand over their heart.[24] Like the flag, this hymn's venerated status is evident in the moral outrage expressed when it is perceived to be desecrated. Such was the case on July 25, 1990, when comedian Roseanne Barr sang the hymn before a San Diego Padres baseball game off-key and finished by spitting and grabbing her crotch. So profane was this activity that it prompted a rebuke by no less than the President of the United States, George H. W. Bush, who called her performance "disgusting" and a "disgrace."[25]

Explosive anger met eleven-year-old Sebastien De La Cruz who sang the national anthem before Game 3 of the 2013 NBA Finals between the Miami Heat and the San Antonio Spurs. Social media erupted with vitriolic comments deriding the selection of a Latino to sing this hymn. About a month later, Marc Anthony evoked similar wrath when he sang "God Bless America" before the 2013 Major League Baseball All-Star game. A 2014 Coca-Cola Super Bowl commercial featuring "America the Beautiful" in multiple languages (English, Spanish, Arabic, etc.) provoked outrage and boycott threats. Stoking such objections is a commitment to a purified (and therefore ethnically exclusive) vision of Americanism.

SACRED DAYS

Americanism has its own holy days. On October 3, 1789, George Washington proclaimed that November 26 would be "a day of public thanksgiving and prayer."[26] Under Lincoln, Thanksgiving became institutionalized as an annual holiday. The holiday links the American family unit to the national cult.[27] Other sacrosanct days—Memorial Day, Veteran's Day, President's Day, presidential inaugurations, Fourth of July, Flag Day—commemorate and inculcate diverse aspects of Americanism.[28]

September 11th is the most recent holy day to be included in this sancti-fied pantheon. Its revered status is evident in its ability—like the flag—to be profaned. Six days after the attacks, Bill Maher obliged by remarking on his television show *Politically Incorrect*:

> We have been the cowards, lobbing cruise missiles from 2,000 miles away. That's cowardly. Staying in the airplane when it hits the building, say what you want about it, it's not cowardly.[29]

Response to Maher was swift and decisive. Sony and Federal Express imme-diately withdrew advertising from the show. Seventeen ABC affiliate stations stopped airing the program. The show was cancelled the following June.

SACRED MYTH OF ORIGINS

America's myth of origins, its own Garden of Eden tale, explains its genesis. In broad strokes, America's myth is that a persecuted people fled Britain and came to America for religious freedom. An alternative understanding of America's origins might begin earlier with indigenous people who dwelled in their own land centuries before the British arrived. These First Nations people are largely erased, or severely marginalized, in the myth—as they were in history. For a myth's primary purpose is not to record and transmit historical accuracy, but to instill and legitimate core values.

Freedom is the primary—and inviolable—value that surfaces as a leitmotif in America's myth(s) of origins. It explains the flight from England to America (religious freedom), the Revolutionary War (economic freedom), and the Civil War (freedom for the slaves, or for the states).[30] Freedom was used to explain the motives of the 9/11 attackers. "Why do they hate us?" Pres-ident George W. Bush asked. "They hate our freedoms."[31]

Freedom's hallowed status is apparent in the willingness to kill and die for it; it is deemed worthy to be purchased in the currency of blood. In these etiologies, violence and freedom are inextricably linked, even mutually depen-dent.[32] As in the national anthem, freemen in the land of the free must conquer. Subsequent U.S. wars, torture, and drone killings are legitimated by framing these activities—and their victims—as necessary in the eternal and divinely decreed quest for freedom.[33]

Criticism of national violence is not tolerated. During the initial phase of the second United States–Iraq War in March 2003, Natalie Maines of the Dixie Chicks stated from a London concert stage: "We do not want this war;

we do not want this violence." She added, "Just so you know, we're ashamed the president of the United States is from Texas."[34] As with Maher, responses were rapid and rabid. WDAF-AM in Kansas City, Missouri encouraged listeners to toss their Dixie Chicks CDs into garbage cans set up outside their studio. WTDR-FM in Talladega, Alabama dropped the band from its playlist, and many other stations followed suit. In Shreveport, Louisiana, protestors smashed Dixie Chicks CDs with a tractor. Maines received death threats. Such a fate was judged fitting for an apostate of the national cult.

Fueling American outrage over the 9/11 attacks was disbelief that freedom-loving, innocent civilians were targets. A curious cultural amnesia cloaked America's own pioneering role in extinguishing civilians in modern warfare (ca. 125,000 Japanese lives in Hiroshima and more than 60,000 lives in Nagasaki). These atomic bombings of civilian populations are difficult to integrate into our nation's mythology because they do not befit the image of a "land of the free and home of the brave." As George Orwell points out, "The nationalist not only does not disapprove of atrocities committed by his own side, he has a remarkable capacity for not even hearing about them."[35] Consider a selective list of U.S. military actions:

1949	consulted in overthrowing the Syrian government
1953	helped overthrow Iran's government and depose the prime minister
1954	helped bring down Guatemala's elected government
1957	helped rig elections in Lebanon
1959	attempted to help topple the Cuban government
1960–63	planned a coup to overthrow the Iraqi government
1961	helped assassinate Patrice Lumumba of Zaire/Congo
1961	helped overthrow the Prime Minister of the Dominican Republic
1963	helped assassinate Diem, the leader of South Vietnam
1964	helped support a coup in Brazil
1973	helped plan a coup to topple Chilean president Salvador Allende
1980	supported a coup in Turkey
1980s	attempted to overthrow the Nicaraguan government
1980s	funneled weapons and $20 billion to the Afghan mujahideen to oppose the Soviets in Afghanistan

General American ignorance of these actions underscores the power of America's sacred myths. Sanitizing history also perpetuates the very ignoble acts that are deemed incompatible with our national character. As the recent Texas and Colorado school board efforts to whitewash American history demonstrate, we adapt our stories to conform to our national myth.[36]

Any religion that survives its infancy develops a zealous and unfettered commitment to self-preservation. Defending one's survival is axiomatic, and any and all acts can be justified in the name of self-preservation. How else to explain Secretary of State Madeline Albright's response on *60 Minutes* when Leslie Stahl noted that U.S. sanctions in Iraq had led to the deaths of half a million Iraqi children? "Is the price worth it?" Stahl asked. Albright was firm: "I think this is a very hard choice, but the price—we think the price is worth it."[37] Like the Vatican's response to sexual abuse, such ardent self-preservation is often pursued at the institution's own peril. A tacit credo of Americanism is not so much that God is on our side, but that we have become godlike, with the accompanying divine right to give and take life.

SACRED VALUE

The American Dream is—like freedom—a sanctified value of American self-worship. It is much more than "our national motto."[38] In theological terms, the American Dream is the primary *soteriological* vision of American religion. It is, in other words, the primary vehicle of personal and communal salvation. Achieving the American Dream, so the promise goes, brings meaning and spiritual fulfillment.[39] It is salvific. Maslow's hierarchy has a new apex.

Defining the American Dream is difficult, not least because of the presence of multiple "dreams."[40] Broadly understood, the American Dream is the championing of success (usually defined materially) and an unbridled optimism about the opportunities to achieve such success.[41] Apparently coined in 1931, author James Truslow Adams describes the American Dream as

> that dream of a land in which life should be *better* and *richer* and *fuller* for everyone, with opportunity for each according to ability or achievement.... It is not a dream of motor cars and high wages merely, but a dream of social order in which each man and each woman shall be able to attain to the fullest stature of which they are innately capable, and be recognized by others for what they are, regardless of the fortuitous circumstances of birth or position.[42]

Adams' ideas remain alive and well. In a 2013 *Harvard Business Review* article, the dean of Harvard's business school writes, "The American Dream is the country's most important asset—more valuable than its extraordinary natural resources, deep financial capacity, or unparalleled workforce."[43] Confidence in the future is identified as its central pillar: "While the American Dream rests on a broad set of virtues . . . its foundation is a spirit of *optimism*."[44] The Dream's inherent goodness is also upheld, with no consideration for any potential drawbacks. The only worry is about its potential demise.[45] It is axiomatic that the American Dream is to be as accessible as possible and pursued with utmost zeal.

Underlying these attitudes are assumptions about the American Dream's sacrosanct nature. This consecrated status helps explain why critiques of the American Dream are nothing less than sacrilege. One example of such blasphemy emanates from Blacks in America who have experienced the Dream's less savory aspects.

THE AMERICAN DREAM: A RACIAL CRITIQUE

In an 1852 speech in Rochester, New York ("What to a Slave is the Fourth of July?"), the emancipated slave Frederick Douglass posed a crucial question about the meaning of the Independence Day holiday for Black people in America: "What have I, or those I represent, to do with your national independence? Are the great principles of political freedom and of natural justice, embodied in that Declaration of Independence, extended to us?" Douglass replies with a resounding "No," and he indicts the American holiday:

> I am not included within the pale of this glorious anniversary! Your high independence only reveals the immeasurable distance between us. The blessings in which you, this day, rejoice, are not enjoyed in common. The rich inheritance of justice, liberty, prosperity and independence, bequeathed by your fathers, is shared by you, not by me. The sunlight that brought life and healing to you, has brought stripes and death to me. This Fourth [of] July is yours, not mine. You may rejoice, I must mourn.

Douglass identifies an irreconcilable hypocrisy between slavery and the noble sentiments lauded on July Fourth:

> What, to the American slave, is your Fourth of July? I answer: a day that reveals to him, more than all other days in the year, the gross injustice and cruelty to which he is the constant victim. To him, your celebration is a sham; your boasted

liberty, an unholy license; your national greatness, swelling vanity; your sounds of rejoicing are empty and heartless; your denunciations of tyrants, brass fronted impudence; your shouts of liberty and equality, hollow mockery; your prayers and hymns, your sermons and thanksgivings, with all your religious parade, and solemnity, are, to him, mere bombast, fraud, deception, impiety, and hypoc-risy—a thin veil to cover up crimes which would disgrace a nation of savages. There is not a nation on the earth guilty of practices, more shocking and bloody, than are the people of these United States, at this very hour.

Douglass views the holiday through the lens of the selling of human beings, an act "co-extensive with the star-spangled banner and American Christianity." "The existence of slavery," he insists, "brands your republicanism as a sham, your humanity as a base pretence, and your Christianity as a lie."

Douglass' denunciation is not, however, total. He finds potentially liberat-ing traces in the Bible and the Constitution:

Standing with God and the crushed and bleeding slave on this occasion, I will, in the name of humanity which is outraged, in the name of liberty which is fet-tered, in the name of the constitution and the Bible, which are disregarded and trampled upon, dare to call in question and to denounce, with all the emphasis I can command, everything that serves to perpetuate slavery-the great sin and shame of America!

If "interpreted as it ought to be interpreted," he maintains, "the Constitution is a GLORIOUS LIBERTY DOCUMENT."[46]

Like Douglass, Martin Luther King Jr. was ambivalent about the Amer-ican Dream. In his "I Have a Dream" speech, King articulates a classic inte-grationist hope, one "deeply rooted in the American dream." Referring to the Constitution and Declaration of Independence, he laments that "America has defaulted on this promissory note insofar as her citizens of color are concerned. Instead of honoring this sacred obligation, America has given the Negro peo-ple a bad check, a check which has come back marked 'insufficient funds.'" "But," he insists, "we refuse to believe that the bank of justice is bankrupt."[47] In his "Mountaintop" speech, delivered the day before he died, King reiterated his confidence: students who launched the sit-in movement "were really stand-ing up for the best in the American dream, and taking the whole nation back to those great wells of democracy which were dug deep by the Founding Fathers in the Declaration of Independence and the Constitution."[48]

At other times King was far less sanguine about the American Dream.[49] His 1964 speech "The American Dream" bemoans the gulf between the Dream's promise and reality. America is "essentially a dream, a dream yet unfulfilled." Even the claim in the Declaration of Independence that all are created equal "is a dream."[50]

Malcolm X maintained, on the contrary, that the freedom enshrined in America's founding documents was meant for—and applied to—Whites only.[51] In his speech "The Ballot or the Bullet" he declared:

> No, I'm not an American. I'm one of the 22 million black people who are the victims of Americanism. One of the 22 million black people who are the victims of democracy, nothing but disguised hypocrisy. So, I'm not standing here speaking to you as an American, or a patriot, or a flag-saluter, or a flag-waver—no, not I! I'm speaking as a victim of this American system. And I see America through the eyes of the victim. I don't see any American dream; I see an American nightmare![52]

Malcolm was succinct: "We're not Americans, we're Africans who happen to be in America. We were kidnapped and brought here against our will from Africa. We didn't land on Plymouth Rock—that rock landed on us."[53]

Near the end of his life, King's views on the American Dream veered closer to Malcolm's.[54] Less than four months before his assassination, King espoused a bleaker vision of the Dream, one which he saw "turn into a nightmare."[55] Evidence for this dire assessment included the bombing of the four girls in Birmingham, the Vietnam War, and the "black brothers and sisters perishing on a lonely island of poverty in the midst of a vast ocean of material prosperity." King concludes bleakly, "Yes, I am personally the victim of deferred dreams, of blasted hopes."[56]

Langston Hughes' poetry—to which King alludes—poignantly and prophetically conveys the collective anguish and hopes of Blacks in America.[57] Scores of his poems lament the failure of dreams in general and the American Dream specifically. "Let America Be America Again" includes the plaintive refrain: "Let America be America again / Let it be the dream it used to be / . . . (America never was America to me.)"[58] The haunting poem vacillates between a plea for America to realize its potential of justice, and a grim recognition that America has yet to do so: "O, let America be America again— / The land that never has been yet— / And yet must be—the land where every man is free."[59] His poem "Harlem [2]" inquires about the unrealized dreams of Blacks in America, wondering if a "dream deferred" ultimately explodes.[60] Lorraine Hansberry's 1959 play *A Raisin in the Sun*—which takes its title from this Hughes poem—depicts African-Americans as perennial outsiders to the national Dream. The play (and subsequent 1961 film) illustrates the psychic despair produced by failing to achieve the Dream, and the innumerable obstacles impeding such achievement.

Black prophetic and poetic critique of Americanism remains relevant and controversial. In the 2008 Democratic primary debate, ABC moderators Gibson and Stephanopoulos devoted nine minutes and forty-four seconds to Obama's relationship with African American pastor Jeremiah Wright. After the economy, Gibson and Stephanopoulos considered Reverend Wright's critique of America to be the most monumental issue for potential voters. (Gun violence was given eight minutes and twenty-three seconds, and the United States–Iraq War merited only six minutes and forty-eight seconds). Stephanopoulos' queries to Obama ("Do you think Reverend Wright loves America as much as you do?" and "You do believe he's as patriotic as you are?") reflect ignorance of the historical role of prophetic critique in the Black church, and also assume that criticism of America is inherently unpatriotic.[61]

Black Americans are not the only ones who have experienced the American Dream as problematic and traumatic. The claim that "America is a nightmare for the poor of *every race*" resonates with Hughes' poem "Let America Be America Again," and points to a more encompassing national deficiency.[62] Psychological insights suggest that the American Dream poses fundamental problems even for those who do achieve it.

THE AMERICAN DREAM: A PSYCHOLOGICAL CRITIQUE

In the first sentence of *Civilization and Its Discontents,* Sigmund Freud critiques a value system that resonates with core elements of the American Dream: "It is impossible to escape the impression that people commonly use false standards of measurement—that they seek power, success and wealth for themselves and admire them in others, and that they underestimate what is of true value in life."[63] Freud ends his book reflecting on whether certain civilizations could be diagnosed as neurotic, and hoping that someone "will venture to embark upon a pathology of cultural communities."[64]

Psychologist Erich Fromm takes up this very challenge in *The Sane Society,* examining relative levels of social health and illness/neurosis.[65] Relying on WHO statistics showing much higher rates of suicide and alcoholism in wealthier countries, Fromm concludes that countries that come closest to realizing "the materially comfortable life, relatively equal distribution of wealth, stable democracy and peace . . . show the most severe signs of mental unbalance!"[66] Instead of engendering psychological health, economic prosperity brings an increase in mental sickness. Adjustment to this system therefore constitutes a kind of insanity.[67]

Fromm diagnoses people who are (not quite) living in modern Western society as alienated relationally, vocationally, politically, and culturally.[68] People are principally passive consumers of products they neither need nor truly enjoy.[69] Such people "live without living."[70] These consumers are also commodities who measure their worth in economic terms.[71] In this Faustian bargain, "happiness becomes identical with consumption of newer and better commodities."[72]

The tragic and tedious fate of such consumers is premature death. Although life ought to be a series of rebirths ("we should be fully born, when we die"), Fromm laments that most people "die before they are born."[73] People seek escape through various pathologies because they cannot "stand any longer the boredom of a meaningless life."[74] Anticipating Gardavský's argument, Fromm maintains that such premature death is humanity's fundamental threat: "In the nineteenth century the problem was that *God is dead*; in the twentieth century the problem is that *man is dead*."[75]

Given how toxic society is to the human spirit, Fromm is surprised so few clergy critique this dehumanizing system.[76] Instead, "all churches . . . use religion to keep man going and satisfied with a profoundly irreligious system. The majority of them do not seem to recognize that this type of religion will eventually degenerate into overt idolatry."[77] Fromm identifies nationalism as the most pernicious form of idolatry, especially dangerous given its omnipresent allure. Nationalism is, he argues, "our form of incest, is our idolatry, is our insanity."[78] The irony of such American idolatry[79] is that a person practices it "bowing to the new idols, yet swearing by the name of the God who commanded him to destroy all idols."[80]

As the responses to Bill Maher and the Dixie Chicks illustrate, fervent devotion to the national cult surfaces most viciously when its holy symbols are threatened:

> Let us picture a man who takes the flag of his country to a street of one of the cities of the Western world, and tramples on it in view of other people. He would be lucky not to be lynched. Almost everybody would feel a sense of furious indignation. . . . The man who desecrated the flag would have done something unspeakable; he would have committed a crime which is not *one* crime among others, but *the* crime, the one unforgivable and unpardonable.[81]

Unpatriotic acts constitute "an attack against 'the sacred.'" "Even if a man should speak disparagingly of God," Fromm argues, "he would hardly arouse the same feeling of indignation as against *the* crime, against the sacrilege which is the violation of the symbols of the country."[82] As Oscar Wilde allegedly quipped, patriotism is the "virtue of the vicious."

The American Dream poses a potential religious threat since meaningful living is a fundamental religious enterprise. Like theologian Paul Tillich's definition of religion as "ultimate concern," Fromm understands the quest for meaning as a basic building block and sign of religiosity. Religions, he asserts, are all efforts to discover what meaningful living entails.[83]

Anticipating Fromm, the psychoanalyst Carl Jung identified the quest for meaning as central to a person's psychological health, describing such activity as religious. The crux of his patients' neuroses, Jung noted, was fundamentally religious and existential.[84] He believed many of his patients came for help "not because they were suffering from a neurosis, but because *they could find no meaning in life.*"[85] These patients had "*not discovered what life means,*" and they were not helped by philosophy or religion.[86] The psychiatrist Viktor Frankl also situated existential concerns at the heart of his treatment. Upending a core premise of Freudian psychology, he argued that what most determines psychological health is not a person's childhood or family of origin, but one's sense of meaning in their life.[87]

THE AMERICAN DREAM'S GOSPEL OF SUCCESS

The religion of Americanism champions a gospel of unfettered and unlimited success. Triumph is the sign of salvation, failure an abomination. Fromm observed this impulse in our cultural religion: "the meaning of our life is to move, to forge ahead, to arrive as near to the top as possible."[88] Sustaining this compulsion, he contends, is "the conviction that *there is no purpose except to invest life successfully and to get it over with without major mishaps.*"[89]

The American Dream and its gospel of success was a chief target of criticism in F. Scott Fitzgerald's *The Great Gatsby*. Like the three films analyzed in this book, his novel appeared during an economic zenith—in 1925, near the height of the "Roaring Twenties" or (to use a term Fitzgerald coined) "The Jazz Age." The novel's critique of American culture is evident in an anecdote about Fitzgerald's final preference for the title. Although an early working title was "Among the Ash Heaps and Millionaires," he cabled his desire on March 19, 1925, noting that he was "crazy" about "Under the Red, White, and Blue." At three weeks prior to publication, however, he was informed that the title could not be changed.[90]

Jay Gatsby, the titular character, is a cipher for the American Dream and those who pursue it. A self-made man in more ways than one, Gatsby invents for himself a persona, history, and even a name. He is as fanciful as the American Dream he symbolizes. Gatsby's "dream" is Daisy, an old flame he is determined to win back by accruing massive amounts of wealth. As in the American Dream, success is his vehicle of procuring happiness and meaning. Daisy is Gatsby's goal, dream, and mirage, and in these ways she too symbolizes aspects of the American Dream:

> There must have been moments even that afternoon when Daisy tumbled short of his dreams—not through her own fault but because of the *colossal vitality of his illusion*. It had gone beyond her, beyond everything. He had thrown himself into it with a creative passion, adding to it all the time, decking it out with every bright feather that drifted his way. *No amount of fire or freshness can challenge what a man will store up in his ghostly heart.*[91]

Gatsby's pursuit of Daisy becomes as grandiose as he makes her out to be in his mind. Chasing this illusion proves costly for Gatsby who "*paid a high price for living too long with a single dream.*" He has difficulty discerning the boundary between reality and fantasy. His "reveries provided an outlet for his imagination; they were a satisfactory hint of the unreality of reality, a promise that the rock of the world was founded securely on a fairy's wing."[92] The painful contrast between the "real" and the "illusion" ends with a foreshadowing of Gatsby's death, perhaps symbolizing the costs paid by those who similarly rush headlong in pursuit of the American Dream.[93]

The novel's final four paragraphs are redolent with polyvalent metaphors about America and its illusionary Dream:

> And as the moon rose higher the inessential houses began to melt away until gradually I became aware of the old island here that flowered once for Dutch sailors' eyes—a fresh, green breast of the new world. Its vanished trees, the trees that had made way for Gatsby's house, had once pandered in *whispers to the last and greatest of all human dreams*; for a transitory enchanted moment man must have held his breath in the presence of this continent, compelled into an aesthetic contemplation he neither understood nor desired, face to face for the last time in history with something commensurate to his capacity for wonder.[94]

Fitzgerald presents America as the final bastion of potential wonder, a land so pregnant with possibility and potential that it elicits dreams from its voyeurs.

> And as I sat there, brooding on the old unknown world, I thought of Gatsby's wonder when he first picked out the green light at the end of Daisy's dock. He had come a long way to this blue lawn and *his dream must have seemed so close that he could hardly fail to grasp it.* He did not know that *it was already behind him,* somewhere back in that vast obscurity beyond the city, where the dark fields of the republic rolled on under the night.[95]

Fitzgerald intimates that the quest for the American Dream is futile since the goal itself (happiness?) is imaginary. If it ever existed it only did so in the past, yet even this might be a charade, birthed by nostalgia. Gatsby thrills to vain pursuit of the past. Repudiating Nick's remark ("You can't repeat the past"), he insists, "Can't repeat the past? . . . Why of course you can!"[96]

> Gatsby believed in the green light, the orgastic future that year by year recedes before us. *It eluded us then, but that's no matter—tomorrow we will run faster, stretch out our arms farther . . . . And one fine morning—*
> *So we beat on, boats against the current, borne back ceaselessly into the past.*[97]

In 1924—one year before *Gatsby's* publication—Fitzgerald offered his own interpretation of the book: "That's the whole burden of this novel—*the loss of those illusions* that give such color to the world so that you don't care whether things are true or false as long as they partake of the magical glory."[98] For Gatsby, the American Dream proves to be absurd, meaningless, and elusive.[99] Yet he (and the readers) join the narrator in chasing after it regardless, running faster, arms outstretched, vainly pursuing the past.

AMERICA'S DENIAL OF DEATH

The corollary of America's love affair with success is a denial of death. The exaltation of success in the American Dream leaves little tolerance for failure, and nothing epitomizes failure more than death. Death is the antithesis of success. In the American Dream, death is anathema. It is that which must not be named. Like Voldemort (French for "theft of death" or "flight from death"), people spend their lives fleeing death's shadow, only to find themselves in its inevitable grasp. In his groundbreaking work, Ernest Becker asserts that people are principally motivated by their "terror of death."[100] "It is the basic fear," he maintains, "that influences all others, a fear from which no one is immune, no matter how disguised it may be."[101] It is "the terror that we carry around in our secret heart."[102]

Corroborating Becker's thesis is a study showing a gradual erasure of death in western civilization in the twentieth century.[103] The epicenter and origin of this revolution was the United States.[104] The trend toward denying death began in the United States at the turn of the century, and "accelerated markedly" in 1930–1950, when the locus of death shifted. Dying at home became too "inconvenient," so instead of dying "in the bosom of one's family," one died "in the hospital, alone."[105] As the new "masters of death," doctors presided over the *absence* of a ritual ceremony in hospital deaths. An acceptable death became that which did not place too grievous or onerous of a burden—emotional or otherwise—on family members.[106]

Practical changes in the funeral ceremony facilitated this cultural exile of death. The family reception line was removed, dark clothing was no longer mandatory attire, the coffin became the "casket," funeral homes were privatized, and embalming (begun in California in 1900) became more common. All these changes reflected and contributed to one major emphasis: "It is above all essential that society—the neighbors, friends, colleagues, and children—notice to the least possible degree that death has occurred."[107] With cremation the corpse was banished: it "is the most radical means of getting rid of the body and of forgetting it, of nullifying it, of being 'too final.'"[108] If the corpse did remain, its deathly pallor was made tolerable through embalming, a practice "almost unknown in Europe and characteristic of the American way of death."[109]

Fueling this cultural conspiracy was a commitment to happiness, a principal tenet of the American Dream.[110] The American revolution in exorcising death's ugliness was an "interdiction of death in order to preserve happiness."[111] This new prevailing ethos privileged a tidy death, one that minimized its unwelcome attendants: pain, agony, and grief. "Too evident sorrow does not inspire pity but repugnance, it is the sign of mental instability or of bad manners: it is *morbid*." On the contrary, "One only has the right to cry if no one else can see or hear. Solitary and shameful mourning is the only recourse, like a sort of masturbation."[112]

The American Dream functions as a sacred cultural vehicle of the denial of death.[113] In the American Dream, death is not only sanitized, but its removal from personal and public life is codified in a tacit dogma. Within its optimistic contours of success, the American Dream offers no space (and no healthy coping mechanisms) for loss, suffering, failure, and death. It is perhaps no accident that this fear and displacement of death would be so acute in the country that enshrined the pursuit of happiness as holy and inviolable. The American Dream is, perhaps, too big (and too potentially happy) to fail.

Since the American Dream operates as a "vehicle of earthly heroism," to question it—let alone dismantle or subvert it—is to attack a source of profound psychological and religious comfort. Such a challenge strikes at our culture's pillars of personal and cosmic meaning. For what crumbles among the debris is nothing less than the Dream's promise of immortality.[114] A person can avoid the threat of personal extinction by "extend[ing] oneself beyond death in symbolic ways," and surrounding death "by larger meanings."[115] The American Dream is one such larger meaning, a "codified hero system" that provides a "living myth of the significance of human life."[116]

Scores of films elevate and enshrine the sacred covenant of the American Dream.[117] In the words of one critic, the "American Dream is alive and well in cinematic fare."[118] Fewer films have examined its darker underbelly. Paul Thomas Anderson's *There Will Be Blood* (2007) did so, personifying American capitalism in Daniel Plainview (Daniel Day-Lewis). Echoing *Citizen Kane* (d. Welles, 1941), Plainview animates the moral and spiritual depravity that results from pursuing wealth and success at all costs. Walter White (Bryan Cranston) in the AMC series *Breaking Bad* (2008–2013) is a more recent incarnation of this endeavor. Like Michael Corleone of *The Godfather* films (d. Coppola, 1972, 1974, 1990), White illustrates the destruction wreaked upon those who plunge headfirst into the material success of the American Dream.

Ernest Becker argued that organized religion failed because the church did not offer a "valid hero system" that was distinct from the discredited heroic system of the broader American culture:

> If traditional culture is discredited as heroics, then the church that supports that culture automatically discredits itself. If the church, on the other hand, chooses to insist on its own special heroics, it might find that in crucial ways it must work against the culture, recruit youth to be anti-heroes to the ways of life of the society they live in. *This is the dilemma of religion in our time.*[119]

In subverting the religion of the American Dream, *Fight Club, American Beauty,* and *About Schmidt* embark upon this very challenge. The main character in each film is, in the words of The National, "half awake in a fake empire." These films propose that an essential step in waking from the American

Dream's stupor is confronting one's own death. Rejecting a fundamental American credo, these films illustrate the counterintuitive insight that denying death engenders spiritual death, and inhibits a meaning-filled life.[120] *Fight Club, American Beauty,* and *About Schmidt* encourage viewers to mourn their eventual death as a key step toward meaningful living.[121]

❊ 2 ❊

FIGHT CLUB
Lamenting God's Abandonment and the American Dream

Storytelling in itself is a holy, human concern.

—David Fincher, director of *Fight Club*[1]

I don't know how much movies should entertain ... I'm always
interested in movies that scar.

—David Fincher[2]

If you haven't already noticed, all my books are about a lonely person
looking for some way to connect with other people. In a way, that is the
opposite of the American Dream.

—Chuck Palahniuk, author of *Fight Club*[3]

Film critic Roger Ebert described *Fight Club* (1999) as "cheerfully fascist ... a celebration of violence in which the heroes write themselves a license to drink, smoke, screw and beat one another up." Ebert called character Tyler Durden "a man who tripped over the Nietzsche display on his way to the coffee bar in Borders. In my opinion, he has no useful truths."[4] For *Los Angeles Times* film critic Kenneth Turan, *Fight Club* was "a witless mishmash of whiny, infantile philosophizing and bone-crunching violence that actually thinks it's saying something of significance."[5] Rex Reed outdid everyone, calling it a "film without a single redeeming quality, which may have to find its audience in hell."[6]

Talk show host Rosie O'Donnell was so unnerved by the film that she had difficulty sleeping; on the day of its release she gave away the film's surprise ending on her nationally televised show, to discourage others from seeing it.[7] Negative reactions to the film may partially explain its poor box office performance; in its nearly five month run in the United States and Canada, the film earned only $37 million (much less than its reported $63 million budget).

The intensity of the film's detractors has been surpassed by the zealous devotion of its fans. As of 2015 (sixteen years after its release), *Fight Club* stands at #10 on the Internet Movie Database (IMDb) list of best films.[8] Of the top 250 films on this list, only three have received more total votes than *Fight Club*.[9] In 2006 the British film magazine *Empire* ranked it as the eighth greatest film of all time, and in 2007 the British film magazine *Total Film* ranked it as the "Greatest Film of our Lifetime."[10] Critics have raved about the film; *Rolling Stone*'s Peter Travers called it "an uncompromising American classic."[11] The film has more than made up in DVD/video sales and rentals ($55 million) what it lacked in box office earnings.

Fight Club has left an indelible mark on American culture, spawning numerous actual fight clubs throughout the United States. Several of these were started by teens (in Texas, New Jersey, and Washington) who posted their fights online.[12] Fight clubs were launched at Princeton University and, in 2000 at a gentleman's club in Menlo Park, California. The son of the mayor of Salt Lake City was involved in one, and on April 3, 2008, St. Paul's College in Auckland suspended six students over starting a fight club. Chuck Palahniuk, author of the 1996 novel on which the film is based, has received letters from young men describing fight clubs they started in New Jersey, London, and Spokane, Washington.[13] Some claim the film is partly responsible for the current popularity of Mixed Martial Arts and other types of free-form (and cage) fighting.[14] The film even generated a Versace fashion line.[15] The film's cultural resonances remain alive and well, and in 2015 Palahniuk released *Fight Club 2* in the form of a graphic novel.[16]

Fight Club has both inspired and—to use director David Fincher's term— scarred.[17] This powerful resonance and repulsion is due to the film's subversive and disorienting lament over an American culture that has erased death, pain, and suffering.[18]

THE RELIGIOUS BANKRUPTCY OF THE AMERICAN DREAM

At the heart of *Fight Club* is the religious development of the film's narrator and unnamed main character (Edward Norton). Although multi-dimensional (e.g., psychological and relational), his journey consists primarily in a quest for meaningful living. Central to his progressive *conversions* are his developing attitudes and behaviors—ultimately his lament—regarding the American Dream.

Initially, the narrator's life is void of significance. An insomniac for six months, he describes his depressing lack of existence as "never really asleep, and never really awake."[19] Alienated from meaningful relationships and work, he embodies the "premature death" in which he dies before he really has died.[20]

His living death is rooted in his embrace of various aspects of the American Dream. At the film's outset he is fully ensconced in its accoutrements. As he flatly intones, "Like so many others, I had become a slave to the IKEA nesting instinct." The narrator elaborates, while the camera zooms in on an empty living room that is gradually filled with furniture items:

> If I saw something clever that looked like a little coffee table in the shape of a yin yang, I had to have it. The Klipsk personal office unit, the Hovetrekke home excer bike, or the Johanneshov sofa with the Strinne green stripe pattern, even the Rislampa/Har wired-lamps of environmentally friendly unbleached paper. I'd flick through catalogues and wonder, *"What kind of dining set defines me as a person?"* I had it all . . .

2.1 Ikea Nesting Instinct

The narrator's subsequent complaint about his insomnia suggests that his enslavement to his possessions is a principal cause of his lethargy. It is not despite "having it all," but *because* he has it all that he finds himself unfulfilled.[21] He is enslaved, not only to the "Ikea nesting instinct," but also to a broader American culture that associates contentment with acquiring certain possessions. The superficiality of these accessories is symbolized by the depressing contents of his refrigerator: a handful of condiment bottles thinly spread out on different racks. This image mirrors the narrator's lack of internal substance. He medicates this void by purchasing an endless array of external trimmings.

Symptomatic of, and contributing to, this emptiness is the narrator's complete lack of any human connection. This relational lacuna is exemplified in his comment, "We used to read pornography; now it was the Horchow collection." Or, as the original screenplay read: "It used to be Playboys; now—Ikea."[22] If pornography represents a shift of relationship from a person to a manufactured image, it presumably still involves a *human* image. Yet the narrator seeks stimulation and meaning from nothing human whatsoever. He seeks to be turned on by the *im*personal. Acquiring material possessions—an integral component of the American Dream—fails to provide him with substantive meaning.

The abandonment of this Dream and its accessories (job, paycheck, home) is integral to the narrator's development. Catalyzing this growth is Tyler Durden (Brad Pitt) who incarnates the antithesis of the narrator's enslavement to his possessions. When the narrator's condo and possessions are destroyed in an explosion, he grieves their loss, regarding it as a traumatic setback:

> When you buy furniture you tell yourself, "That's it, that's the last sofa I'm gonna need. Whatever else happens, I got that sofa problem handled." I had it all—I had a stereo that was very decent, a wardrobe that was getting very respectable—*I was close to being complete.*

Tyler could not disagree more, and he rejects equating personal identity with one's possessions:

> What are we then? . . . We're consumers. We're byproducts of a lifestyle obsession. Murder, crime, poverty—these things don't concern me. What concerns me are celebrity magazines, television with 500 channels, some guy's name on my underwear. Rogaine, Viagra, Olestra.

Tyler views the world as a Huxlean dystopia in which people amuse themselves to death.[23] For Tyler this *living* death is perpetuated by enslavement to possessions, one that stymies concern for weightier issues (crime and poverty). Channeling Emerson, Tyler opines, "The things you own end up owning you." He succinctly condemns an inevitable consequence of a culture that insists on identifying oneself with material goods, a system that produces middle class "slaves with white collars."[24]

The American Dream poses a fundamental threat to the narrator's religious life. Tyler's homilies often address the spiritual vacuity of American culture:

> I see in fight club the strongest and smartest men who've ever lived. I see all this potential, and I see it squandered. Goddammit, an entire generation pumping gas, waiting tables—slaves with white collars. Advertising has us chasing cars and clothes, working jobs we hate so we can buy shit we don't need. We're the middle children of history . . . no purpose or place. We have no great war, no great depression. Our great war is a *spiritual war*. Our great depression is our lives.

The toxicity of the American Dream thus constitutes an existential and a spiritual threat. Dwelling in life-numbing jobs and pursuing petty possessions amounts to a "spiritual war." The battlefield—and collateral damage—is the great depression of unfulfilled lives.

Describing the bankruptcy of the American Dream in spiritual terms fits with the general religious nature of the narrator's development. Of his time spent in support groups, he remarks, "Every evening I died, and every evening *I was born again—resurrected*." He also recounts the experience of fight clubs with explicit religious language:

> Fight club wasn't about winning or losing. It wasn't about words. The hysterical shouting was in tongues, like in a Pentecostal church. When the fight was over, nothing was solved, but nothing mattered. Afterwards, *we all felt saved*.

Tyler interprets the destruction of the narrator's condo as a spiritual event: "But maybe, just maybe, *you've been delivered*." Such language draws attention to the *religious* texture of the narrator's development. Palahniuk himself has reflected on the important religious function of communities such as support groups and fight clubs:

> In so many ways, these places—support groups, twelve-step recovery groups, demolition derbies—*they've come to serve the role that organized religion used to*. We used to go to church to reveal the worst aspects of ourselves, our sin. To tell our stories. To be recognized. To be forgiven. And to be redeemed, accepted back into our community. This ritual was our way to stay connected to people,

and to resolve our anxiety before it could take us so far from humanity that we would be lost.[25]

Nothing less than the narrator's religious health is at stake, and it is put in peril by his enslavement to the American Dream.

LAMENT LANGUAGE AND LITERATURE

Fight Club employs the specific genre of lament to protest the religious bankruptcy of the American Dream. Biblical laments provide a helpful framework for understanding how *Fight Club* functions as a lament of divine abandonment and the American Dream.

Found primarily in the Psalms, lament also occurs in Job, Lamentations, and in one noteworthy New Testament text. Laments are primarily appeals to God to remove suffering.[26] Rooted in painful experiences, they give voice to a variety of grief, mourning, anger, rage, fear, and disappointment.[27] Articulating emotions and experiences that are typically silenced or ignored, laments direct these volatile emotions to God.[28] Laments complain to God *about God*.[29] Lament psalms blame God for troubles, accuse God of failing to help, plead with God to remove misery, and question God's distance or absence.[30] Psalms of lament thus differ from psalms of praise or thanks. Whereas the latter affirm, thank, or praise God, laments accuse God of failing to be what psalms of praise or thanks declare. In laments, God fails to deliver, rescue, or support, and God can be the source of pain, suffering, and death. Psalm 88 contains many elements of lament:

> You have put me in the depths of the Pit,
>   in the regions dark and deep.
> Your wrath lies heavy upon me,
>   and you overwhelm me with all your waves.
> You have caused my companions to shun me;
>   you have made me a thing of horror to them.
> I am shut in so that I cannot escape;
>   my eye grows dim through sorrow.
>
> (Ps 88:6-9a, NRSV)

Although most lament psalms eventually transition to praise (e.g. Pss 13; 22), Psalm 88 retains its lament to the very end:

O LORD, why do you cast me off?
   Why do you hide your face from me?
Wretched and close to death from my youth up,
   I suffer your terrors; I am desperate.
Your wrath has swept over me;
   your dread assaults destroy me.
They surround me like a flood all day long;
   from all sides they close in on me.
You have caused friend and neighbor to shun me;
   my companions are in darkness.

(Ps 88:14-18, NRSV)

Perhaps the most famous biblical lament is Jesus' final cry from the cross in Mark and Matthew: "My God, my God, why have you abandoned me?" (Mark 15:34; Matt 27:46).[31] As in Hebrew Bible laments, God is accused, questioned, and blamed.[32] In his Gethsemane prayer (Mark 14:35-36) and—much more so—in his cry from the cross, Jesus models a response to suffering that is far from passive or resigned. Jesus laments his suffering, and protests God's abandonment—and perhaps complicity—in it.[33] Jesus ends his life accusing God of forsaking him. Discomfort with this accusation of divine abandonment is a likely reason why the author of Luke's Gospel omits Jesus' line, replacing it with: "Father, into your hands I commit my spirit" (Luke 23:46).[34] For many, Luke offers a more palatable Jesus who dies entrusting himself to divine care.

German theologian and pastor Dietrich Bonhoeffer's reflection on Jesus' cry of abandonment (Mark 15:34) approximates a kind of lament:

> God would have us know that we must live as men [and women] who manage our lives without [God]. The God who is with us is the God who forsakes us.... Before God and with God we live without God. God lets himself be pushed out of the world on to the cross. He is weak and powerless in the world, and that is precisely the way, the only way, in which [God] is with us and helps us.[35]

Bonhoeffer's claim—made amidst God's deafening silence during the Holocaust—might help explain the author's choices to oppose, critique, and seek to end Hitler's reign. If divine aid is impossible with a God who does not intervene, intervention requires that people offer themselves as instruments of divine aid. Lament can thus empower justice.[36]

Despite being affirmed in biblical texts and by theologians as a meaningful and liberating expression of faith, lament is largely absent in contemporary American churches.[37] This deficiency reflects a broader cultural distaste for lament, especially lament over divine abandonment. The creation of lament in American culture is largely the domain of artists such as Mary Doria Russell, whose novel *The Sparrow* is a narrativized lament, and Terrence Malick, whose films *The Tree of Life* (2011) and *To the Wonder* (2012) are cinematic laments.[38]

A notable lament in television appears in "Two Cathedrals," the season two finale of NBC's series *The West Wing*.[39] U.S. President Jed Bartlet (Martin Sheen) is a committed Catholic whose religious identity influences many of his personal and political decisions.[40] After attending a funeral for his secretary Mrs. Landingham—killed by a drunk driver while driving her very first car—he speaks to God while walking up the aisle in the National Cathedral:

> You're a son of a bitch, you know that? She bought her first new car and you hit her with a drunk driver. What, was that supposed to be funny? "You can't conceive, nor can I, the appalling strangeness of the mercy of God," says Graham Greene. I don't know whose ass he was kissing there 'cause I think you're just vindictive. What was Josh Lyman? A warning shot? That was my son. What did I ever do to yours but praise his glory and praise his name? There's a tropical storm that's gaining speed and power. They say we haven't had a storm this bad since you took out that tender ship of mine in the North Atlantic last year . . . sixty-eight crew. You know what a tender ship does? Fixes the other ships. Doesn't even carry guns. Just goes around, fixes the other ships and delivers the mail. That's all it can do.

He continues as he ascends the stairs to the Inner Sanctuary:

> *Gratias tibi ago, Domine.* Yes, I lied. It was a sin. I've committed many sins. Have I displeased you, you feckless thug? 3.8 million new jobs, that wasn't good? Bailed out Mexico, increased foreign trade, 30 million new acres of land for conservation, put Mendoza on the bench, we're not fighting a war, I've raised three children—that's not enough to buy me out of the doghouse?

Pausing at the top of the stairs, Bartley holds out his arms, and continues in Latin:

> *Haec credam a deo pio? A deo iusto? A deo scito? Cruciatus in crucem! Tuus in terra servus nuntius fui officium perfeci. Cruciatus in crucem. Eas in crucem!*

The translation of his Latin emphasizes his lament:

> Should I believe these acts are from a loving God? A just God? A discerning God? To hell with your torments! I am your servant on Earth; I have been

your messenger; I have carried out my duty. To hell with your torments. To hell with you!

Despite echoing biblical laments, many viewers were displeased with Bartlet's oration. In response to a rerun of this episode (on September 19, 2001), the special projects coordinator for the American Family Association filed an indecency complaint with the FCC.[41] Screenwriter Aaron Sorkin, perhaps with such criticisms in mind, commented, "It's never my intention to offend anybody or be reckless with things that are important to others. I meant the episode as a tribute to faith."[42] Acknowledging that Bartlet's faith commitment is a pervasive theme throughout the series, Sorkin pointed out, "but nowhere do I think [his faith] was more strongly expressed than in Two Cathedrals."[43]

Laments signify a more mature faith expression than praise or thanks in that they demand a divine response. Laments allow God to be "newly engaged in the crisis in a way that puts God at risk" because of the anticipation embedded in laments that God will end suffering.[44] Language of praise or thanks affirms who God is or what God has done, but it does not expect God to *do* anything. In calling God to show up, laments envision a God capable of acting to change circumstances. Hoping against hope, laments entail a certain trust in God that is lacking in expressions of praise or thanks.

FIGHT CLUB AS CINEMATIC LAMENT

Fight Club articulates a theological lament of divine abandonment and a sociopolitical lament of the American Dream. The film's most explicit lament comes from Tyler who pontificates while inflicting a chemical burn on the narrator's hand:

> Our fathers were our models for God. If our fathers bailed, what does that tell you about God? You have to consider the possibility that God does not like you. He never wanted you. In all probability, he hates you. This is not the worst thing that can happen. We don't need him! Fuck damnation, man! Fuck redemption! We are God's unwanted children? So be it!

At the heart of Tyler's lament—like that of Jesus in Mark 15:34—is an accusation of divine abandonment.[45]

This lament signals a crucial phase in the narrator's religious progression. For laments facilitate personal development by enabling the one lamenting to become individuated in one's relationship with God.[46] Through a lament a person can "take initiative with God and so develop over against God the ego-strength that is necessary for responsible faith."⁴⁷ No longer perceived as an omnipotent being who must be praised, God can be engaged in a genuine relationship characterized by authenticity and vulnerability. As Fromm argues, a relationship with God marked by slavish obedience springs from a lack of freedom, a need to please, and a refusal to become an adult.⁴⁸ Like children who are incapable of displaying anger toward or disappointment in their parents, people who only thank or praise God remain in an infantile faith stage.⁴⁹

The narrator's initial zombiesque ennui epitomizes the kind of passivity that thrives in the absence of lament. His journey from psycho-spiritual death to vitality coincides with his ability to lament his status as God's unwanted child.

Laments also address concrete political realities and power relationships embedded in social structures, seeking to redress inequities by redistributing power.⁵⁰ For this reason, those in authority have a vested interest in minimizing or eliminating expressions of lament. For lament insists that the current social order is fundamentally awry. Refusals to permit lament (and only allow expressions of praise or thanks) legitimate the status quo, thereby "sanction[ing] social control."⁵¹ When lament is silenced, a "theological monopoly is reinforced, docility and submissiveness are engendered, and the outcome in terms of social practice is to reinforce and consolidate the political-economic monopoly of the status quo."⁵² Lament can thus have potentially significant socio-political—in addition to theological and religious—ramifications.

The film's repudiation of the American Dream exemplifies these social dynamics of lament. For laments challenge "a system that does not deliver. That system is visible on earth and addressed in heaven with the passionate conviction that it can, must, and will be changed."⁵³ Propelling the narrator's conversion is his rejection of a cultural system that fails to deliver. Lament is a primary tool in his endeavor. In lamenting the bankruptcy and meaninglessness of the American Dream, the film subverts a cherished myth of American religion. The visual disturbance of the occasional shaking of the camera, the frequent use of grainy filters, and the periodic interspersing of single frames mirrors and intensifies the disorientation of the film's assault on a sacred cultural ethos.

The narrator laments God's abandonment and the American Dream, and each lament facilitates and contributes to his religious conversion; the theological and socio-political laments are vitally linked in his spiritual growth and his emancipation from the shackles of the American Dream's bereft promises. A supplemental *Fight Club* DVD advertising spot elucidates Tyler's sermon on divine abandonment; the narrator speaks directly to the camera:

> If you could be either God's worst enemy or nothing, which would you choose? We're the middle children in history. We have no special purpose or place. Unless we get God's attention we'll have no chance of damnation or redemption . . . Which is worse: hell or nothing? Burn the museums, wipe your ass with the Mona Lisa. At least this way *God will know your name.*[54]

The above clip (developed by Fincher to advertise the film, but rejected by Fox executives) is based on Tyler's speech in Palahniuk's novel:

> If you're male, and you're Christian and living in America, your father is your model for God. And if you never know your father, if your father bails out or dies or is never at home, what do you believe about God? What you end up doing . . . is you spend your life searching for a father and God . . . How Tyler saw it was that getting God's attention for being bad was better than getting no attention at all. Maybe because God's hate is better than His indifference. If you could be either God's worst enemy or nothing, which would you choose? . . . Unless we get God's attention, we have no hope of damnation or redemption. Which is worse, hell or nothing? Only if we're caught can we be saved. Burn the *Louvre,* . . . and wipe your ass with the Mona Lisa. This way at least, God would know our names . . . The lower you fall, the higher you'll fly. The farther you run, the more God wants you back. If the prodigal son had never left home . . . the fatted calf would still be alive.[55]

Tyler's speech illuminates some of the fundamental motives behind the violence of *Fight Club* and the antics of Project Mayhem. Tyler's anarchic behavior springs not from nihilism (*contra* many critics of the film), but rather from a desperate yearning for divine attention. He would rather be damned than neglected, for the cost of damnation is outweighed by the benefit of being known by God. Like any good (or poor) preacher, Tyler offers a proof text as a warrant: Jesus' parable of the "Prodigal Son" (Luke 15:11-32) suggests that the more destructive a person becomes, the more one can experience divine love. Self-destruction is, Tyler repeatedly insists, a prerequisite for authentic living. "Only after disaster," he claims, "can we be resurrected."

LAMENTING DEATH'S ERASURE

America is, however, collectively averse to the disaster necessary for resurrection. *Fight Club* faults American culture for demonizing death, exorcising failure, and silencing suffering. It is this American denial of human fragility that the film laments, protesting the American Dream's obsession with success, and its corresponding erasure of pain, grief, and anguish. *Fight Club* laments America's absence of lament.

There is therefore a decisive difference between lament in *Fight Club* and biblical texts. Whereas biblical laments are rooted in—and consist of pleas to remove—pain, *Fight Club*, anchored in an anesthetized culture, yearns for suffering. Biblical laments seek relief *from* agony; *Fight Club* finds relief *in* affliction, since such pain relieves and rescues one from a sedated life devoid of feeling and (therefore) meaning. *Fight Club* thus inverts the traditional aim of lament, and in doing so highlights the desperate and pervasive tendency in American culture to escape pain, and keep death at bay.[56]

Railing against a fundamental tenet of the American Dream, Tyler proposes that life is to be found not in success, but in descending from completion towards destruction. He repudiates the narrator's ethos, and declares, "So fuck off with your sofa units and Strinne green stripe patterns. I say: 'Never be complete.' I say: 'Stop being perfect.' I say: 'Let's evolve. Let the chips fall where they may.'" Unlike the narrator, Tyler views the destruction of his condo and possessions as a golden opportunity since it represents a first step toward embracing failure and (therefore) death. This departure from perfection accelerates when the narrator moves in with Tyler, who resides in a dilapidated house in a neglected part of town. The leaky ceilings, watery floors, and faucets spewing murky water symbolize the abrupt shift from completion toward deterioration.

Destruction is valuable because, among other things, it cultivates awareness of one's mortality. The narrator's religious conversion in the film is wedded to (and the result of) a series of steps which brings him ever nearer to death. This progression, foreign to an American culture that denies and despises death, provides the narrator with increasing psychological and spiritual fulfillment. Death becomes his doorway to true life.

The first stage of the narrator's conversion fittingly occurs after following a physician's suggestion: "You want to see *pain*? Swing by First Methodist Tuesday nights; see the guys with testicular cancer—that's *pain*." At this support group the narrator experiences a cultural taboo: lament. He witnesses searing turmoil as men vulnerably expose their grief over losses associated with their cancer. To the narrator, such uncensored outpourings of feelings are a foreign language, but he relishes the emotional intensity and is enlivened in turn. The communal lament invigorates and refreshes him. The night after his initial visit he sleeps peacefully for the first time in months. Enamored with this catharsis, he begins attending multiple support groups, for diseases he does not have. The raw agony shocks him out of his coma, and into life. His religious blossoming begins here, and he describes these groups as a nightly experience of dying, being born again, and resurrecting.[57] The support groups, however, only go so far.

The fight clubs that the narrator and Tyler launch are a second (and closer) step toward confronting death, for they provide the *physicality* of pain. A newfound heightened sense of aliveness pervades the entire fighting experience. All else pales in comparison to the ecstasy produced by the animalistic encounters in which men discover what they are made of and how much pain they can tolerate.

Fight club does for the flesh what the support groups do for the heart. For a central ethos of fight club—far from hurting others—is a willingness to receive and embrace pain in one's own body. Tyler's first homework assignment for fight club members is to pick a fight with a stranger *and lose*. One turns not merely one's cheek but one's entire body, offering it as a target for physical assault. Tyler models this kind of masochism when he repeatedly lets Lou beat his face to a pulp, rather than let him shut down their club. The narrator takes this reception of physical pain a step further by beating himself senseless in an effort to blackmail his supervisor. Amidst the film's flurry of violence—repellent to many viewers—is a commitment to a certain kind of non-violence toward others.

This embrace of physical pain is essential for the narrator's development. The genesis of fight club occurs when Tyler tells him, "I want you to do me a favor: I want you to hit me as hard as you can." Thus begins a combat ritual between the two; other men later notice and join in, birthing fight club. Viewers realize later that in these early fights, the narrator is fighting himself and not Tyler. One might say that the first rule of fight club is to hurt yourself and not others. Masochism, not sadism, is the cardinal virtue. This value for self-inflicted pain underlies the film's condemnation of the narrator's relentless pummeling of Angel Face (Jared Leto).

Tyler's chemical burn ceremony is a key rite of passage in the narrator's embrace of pain and acceptance of his own mortality. During the burn ritual—yet another self-inflicted wound—Tyler expounds on his philosophy regarding pain.[58] After pouring lye on the narrator's hand, he chastises him for trying to escape the pain through meditation:

> Stay with the pain; don't shut this out.... Without pain, without sacrifice we would have nothing.... *This* is your pain; *this* is your burning hand, it's right here.... Don't deal with it the way those dead people do![59] ... This is the greatest moment of your life, man, and you're off somewhere missing it!

2.2 Chemical Burn

Tyler roots the narrator's inability to remain in his pain with his reluctance to accept his own death: "First you have to give up; first you have to know—not fear, *know*—that someday *you're going to die*."[60] The pain's acute intensity is a visceral reminder of death's inevitability, and "staying with" the pain is a way of facing one's inevitable demise. The narrator finally relents, allowing himself to be still, even as the flesh of his hand sizzles and smokes. Tyler's subsequent quip ("It's only after we've lost everything that we're free to do anything") intimates that accepting physical pain is an integral step toward facing one's death, and that this journey engenders freedom. After the narrator collapses on the floor, Tyler affirms, "Congratulations, you're one step closer to hitting bottom."

Accepting physical pain and confronting one's mortality inverts the prevailing American propensity to avoid suffering and death. As author Bret Easton Ellis notes, the film "rages against the hypocrisy of a society that continually promises us the impossible: fame, beauty, wealth, immortality, life without pain."[61] For Tyler, evading suffering and death is a sign that one is already dead. Tyler echoes a central argument in the biblical text Qoheleth (Ecclesiastes), that meaningful living depends on one's ability to come to terms with death.[62] As the narrator notes in the novel (prior to the lye burn):

> Tyler says I'm nowhere near hitting the bottom, yet. And if I don't fall all the way, I can't be saved. Jesus did it with his crucifixion thing. I shouldn't just abandon money and property and knowledge. . . . I should run from self-improvement, and I should be running toward disaster.[63]

The narrator rushes headlong into the paradoxical kind of enhanced life that results from self-destruction. In losing his life, he saves it.

Tyler wants people to grapple with their inevitable death because he believes that death's nearness will lead them to consider matters of existential significance, and that they will reorient their lives in light of this epiphany. He bewails how the omnipresent bombardment of entertainment precludes dwelling on such important matters. During a car ride, he intentionally veers into the oncoming lane of traffic, and removes his hand from the steering wheel. He asks two passengers in the back what they wish they would have done before dying. After they reply ("Paint a self-portrait," "Build a house"), Tyler asks the narrator, "And you?" Fearful of hitting oncoming cars, he responds ("I don't know; nothing, nothing!") and quickly seizes the steering wheel. Tyler, however, is insistent: "You have to know the answer to this question: If you were to die right now, how would you feel about your life?" "I don't know," the narrator responds angrily, "I wouldn't feel anything good about my life; is that what you want to hear me say?" Tyler rejects his answer and his effort to grab the steering wheel: "Not good enough."

For Tyler, death's proximity augments the essential and relativizes the trivial. By steering into oncoming traffic, he embodies his proposition, shifting the question about what one would like to do before dying from the hypothetical to the concrete and immediate present. For two passengers, contemplating death enables quick consideration of what matters most (painting, building a house). The narrator fails to articulate what is most important to him, and his inability is bound to a refusal to let go of control (literally and figuratively) and risk embracing his demise. Tyler registers his dismay when the narrator again grips the wheel after the car careens unguided down the highway:

> Look at you! Look at you! You're fucking pathetic! Why do you think I blew up your condo? . . . Hitting bottom isn't a weekend retreat; it's not a goddamn seminar. *Stop trying to control everything, and just let go! Let go!*

Finally relenting, the narrator releases the wheel, leading the car—as Tyler accelerates—to crash into a parked car, and tumble down an embankment. After the crash, Tyler laughs and exclaims, "Goddamn! We've just had a *near-life* experience."

Since facing death engenders meaningful living, efforts to seize control and stave off one's death hinder such activity. Self-protection only insulates a person from fully living. Tyler's question about blowing up the narrator's condo suggests, moreover, that acquiring material possessions is a primary hindrance to such meaningful living, and a means of maintaining an illusory sense of control over life (and death). American culture fosters a denial of death by encouraging the illusion that consumption is a means of exerting control over one's destiny. People buy the lie that they can purchase their way out of mortality.

One of Tyler's "homework assignments" illustrates his philosophy regarding the intimate link between facing death and living meaningfully. At gunpoint, Tyler forces an employee out of a liquor store, and onto his knees in a parking lot. Pointing the gun at his head, Tyler takes the man's wallet and reads his license. Tyler announces, "Raymond, you're going to die." Already flustered, Raymond begins sobbing. Noticing an expired community college ID in the wallet, Tyler asks Raymond what he studied. Dissatisfied with Raymond's vague replies, Tyler cocks the gun, frightening Raymond even more, and repeats himself: "The question, Raymond, is what did you want to be?" Raymond finally sputters, "Veterinarian. Veterinarian." When Tyler notes that this would require more schooling, Raymond agrees, muttering, "Too much school." "Would you rather be dead?" Tyler retorts. "Would you rather die, here, on your knees, in the back of a convenience store?" Tyler uncocks the gun, places it in his waistband, and declares, "I'm keeping your license; I'm going to check in on you. I know where you live. If you're not on your way to becoming a veterinarian in six weeks, you will be dead." Tyler flips his wallet on the ground in front of a crying Raymond, and tells him to run home.

Although many viewers share the narrator's disgust with this episode, Tyler sees his deed as salvific: "Tomorrow will be the most beautiful day of Raymond K. Hessel's life. His breakfast will taste better than any meal you or I have ever tasted." Confronting death instills a genuine gratitude that is rooted in recognizing life's frailty. As the narrator reflects on this incident (and notices there were no bullets in the gun), he seems swayed by Tyler's logic: "You had to give it to him. He had a plan, and it started to make sense, in a Tyler sort of way. No fear. No distractions. The ability to let that which does not matter, truly slide."

In compelling Raymond and the narrator to face death and (thereby) come to terms with their own mortality, Tyler militates against an American culture whose dominant neurosis—as Becker diagnosed—is its denial of death. *Fight Club* relentlessly assaults this social illness by reminding viewers of their own future death. As the narrator oft notes, "On a long enough time line, the survival rate for everyone drops to zero." The irony of this American disavowal of death is that it produces—as the narrator illustrates at the film's outset—spiritual sterility. Tyler's counterintuitive insight is that meaningful living is predicated upon a twinned willingness to draw near to death and embrace one's inevitable expiration. Doing so awakens one to matters of personal and social significance, and propels one toward a life of purpose. Tyler thus exposes people to death, often creatively, such as when he replaces "Emergency Procedure" cards in airplanes (depicting unperturbed passengers placidly putting on oxygen masks) with terrifying images of passengers screaming in panic as the plane crashes and bursts into flames.

In the final phase of his development, the narrator comes as close to death as possible: he places a gun in his mouth and pulls the trigger. Having discovered that Tyler exists only in his own psyche, he recognizes he can put an end to Tyler by destroying himself. With this attempted suicide, the narrator completes his path toward self-destruction. In erasing Tyler he embraces Tyler's ethos of wooing death. This proximity to death represents the final step of his psycho-spiritual growth, which ultimately and ironically requires that he kill the primary catalyst of his own religious awakening.

Fight Club acknowledges that self-inflicted violence may (inevitably?) erupt into harm against others. Acts by Project Mayhem are not limited to vandalism (smashing VW Beetles, sabotaging art pieces), but also include threatening a police chief with castration, and the death of club member Robert Paulson. It is thus significant that the narrator opts at the end of the film to return to the original vision of acceptable violence, that which is directed toward oneself. He ultimately recognizes that his worst enemy lurks within the recesses of his psyche.

RELATIONAL ALIENATION AND INTIMACY

Fight Club not only laments the religious bankruptcy of the American Dream, but also identifies alternative sources of existential meaning. The film both *de*constructs and *re*constructs; it *dis*orients and *re*orients. In addition to death and destruction, the film locates meaning in personal relationship and economic liberation.

The American Dream's preoccupation with material acquisition not only shields the narrator from death and (therefore) meaningful living, but also alienates him from personal relationships. In the beginning of the film such relationships are nonexistent. This relational vacuum is a central thread in many of Palahniuk's works. As he explains in the opening sentence of *Non-Fiction*: "If you haven't already noticed, all my books are about a lonely person looking for some way to connect with other people. In a way, that is *the opposite of the American Dream . . .*" Palahniuk cites Howard Hughes and William Randolph Hearst as epitomizing the American yearning to find "an environment you can control, free from conflict and pain. Where you rule." Such a life is not limited to the ultrawealthy: "Whether it's a ranch in Montana or a basement apartment with ten thousand DVDs and high-speed Internet access, it never fails. We get there, and we're alone. And we're lonely."[64] Palahniuk refers to "the narrator in his *Fight Club* condo" as an example of someone who becomes "miserable enough" to venture out "back into the larger world."[65]

Venturing out leads the narrator to Marla Singer (Helena Bonham Carter). Aside from his own split psyche, the narrator's most significant and complex relationship is with Marla. From the outset he detests her because she mirrors his own hypocrisy. Like him, she attends multiple terminal illness support groups for diseases she does not have. Her pretense threatens his enjoyment of these groups because she exposes his own fraud: "Marla, the big tourist. Her lie reflected my lie." Unable to bear her reflection of his own duplicity, he decides they will divide up the support groups so he can avoid her. He thus rejects an opportunity for intimacy and connection when faced with a woman who reinforces his own weakness.

His fear of relational intimacy quickens the emergence of Tyler. In what may be the film's most pivotal scene, the narrator calls Marla from a payphone after discovering that his condo exploded. When she answers, he is speechless and hangs up. At this point he makes a crucial decision: he calls Tyler. Tyler does not answer, but as the narrator leaves the pay phone, the phone rings. He picks it up, and Tyler is on the other line. This scene is the first time he deliberately and consciously chooses to pursue a relationship with a personality existing only in his own psyche.[66] Several cinematic devices heighten the scene's significance: introducing a somber sound, slowing the camera speed, and zooming in on the phone and the narrator immediately before he calls Tyler. The psychic damage to the narrator caused by choosing to call Tyler is symbolized in the image of the narrator's condo exploding that plays on the screen right before he hangs up on Marla. His psychosis has reached a destructive tipping point that induces the emergence of a separate personality.

The narrator's pursuit and creation of Tyler occurs at the precise moment— and because—he is unwilling to engage with Marla, an *actual* human being. Cocooning himself in his Ikea-laden apartment has stunted his capacity for relational intimacy. He can only achieve sexual intimacy with Marla as his alter ego Tyler. Prior to calling Tyler in the phone booth, the narrator's voiceover remarks, "If you ask me now, I couldn't tell you why I called him." But viewers can offer an explanation: he pursues (and therefore creates) Tyler in order to avoid intimacy with Marla. Another indication of this scene's crucial nature is the novel's penultimate page, when the narrator remarks upon this moment with poignant regret:

> And if there were a telephone in Heaven, I would call Marla from Heaven and the moment she says, "Hello," I wouldn't hang up. I'd say, "Hi. What's happening? Tell me every little thing."[67]

The narrator's anxious ambivalence regarding intimacy with Marla underscores the importance of his final choices. Recognizing how much danger she is in, he tries to protect her by putting her on a bus out of town. After she is captured, he makes a far more desperate choice to save her. By shooting himself, he unambiguously chooses—for the first time—Marla over Tyler. It is significant that the film's final (well, penultimate) image shows the narrator and Marla holding hands as they watch credit card buildings across Los Angeles explode and crumble. The narrator finally, albeit for a brief sliver of a moment, connects with Marla as his genuine self. Their connection illustrates one of Palahniuk's recurring themes: "I have been called a nihilist, but I would describe myself as a romantic. I'm always looking for narratives that bring people together. I like my books to have a wedding at the end, rather than a death."[68]

2.3 Ground Zero

ECONOMIC LIBERATION

Threaded throughout Ecclesiastes is an argument (repeated seven times) that enjoyment is the optimal experience for human beings. There is, the text claims, "nothing better" a person can do than enjoy food and drink. Like *Fight Club*, Ecclesiastes insists on the importance of facing death as the primary means toward enjoyment. The former enables the latter. Yet for *Fight Club*, enjoyment is not nearly good enough. The film maintains, on the contrary, that enjoyment is a low rung on the existential ladder of meaningful living, and even a potential impediment in this journey.

Tyler seeks psychic liberation from his culture's insistence—ubiquitous in advertising—on equating personal identity with monetary status. Such liberation begins with the narrator's destruction of his condo and personal possessions, the chief signifiers of his identity (*"What kind of dining set defines me as a person?"*). Jobs, salaries, and other signs of economic status are invisible in fight clubs, and therefore not used to differentiate one man from another. As Tyler declares, while speaking directly to the camera (and therefore the viewer): "You are not your job. You are not how much money you have in the bank. You're not the car you drive. You are not the contents of your wallet. You're not your fucking khakis."[69] This effort to eliminate economic barriers is clear in the novel: "another new fight club rule is that fight club will always be free. It will never cost to get in. . . . We want you, not your money."[70]

The fight clubs eliminate socio-economic hierarchies, and Project Mayhem is Tyler's vehicle for applying this financial parity to society at large. Manifest in the evolution of fight clubs into Project Mayhem is a transition from personal to socio-political lament; acts of vandalism (targeting advertisers and consumer culture icons) culminate in an effort to establish economic equality by obliterating all monetary debt. To achieve this end, Tyler plans (and ultimately succeeds) in blowing up buildings of credit card companies. *Fight Club's* vision of redemption is thus both personal and social. The film's lament of the American Dream's spiritual emptiness animates and catalyzes an organized resistance that seeks to reconstruct and level the economic playing field. The narrator's condo and possessions were destroyed to free him from personal enslavement to possessions. Demolishing credit card buildings is meant to liberate an entire society from systemic slavery.

CRAFTING A NEW REALITY

Viewers respond passionately and viscerally to *Fight Club* because the film assaults a sacred American myth. This religious myth consists in the belief that personal fulfillment is found in acquiring a financially sound and respectable career, a stable paycheck, and the proper possessions (home, furniture, automobile, etc.). The dissociation of the narrator's psyche reflects the psychic trauma associated with rejecting a sacred cultural ethos, one which functions as a vehicle of personal and communal salvation. The film more than hints at this psychosis in the opening credit sequence, which plays over a camera shot emerging from the neural connections in the narrator's brain.

As a narrativized lament, *Fight Club* suggests that there is an integral connection between the spiritual bankruptcy of the American Dream and God's abandonment of people, that perhaps the American Dream and God's presence are incompatible, and that lament is a fitting response to this divine neglect. Lament insists that things are not right as they are, and demands a radical change. *Fight Club* diagnoses the illnesses of the American Dream, and prescribes alternatives to this neurosis.

In the same way that Marla mirrors the narrator, the film images American culture. Many Americans who peer into the mirror of *Fight Club* do not like what they see, neither what the film critiques as meaningless, nor what it proposes as meaningful. This critique and proposal explains why the film resonates so powerfully with its fans. For many, the film confirms their experience of the American Dream as something that removes them from humanity, and articulates their own desperate longing to find spiritual vitality elsewhere. *Fight Club* imagines that people can make radical choices to construct and create meaning in an otherwise meaningless culture. Palahniuk hints at a similar notion:

> All that's left is a book, and now a movie, a funny, exciting movie. A wild, excellent movie. What for other people will be a whiplash carnival ride, for my friends and me, is a nostalgic scrapbook. A reminder. Amazing reassuring proof that our anger, our disappointment, our striving and resentment unite us with each other, and now with the world. What's left is the proof we can create reality.[71]

✳ 3 ✳

AMERICAN BEAUTY
Death as Divine Beauty

I really love storytelling, and I love the stories as they reveal themselves.
It's an incredibly nourishing process, it's probably the closest I come to
having a religion.

—Alan Ball, screenwriter of *American Beauty*[1]

We would rather be ruined than changed. We would rather die in our
dread than climb the cross of the moment and let our illusions die.

—W. H. Auden[2]

All along I thought I was learning how to take
How to bend not how to break
How to live not how to cry
But really I've been learning how to die
I've been learning how to die.

—Jon Foreman[3]

*A*merican Beauty (d. Sam Mendes, 1999) joins *Fight Club* in railing against the religious toxicity of the American Dream.[4] American culture's spiritual failure is chiefly conveyed through the main character's religious journey. Like *Fight Club's* narrator, Lester Burnham (Kevin Spacey) suffers from a premature, internal death. Preceding his physical death is a more tragic collapse of his spirit. He introduces himself in a voiceover:

"This is my life: I'm 42 years old. In less than a year, I'll be dead. Of course, I don't know that yet. And in a way, *I'm dead already*."[5]

Every introductory scene portrays Lester's joyless existence. While masturbating in the shower his melancholic voiceover confesses, "This will be the high point of my day. It's all downhill from here." His wife Carolyn (Annette Bening) regards Lester with contempt, staring at him with disdain while he picks up the contents of his briefcase that he spilled all over the walkway.[6] His frequent voiceovers—a throwback to *Sunset Blvd.* (also narrated by a dead character)—accentuate his relational isolation.[7]

Lester's resignation from life is depicted in sleeping—crumpled in a corner of the back seat, his hand crammed against his face—while Carolyn drives him to work. This visual metaphor of his acquiescence (and Carolyn's control) recurs later; Lester is a passenger (and Carolyn drives) when they are in a vehicle. Content to let another drive (literally and metaphorically), he is a sleeping passenger through life. As with Neo in *The Matrix* and *Fight Club*'s narrator, sleep is a primary symbol for the internal deadness of the main character.

Lester is "exhibit A" for Oscar Wilde's claim: "To live is the rarest thing in the world. Most people exist, that is all."[8] Existing is even a stretch for Lester. He describes the past twenty years of his life as a "coma." As he sleeps in the back seat, his voiceover summarizes his lack of existence:

> Both my wife and daughter think I'm this gigantic loser, and they're right. I have lost something. I'm not exactly sure what it is, but I know I didn't always feel this . . . *sedated*. But you know what, it's never too late to get it back.

Lester's final line above articulates a central thesis of the film: it *is* possible to recover a meaningful life that has been lost. Supporting this optimism is the upward camera tilt during this last line to the blue sky. That something has been lost is clear. About Carolyn he remarks, "She wasn't always like this; she used to be happy; we used to be happy." Far from a fixed constant, her discontent and Lester's misery are a departure from a previous state of joy. Lester's distance with his daughter is similarly a devolvement from a prior period of happiness ("Janie, what happened? We used to be pals"). Substantiating Lester's claim is the close up shot of a family photograph on the kitchen counter in which he, Carolyn, and Jane all appear to be having an authentically delightful time.[9] The film proposes that reliving such joy is possible, and it proceeds to diagnose the precise illness facing Lester and prescribe a path to spiritual and relational recovery.

THE PRISON OF THE AMERICAN DREAM

The film indicts the American Dream as the chief culprit responsible for choking Lester's spiritual vitality, and sabotaging his family relationships. Lester has acquired essential ingredients of the American Dream: a fairly secure job and a steady salary; a picturesque suburban house; a family. The latter makes him more firmly ensconced in the American Dream than *Fight Club*'s narrator. Yet despite (or because of?) these elements he finds himself imprisoned in a meaningless life. If the film is, as critic Roger Ebert remarks, a "story of [Lester's] rebellion," the American Dream is his principal target.[10]

Four introductory scenes show Lester as a prisoner: wedged in the shower; watching Carolyn from behind a window with bars; cramped in the car's back seat; and sitting in his cubicle. In each case he is trapped in a small space; in two he is depicted behind "bars." Mendes calls the shower scene the "first of a series of jail cells," and comments similarly about the three subsequent scenes.[11] Lester's cubicle is the most explicit; reflected in a computer monitor with a series of vertical bars, his face appears in a virtual prison.[12] Lester is entrapped in the three main pillars of the American Dream: home, family, and career.[13]

3.1 Lester Imprisoned

Each area diminishes Lester's humanity and saps his spirituality. His superficial job of selling advertising not only lacks purpose, it is spiritually harmful. The color grey that dominates the carpet, cubicles, walls, and columns reflects his job's lifelessness. When informed about a new requirement that every employee detail their contributions, Lester protests about a manager who racked up $50,000 on a company credit card to pay for a prostitute and her three-month hotel stay. His outrage at such hypocrisy points to a moral and ethical abyss at the heart of his workplace. When Carolyn insists that he comply with the new requirement, he erupts, "All right, let's just sell our souls and work for Satan because it's more convenient that way!" Although exaggerated, his outburst indicts a system whose price for conformity is the sacrifice of one's soul. His career is a Faustian bargain. Like *Fight Club*'s narrator—who places a monetary value on human life—Lester loses his soul in the American workplace.[14]

Lester's home is a prison that suffocates his authentic expression and spiritual vitality. He even claims that Carolyn would prefer that he be a "fucking prisoner." The first of two dinner scenes is preceded by shots of traditional stock family photographs, canned pictures that set the stage for the emotional distance and relational coldness at mealtime.[15] The bland music and exquisitely decorated table and dining room mask (and compensate for?) a lack of vulnerability and emotional intimacy. Underscoring this relational gulf is the physical distance between Lester, Carolyn, and Jane.[16] Conversations are spartan and forced, with sarcasm and bitterness the default modes of expression. The homage to *Ordinary People* (d. Redford, 1980) in the initial wide-shot of the dinner table anticipates some of this dysfunction.

AWAKENING (AND AROUSED) FROM DEATH TO LIFE

Eroticism—to the dismay of many viewers—is the first catalyst in Lester's exodus from spiritual death. A high school cheerleading routine ("On Broadway") is transformed into the first of four sexual fantasies featuring his daughter's high school friend, Angela Hayes (Mena Suvari). From this point on, Lester is a new man. Lying in bed that night, he smiles and watches spellbound as an image of Angela waves provocatively to him from the ceiling. "It's the weirdest thing, I feel like I've been in a coma for about twenty years. And I'm just now waking up . . . Spec-tac-ular!" Fantasizing arouses Lester from his sedation; Angela is the first signal that it is indeed "not too late to get it back."

Lester's sexual fantasies—befitting the nature of his journey—have a distinctly religious texture. A fantasy of Angela in the bathtub is suffused with religious imagery. The tub is centered and elevated on an altar-like dais, and light streams through the windows, evoking an antique European church. Steam fills the frame, expanding the sense of mystery.[17] The finishing touch is Lester's kneeling before the tub. His posture of veneration fits Ball's original vision: "Lester kneels by the bathtub like a man in church."[18] Mendes built the set so that it would "feel almost *like a religious altar*."[19] The religious qual-ity of this fantasy weds the sacred and the erotic, a pairing whose potential disturbance is exacerbated by the age and power differential between Lester and Angela.

Another controversial catalyst in Lester's development arrives in his drug-peddling neighbor, Ricky Fitts (Wes Bentley). When Ricky unabashedly smokes pot in front of his employer and abruptly quits his job, Lester stands in awe: "I think you just became my personal hero." Ricky models for Lester a foreign but appealing brand of honesty.

Lester's new lifestyle (running, weightlifting, smoking pot, listening to older music, fantasizing about Angela) is characterized by actualizing his desires, with little concern for the consequences. He adopts a blunt candor and—coupled with his sexual awakening—wakes from his coma into a new persona. Both these transformations spur conflict with Carolyn. When she accuses him one night of masturbating, he admits it. When she then exclaims she's unwilling to live in such a marriage, he insists the "new Lester" will satisfy himself sexually since she has been unhelpful in that department. When she threatens divorce, he retorts that he would be entitled to half her earnings. He ends his speech abruptly: "So, turn out the light when you come to bed. OK?" A close-up on his face as he turns and tucks himself in shows a slowly widening grin.

This moment marks a breakthrough; it is the first time he is this frank with Carolyn, and he relishes his new honesty.[20] His following voiceover captures his reborn self: "It's a great thing when you realize you still have the ability to surprise yourself. Makes you wonder what else you can do that you've forgot-ten about." Lester's honesty with Carolyn reaches a peak during the family's second dinner scene. In sharp contrast to the first dinner, Lester holds a beer, and his shirt is unbuttoned.[21] He ends the meal by standing up and throwing a plate of asparagus that smashes against the wall. Giving full vent to his anger represents a radical shift from the first dinner in which he sheepishly abided by Carolyn's direction. No longer content to be a mere passenger, Lester has taken hold of the wheel and is steering his own course.[22]

Physicality (exercise and sexuality) is central to his awakening. Wanting to impress Angela launches him on an exercise regimen of lifting weights and (so he can "look good naked") jogging. His road to salvation is paved with sen-suality; Foucault's quip ("the soul is the prison of the body") does not apply to him.[23] He even smiles while running on the last day of his life.[24]

Lester's development toward spiritual vitality requires escaping from certain shackles of the American Dream.[25] He unleashes his unbridled honesty at his workplace, evident in his self-assessment which Brad reads aloud to Lester:

> BRAD: My job consists of basically masking my contempt for the assholes in charge, and, at least once a day, retiring to the men's room so I can jerk off while I fantasize about a life that doesn't so closely resemble hell.
>
> BRAD: You obviously have no interest in saving yourself.
>
> LESTER: Brad, for fourteen years I've been a whore for the advertising industry. The only way I could save myself now is if I start firebombing.

Demanding a one-year salary with benefits, Lester blackmails Brad, threatens to divulge the company's prostitution expense, and fabricates a claim of sexual harassment. When Brad protests ("Man, you are one twisted fuck"), Lester counters, "Nope, I'm just an ordinary guy with nothing to lose."

Lester's celebratory glide through the office (thrusting his arm forward, joyfully uttering, "Yeah!") parallels the scene in *Fight Club* when the narrator quits his job, successfully blackmails his boss, and triumphantly exits the office. Underlying both sequences is a wish not only to rebel against workplace authority structures, but also to employ unethical tactics to procure some modicum of financial freedom. These blackmail strategies undercut the amoral practices of the workplace. Lester describes himself as a prostitute for an industry whose job consists of creating and maintaining images. He sees his job as so despicable that only acts of violence ("firebombing") can redeem him.

Brad and Lester's use of "salvation" language ("saving yourself" / "save myself") alludes to a religious character of the workplace. Within the American Dream one's career serves as a primary vehicle of existential salvation, in that it holds the possibility and promise of providing financial security and a sense of meaning or purpose. Yet Lester's career—like the *Fight Club* narrator's—is spiritually toxic. Both characters find redemption in reversing the trajectory of success and descending the socio-economic ladder. For Lester it is getting a job flipping burgers and working the counter at Mr. Smiley's, a fast-food joint. Such downward mobility (tinged with nostalgia in Lester's case) is integral to his spiritual growth since it frees him from the American obsession (epitomized by Carolyn) with financial and career success.

LOOKING CLOSER: ILLUSIONS OF BEAUTY

American Beauty's official tagline—displayed overtly on the DVD cover and subtly hidden among the many signs in Lester's cubicle—is *"Look Closer."* This line invites viewers to adopt a posture of attentiveness, for little is as it appears. Veneers obstruct multiple truths whose discovery requires a willingness to suspend one's initial judgment and to see in potentially provocative ways. On one level, the film encourages its audience to look closer at characters, and not settle for initial (and superficial) impressions. Over a dozen reflections of characters in mirrors or windows signal the need to contemplate these characters more carefully.[26] The characters themselves are summoned to this same careful reflection, but only some respond accordingly.[27]

3.2 Look Closer

"Looking closer" also involves reexamining deeply ingrained cultural assumptions about what constitutes beauty and where beauty resides. The film rejects privileging beauty in picturesque homes, the stereotypical (blond and blue-eyed) cheerleader, or red roses. A recurring image throughout the film, red roses appear in about seventeen scenes. Their significance is evident in Ball's original title for the film: *American Rose.* Almost every scene with roses is associated with either Carolyn or Angela, and with both women roses signify illusions.

The prevalence of roses in and around the Burnham home symbolizes the mirage of the family as idyllic and Rockwellesque. This façade is shattered (literally) during the dinner scenes—at which roses are featured as table centerpieces—and in two other conflicts between Carolyn and Lester.[28]

Roses consistently emphasize the illusory quality of Carolyn's projection of success, suggesting, on the contrary, the toxic nature of her efforts to maintain control.

Carolyn's introduction is immediately preceded by an image of a single red rose filling the entire screen. She cuts the rose, holds it up, and admires it reverently. Her front yard is ringed with red roses, and her neighbor Jim, astonished at their beauty, inquires how she gets them to flourish. Roses are a fixture inside her home, where bouquets are prominently displayed on the dining room and kitchen tables. Roses are Carolyn's consistent aesthetic accessory in her pursuit and maintenance of an unblemished ideal of perfection. "As you know," she tells Lester, "my business is selling an image, and part of my job is to live that image." She embodies that image in her inerrant physical appearance and immaculately manicured "Home and Garden" lawn. Her sole comment to her next-door neighbor Jim is about his fashion selection ("I *love* your tie—that color!"). Appearance is everything, and it wearies Lester: "Man, I get exhausted just watching her."

The rose's symbolism is on display during Carolyn's depressing failure to sell a home. Cleaning furiously and fastidiously, she repeats a mantra four times: "I will sell this house today!" A finishing touch is a small bouquet of roses on a table in the house's entrance. Yet every potential buyer is turned off by the house's derelict condition. The incongruence between Carolyn's description of the house and its more decrepit reality exemplifies her perennial commitment to selling an image of success. After failing to sell the house, she slumps against a wall and begins crying. She suddenly stomps her foot, slaps herself in the face, and demands, "Shut up! Stop it, you weak, you baby! Shut up! Shut up! Shut up!" She dries her tears off her face, tries to rearrange her makeup, and exits the house.

Like the American Dream she worships, success is the sole option Carolyn envisions, and when it fails to materialize her only coping mechanisms are destructive. Failure is the one reality with which she cannot cope. Looking closer at Carolyn reveals the hidden psychic turmoil underlying her (and American culture's) unfettered dedication to an image of beauty and success. Carolyn's commitment to maintaining an image of success at all times is toxic to those around her. Her daughter Jane's insecure body image is fueled by Carolyn's rigorous expectations. Seeing Jane one morning, Carolyn barks, "Jane, honey, are you *trying* to look unattractive?" When Jane (Thora Birch) shrugs, "Yes," Carolyn barks back, "Congratulations, you've succeeded admirably!"

If projecting an image of success were incarnated it would take the form of Buddy Kane (Peter Gallagher). The self-proclaimed "Real Estate King," Buddy is handsome and debonair. Exuding confidence and success, he dresses impressively, has a young, blond trophy wife, and drives a Jaguar with the license plate "R. E. King." His face is plastered on real estate advertisements across the city. He is all that Carolyn craves, and everything that Lester is not. Buddy's own philosophy resonates with Carolyn: "Well, call me crazy, but it is my philosophy that in order to be successful, one must project an image of success *at all times*." Buddy *lives* her core value. Carolyn is instantly smitten; Ball describes her at this point as "enraptured, like a fervent Christian who's just come face to face with Jesus."[29]

Carolyn's fling with Buddy—consummated in a motel—provides her with a similar kind of erotic boost that Lester receives from his fantasies. Her ecstasy reaches its zenith while she drives home singing aloud to Bobby Darin's "Don't Rain on My Parade." Paralleling Lester's rendition of "American Woman," this scene reveals a newly released Carolyn who relishes her personal empowerment and independent agency.

The film indicts America's obsession with image as a hindrance to authentic intimacy. Carolyn's fetish for maintaining appearances mars a potentially erotic and intimate moment with Lester. When he initiates physically by kissing her on the couch, her pleasure gives way to alarm when she notices his beer is perched precariously over the sofa. Her abrupt shift in tone ("Lester, you're gonna spill beer on the couch!") instantly kills the erotic mood.

> LESTER: So what? It's just a couch.
> CAROLYN: This is a $4,000 sofa upholstered in Italian silk! This is *not* just a couch.

Picking up the pillow, Lester slams it down, each time punctuating one of his four words: "IT'S JUST A COUCH!" Exasperated, he points around at the living room furnishings: "This isn't life. This is just stuff, and it's become more important to you than living. Well, honey, that's just nuts."

Their inability to sustain an intimate connection is all the more tragic given their proximity to a genuinely erotic moment. Fueling their potential romance is the sexual awakening each enjoys in their respective journeys. Sex with Buddy relaxes Carolyn, and Lester's fantasies enliven him. Sexuality renews both of them into more joyful versions of themselves. Yet they fail to channel this newfound energy into their marriage. Carolyn's insistence on controlling her aesthetic environment prohibits pleasure with Lester. Like the *Fight Club* narrator—and despite her claim ("Joyless? I'm not joyless . . . *There's plenty of joy in my life*")—rooting her identity in possessions stymies relational and sexual intimacy. Contrary to his homiletic insistence, Lester does not register how purchasing his dream car also appears to elevate "stuff" over "living."[30] Regardless, Lester and Carolyn are unable to re-kindle their previous happiness. It appears—at least with Carolyn—that Lester may not be able to "get it back."

LOOKING BEYOND THE FANTASY

Red roses are regularly associated with Angela, and they are a prominent fixture in Lester's four fantasies. In the first, Angela unzips her cheerleading top to reveal a flood of rose petals emanating from her bosom. In the second, a naked Angela is conspicuously covered in red rose petals which fill up the entire ceiling and slowly descend upon Lester. After he kisses Angela in the third fantasy, he puts his fingers to his lips and slowly removes a single red rose petal from his mouth. In his fourth and final fantasy, Lester finds Angela in a bathtub with red rose petals covering the top of the water, again conspicuously hiding her genitals. On an obvious level, these roses symbolize erotic stimulation and sexual enticement.[31]

The omnipresence of rose petals also signifies the fictive quality of Lester's fantasies. As with Carolyn, the roses accompanying Angela indicate a façade. The only CGI techniques employed in the film are for these fantasy sequences involving roses. In these scenes the method *is* the meaning; form is function. The *how* is a charade, and not only because of the use of CGI.

Sam Mendes and cinematographer Conrad Hall filmed the fantasies in ways that heighten their illusive quality. Mendes and Hall employ a "jump cutting" technique in which a camera shot rapidly replays the previous shot, but from a different angle and at a different speed. In the first fantasy, the camera "jump cuts" on Angela's hands caressing her body during her cheerleading routine. The same technique is used in the third fantasy when she reaches her hand toward the refrigerator, brushing up against Lester. The camera cuts three times to replay (at three different frames per second: 24fps, 48fps, and 72fps) the brushing of her hand on Lester's arm and shoulder. The rapid jump cuts enhance the scene's eroticism by making it a performance, for Lester and the audience. Contributing to the hypnotic nature of the fantasies are the jazzy syncopated rhythms playing during these jump cuts. As with the CGI, these jump-cutting techniques and attendant music are only used during these fantasy sequences. They enrich the depiction of Angela as an incarnate hallucinogenic who awakens and seduces Lester from his sedated stupor.

These fantasies enliven Lester, but the Angela who stars in them is a fabrication—created *imago Lester*—existing solely to perform for him and do his bidding. *Fight Club*'s narrator meets his sexual needs by becoming someone else; Lester meets his by manufacturing an image tailor-made to his desire. In the case of both Carolyn and Angela, the roses symbolize an American ideal—an infallible illusion of perfection and beauty—in which failure does not exist.

Lester's fantasies are a fitting metaphor for the illusive and elusive nature of the American Dream. Like his images of Angela, the American Dream is constructed by media and advertising intent on selling an intoxicating elixir of bliss. Anesthetizing an American public requires—like the CGI, jump cuts, and music—crafting the myth into hyper-mythic proportions. Perpetuating the allure of the idyllic American Dream is a photoshopped façade. The retouched original—if indeed there ever was such a thing—has long been hidden beneath the masquerade. As with the frequent and intentional blurring between Lester's "real" world and his fantasies,[32] it can be difficult to discern where the fantasy of the American Dream begins and ends. It is much like Gatsby's green light, a dream already behind us, but after which "we beat on, boats against the current, borne back ceaselessly into the past."[33] We lack a sure sign—the red rose in Lester's case—that signals we have been lulled into the deceptive realm of deceit.

To its credit, the film acknowledges and even amplifies the fanciful nature of Lester's fantasies. Their phantasmal character is reinforced not only by the music, CGI, and jump cuts, but also by their abrupt end and transition to entirely routine matters. Mendes intentionally shot the basketball scenes preceding Lester's first fantasy "underwhelmingly" in order to convey a sense of the mundane.[34] Lester's fantasy of kissing Angela shifts to his "real mundane point of view" of Angela and Jane standing in the kitchen.[35] The fantasy of Angela in the bathtub ends by cutting to Lester masturbating in bed. These rapid shifts originate in Ball's screenplay; three of the four fantasies conclude with his note, "SMASH CUT TO:"[36]

What the camera abruptly shifts *to* after the fantasies also sharpens the contrast between the real Angela and the simulacrum that Lester constructs. The vision of Angela on the ceiling of Lester's bedroom cuts to Jane and Angela giggling and laughing in a car. This Angela—a somewhat goofy adolescent—destabilizes the viewer who might be caught up in Lester's intoxicating reverie. Lester's fantasy of kissing Angela in the kitchen cuts to Angela who is drinking root beer. This childlike activity marks another stark departure from the adult-rated Angela of the fantasy.[37]

Juxtaposing the fantasy with the adolescent reality undercuts Lester's objectification and distortion of Angela.[38] The film rejects Lester's view of Angela, and it refuses to grant the viewer the ease of indulging in Lester's fantasy because it forces the audience to face Angela the adolescent.[39] The film also problematizes Lester's fantasies through the disgust Jane exudes, both at her father's lascivious obsession and Angela's flirtation. Like *Donnie Darko* (d. Kelly, 2001) and *Little Miss Sunshine* (d. Dayton and Faris, 2006), *American Beauty* critiques the American habit of sexualizing young girls. Unlike these other films, *American Beauty* allows (male) viewers to revel in Lester's fantasies, and then undermines this indulgence.[40]

Lester's fantasies approach a literal climax near the end of the film when he is about to have intercourse with Angela.[41] Yet after she reveals that she is a virgin, Lester makes his most crucial choice, and declines this opportunity to have sex with her. This is perhaps the most pivotal moment in his journey. He halts the entire trajectory of actualizing his sexual desires; he abandons control and decides (for the first time) to put another's needs before his own desires.[42]

Foregoing sex with Angela represents a rejection of the example in Vladimir Nabokov's novel *Lolita*.[43] Both texts feature a 42-year-old man who falls in lust with a *much* younger girl, and Angela *Hayes* is a likely reference to Dolores (Lolita) *Haze*, the twelve-year-old fetish of Humbert's compulsion.[44] Although some critics view Lester as a pedophile in the mold of Humbert,[45] understanding him in this way clashes with the film's perspective, especially since Lester chooses not to consummate his relationship with his nymphet.[46]

Even more suggestive is that "Lester Burnham" is an anagram for "Humbert *learns*," and this reconfiguration highlights Lester's ability to "look closer" and see Angela as an insecure virgin rather than the sultry siren of his fantasies.[47] The chimera becomes a person, and he sees Angela as a child.[48] The revelation prompts him to adopt almost immediately a posture of parental nurture: he wraps her in a blanket, gives her a hug, affirms her value and worth, and makes her a meal.[49] His paternal bearing is also manifest in the questions he asks about Jane's wellbeing. Looking closer saves him and Angela from the kind of predatory encounter that Alan Ball later depicted in his film *Towel-head* (2007).[50]

Lester's fantasies thus play a paradoxical role; they are deceptive and duplicitous but also catalytic for his spiritual development.[51] For Lester to con-tinue progressing in his religious journey he must—as the narrator did with Tyler in *Fight Club*—discard the very element that sparked and facilitated his initial growth. While acknowledging that Angela is the catalyst for Lester regaining his passion for living, Ball clarifies, "But he thinks she's the goal and she's really just the knock on the door. At the risk of sounding incredibly lofty and pretentious, he needs to get back in touch with his spiritual connection to living."[52]

LOOKING CLOSER: A SUBVERSIVE AND SACRED BEAUTY

Ricky Fitts, Lester's next-door neighbor, embodies the film's charge to "look closer." He does so through his video camera, carried so often it is a near con-stant appendage. Twelve scenes feature Ricky filming, and *American Beauty* is framed between an inclusio of two videos he shoots. We frequently see through the lens of his camera, and on these occasions Mendes adjusts the audience's point of view from the typical film filter to the grainier and rougher filter of Ricky's camera. With such optical shifts we see *what* and *as* he sees.[53] Ricky's perspective provides viewers with an aesthetic vision that clashes with prevailing American cultural values. By looking closer Ricky discovers beauty in three unexpected places: Jane, a plastic bag, and death. Like his filter, beauty resides not in the pristine, but in the messier material of the rough and grainy.

Ricky films Jane seven times, and in four of these scenes he opts to focus (literally) on her rather than Angela. His preference for Jane over Angela becomes increasingly explicit: (1) When Jane exits Angela's car, Ricky leaves Angela behind and tracks Jane all the way to her house. (2) After Jane real-izes that her father called Angela, Ricky's camera zooms in on Jane. (3) When Angela dances seductively in the window, vying for his attention, Ricky zooms past her, searching for Jane. Unable to see her, he rests on Jane's face in a mir-ror, preferring her reflection to Angela. Mendes, who filmed this himself, calls it one of his favorite shots, and a "microcosm of the whole film" since "you zoom past the thing that you think is beautiful, the thing that you think is interesting and sexy. Here [Jane] is something infinitely more interesting."[54] (4) Approached by Jane and Angela at school, Ricky raises his camera and zooms past Angela to concentrate on Jane's face.[55]

In consistently preferring Jane to Angela, Ricky rejects a dominant American aesthetic script.[56] As a blond and blue-eyed cheerleader, Angela typifies an American beauty ideal. She is, as Ball notes, "the archetypal American dream girl."[57] She is an ultimate object of desire, and appears as such in Lester's four fantasies. The beauty ideal to which Angela aspires is reflected in the magazine cutouts of female celebrities that adorn every inch of her bedroom walls.

Jane, by contrast, is a prototypical "ordinary" girl who does not conform to the American cultural script for feminine adolescent beauty. Her displeasure with her appearance is the first thing we learn about her, as she peruses a website for breast augmentation and—immediately afterward—disapprovingly examines her body in a full-length mirror. Lester introduces Jane by noting that she is "a pretty typical teenager: angry, insecure, confused." Her insecurity is viciously reinforced by her mother Carolyn.

Given Jane's insecurity, it is significant that three of the four times Ricky prefers Jane over Angela immediately follow a scene where Angela flaunts her sexual prowess to Jane. Ricky follows Jane out of the car after Angela shares how she likes guys "drooling over" her because it gives her "a shot at being a model." Ricky zooms in on Jane immediately after she discovers that her dad has looked through her address book and called Angela, thus juxtaposing Lester's pursuit of Angela with Ricky's interest in Jane. Ricky's zooming past the dancing Angela and fixating on Jane's mirrored reflection follows Angela's description of sex acts she would like to perform with Jane's dad. Ricky's countercultural preference for Jane rejects prevailing American aesthetic norms. By looking closer, he gives Jane attention that her culture and own father fail to provide.

Ricky's filming subverts another American aesthetic sensibility. He shows Jane a video of "the most beautiful thing" he's ever filmed: a plastic bag floating in gusts of wind. Ricky comments as they gaze at the bag:

> It was one of those days where it's a minute away from snowing. And there was this electricity in the air. You can almost hear it. Right? And this bag was just—dancing with me, like a little kid begging me to play with it. For fifteen minutes.
>
> That's the day I realized there was this entire life behind things. And this incredibly benevolent force, who wanted me to know that there was no reason to be afraid. Ever. Video's a poor excuse, I know, but it helps me remember. I need to remember.

On the verge of crying, Ricky concludes, "Sometimes there's so much beauty in the world, I feel like I can't take it. And my heart is just going to—cave in."

His vulnerability engenders a moment of genuine intimacy as Jane reaches over and gently takes hold of his hand. They stare into each other's eyes, and Jane leans in to kiss him.

"Looking closer" enables Ricky to experience the sacred in the mundane; in the trivial, he discovers a moment of profane revelation. The dancing debris conveys the existence of a benevolent life force that wants him to never be afraid. This whisper of divine kindness is a far cry from the forsaking God of *Fight Club*. In *American Beauty*, the sacred is a protective force that elicits in Ricky poignant gratitude and wonder.

Finding a sacred beauty in a discarded piece of refuse represents another rejection of what America prizes as beautiful. Ricky's sacramental sensitivity opens him up to beauty in other (unlikely) facets of life, and such beauty overwhelms and sustains him. His mystical attentiveness parallels an insight about Zen meditation:

> the sacred is *in* the ordinary... in one's daily life, in one's neighbors, friends, and family, in one's back yard, ... travel may be a *flight* from confronting the sacred ... To be looking elsewhere for miracles is to me a sure sign of ignorance that *everything* is miraculous.[58]

The plastic bag signifies a sense of freedom and a corresponding absence of overt control. Like the vapor (*hebel*) that pervades Qoheleth/Ecclesiastes, the floating bag illustrates a way of being that eschews force or manipulation.[59] This image is a stark contrast to the terrifying control wielded by Ricky's father, Colonel Fitts (Chris Cooper). His volatile efforts to dominate explode in physical beatings of Ricky, and are likely responsible for the near-catatonic state of Ricky's mother (Allison Janney). Obsessed with controlling his latent homosexuality, the Colonel demonizes its perceived presence in his neighbors, his son Ricky, and Lester.[60] Looking closer at the Colonel reveals a deeply wounded man whose hatred of his own orientation results in torrents of violence on those around him.[61]

A zealous effort to control also drives Carolyn, and underlies her inability to cope with failure. When Buddy ends their fling, she fights back tears, and pathetically parrots their mantra: "No, no, I understand. Completely. In order to be successful, one must project an image of success at all times." After starting to cry when Buddy exits the car, she reprises her breakdown when failing to sell the house: "Stop it. Stop it," she screams. Her controlling compulsion is also apparent in the self-help tapes she dutifully absorbs. Ball—who considers

Carolyn and the Colonel the "two most tragic characters in the movie"—claims they cannot experience a transformation because "they can't let go of the need to control their lives."[62]

Firearms symbolize the control Carolyn and the Colonel so desperately try to wield. They and Buddy are the only characters associated with guns, and their use of these weapons anticipates the destruction and death that follow their insistence on controlling others. Buddy turns Carolyn on literally, but also to handguns, telling her post-coitus, "Nothing makes you feel more powerful." The regular association of her pistol with her self-help tapes points to their role in her effort to gain control over her life. She clutches her gun while twice repeating the mantra: "I refuse to be a victim." The film suggests that America's obsession with guns covers a fear-fueled and futile effort to assert control.

LOOKING CLOSER: FINDING DIVINE BEAUTY IN DEATH

American Beauty not only—like *Fight Club*—displays death's transformative power, but also illustrates the aesthetic power of death as a source of divine encounter. Death is the third place Ricky experiences beauty. He films a dead bird "because it's beautiful." He expands on his sacramental thanatology while he and Jane walk home. After saying that he once videotaped a homeless woman who had frozen to death, a funeral procession turns and slowly makes its way toward them. They move to the sidewalk and converse as it passes. Jane asks why he would film the dead homeless woman:

> RICKY: Cause it was amazing.
>
> JANE: What's amazing about it?
>
> RICKY: When you see something like that, it's like God is looking right at you—just for a second. And if you're careful, you can look right back.
>
> JANE: And what do you see?
>
> RICKY: Beauty.

Ricky's thanatological aesthetic subverts typical American tastes. In discerning a sacred beauty in death and the plastic bag, he rejects the dualistic vision so common in apocalyptic worldviews that divides the sacred and secular into discrete and impermeable arenas. Ricky animates Victor Hugo's thesis that true art is a juxtaposition of the sublime and grotesque.[63] As Ball remarks,

"And although the puritanical would have us believe otherwise, there is room for beauty in every facet of existence."[64] It is one thing, however, to see earth "crammed with heaven and every common bush afire with God."[65] It is quite another to encounter God in the corpse. The film's radical proposal is that death is a site of sacred and divine beauty.

Ricky has a sacred encounter because of Lester's death. When he finds Lester's body, Ricky lowers himself so he is at eye level with Lester's head. He stares at Lester, transfixed. In what could be interpreted as perversity, Ricky smiles slightly as his eyes lock on Lester's. His previous admission to Jane suggests that this is for Ricky a holy moment in which God is looking at him and he is viewing beauty. His posture of kneeling before Lester (as Lester did before the tub) signals the religious nature of his experience. After staring at Lester for a while, Ricky takes in the broader scene of blood, and utters—in an awed whisper—"Wow." His sacred moment is at death's door.

Lester also experiences a sacred encounter with beauty in his death.[66] Shortly before he is killed, he expresses genuine concern for how Jane is doing and authentic pleasure when he hears that she thinks she is in love. When Angela asks how he is, Lester replies, "It's been a long time since anybody asked me that—I'm great." After she exits, he smiles with sincere appreciation. "I'm great," he repeats, relishing the moment. He picks up the photograph we saw earlier of him, Carolyn, and a much younger Jane all laughing and smiling. He sits and admires the picture with the same kind of awe Carolyn had for her rose. The picture—and the memory—is Lester's rose. Softly, and with gratitude, he whispers, "Man oh man. Man oh man oh man." The camera pans back to reveal a pistol pointed at his head. As he lays the photograph down by the red roses, a gunshot explodes, and blood (matching the crimson of the roses) splatters on the tiled kitchen wall.

Lester's religious journey crescendos into a fleeting moment of genuine gratitude, and it coincides with and ends in death. This moment of actualization at his death is anticipated earlier when—while jogging on his final day—he sings The Who's "The Seeker": "They call me the seeker / I been searchin' low and high / I won't get to get what I'm after / Till the day I die." The film's bittersweet conclusion affirms Lester's declaration at the beginning, that it *is* possible to get "it" back. In granting Lester this epiphany at his death, the film realizes Hugo's vision of coalescing the sublime and grotesque.[67] This juxtaposition impressed Mendes: "And it's always struck me as one of the most breathtaking pieces of writing that in this moment that he understands every-thing, he dies. . . . That to me is what makes it a genuinely moving story."[68]

Lester's final voiceover—from beyond the grave—reinforces the inter-play of death and beauty. Interspersed among a series of memories in black and white is the recurring sound of the gunshot that killed Lester:

> I had always heard your entire life flashes in front of your eyes the sec-ond before you die. First of all, that one second isn't a second at all. It stretches on forever, like an ocean of time.
> For me, it was lying on my back at Boy Scout camp, watching falling stars.
> And yellow leaves from the maple trees that lined our street.
> Or my grandmother's hands, and the way her skin seemed like paper.
> And the first time I saw my cousin Tony's brand new Firebird.
> And Janie.

An image of Jane stands at the front door of the Burnham house. The door shuts and Jane is now a four-year-old in a fairy costume, holding a lit sparkler in one hand.

> And Janie.
> And Carolyn.

An exuberant Carolyn, years earlier on an amusement park ride, is laughing, smiling, and fully enjoying herself.[69] The film shifts to its penultimate image: Ricky's video of the floating plastic bag.

These visual images convey the aesthetic, relational, and nostalgic nature of Lester's epiphany. His final memories—of Jane and Carolyn—reinforce the gratitude and wonder he expresses while earlier holding the family photograph. His renewed attitude toward his family is evident in the authentic joy he feels when he hears Jane is in love. All of Lester's images (with the exception of the plastic bag) are from his past, intimating that a certain kind of nostalgia is effec-tive in providing genuine meaning.[70] Despite the controversy it engendered, the film ends upholding a fairly traditional message about family as a primary source of fulfillment. What is subversive—in addition to the route Lester takes here—is the claim that beauty, the sacred, and genuine gratitude correlate not with success or achievement but rather in death, the epitome of failure.

ALAN BALL: DEATH AND MEANINGFUL LIVING

American Beauty's Hugoesque interplay of the sublime and grotesque is partially rooted in screenwriter Allan Ball's own personal tragedy. As he tells
the story:

> When I was thirteen years old, my sister Mary Ann was driving me to my piano
> lesson when she pulled out from a blind intersection into the path of an oncom-
> ing car. It slammed into her side of our 1973 Ford Pinto, breaking her neck and
> killing her instantly.[71]

It was Mary Ann's twenty-second birthday. Ball notes that the event
"cleanly slic[ed] my life in two: everything before the accident, and everything after. And the brief, eternal instant between those two lives where old,
familiar possibilities end forever, and new, unimagined possibilities are pain-
fully born."[72]

Mary Ann's death would have a profound effect upon Ball's subsequent
art. As he relates in a 2007 interview:[73]

> ROSEN: You repeatedly explore the intersection of pain and beauty in
>   your work—how much does that come from your own expe-
>   rience of grief?
>
> BALL: All of it.
>
> ROSEN: *All* of it?
>
> BALL: I mean, when I was 13, I was in a car accident with my sister. I
>   saw her die in front of me. I got her blood all over me, and that
>   changed me. It changed everything.
>
> ROSEN: How?
>
> BALL: I don't think I would have been a writer, even. I just think that
>   experience fucked me up beyond belief—it also made me a
>   deeper person than I ever would have been. I'm going to start
>   speaking in cross-stitch homilies now: It opened my eyes to
>   how truly important life is, and how truly important it is to
>   see it in *all* of its complexity and not pretend it's just the nice
>   parts. If you pretend it's just the nice parts, you're not really
>   honoring life.

Honoring life—in all its parts—has become one of Ball's trademarks.
Like Ricky Fitts, his art gives sustained attention to the ugliness that inhabits

what is for Ball a broken and beautiful world. (Ball's father died of lung cancer six years after the death of his sister).

Ball's keen interest in death permeates his HBO show *Six Feet Under* (2001–2005). The main characters, the Fischer family, own and operate a funeral home, and every episode begins with someone dying. Ball thus confronts viewers regularly with the reality of mortality and death's potential imminence. Like *American Beauty*, the show compels viewers to reflect on and face their own inevitable demise.

With its series finale, *Six Feet Under* became the first show in television history to depict the death of every single main character. In a poignant montage, Ball traces the future lives of each main character, showing how they age and die. The successive character deaths produce a tidal wave of grief. The finale demands that viewers face their own future death and the death of all their loved ones. "The point," Ball remarks about the show, "is that we live in a culture that goes out of its way to deny mortality."[74] Ball claims that he set the show in Los Angeles because he considers the city the "world capital of the denial of death."[75] One reviewer of the show identified its treatment of death as potentially offensive:

> That . . . Whomever Is in Charge Here has a dark sense of humor can be off-putting to triumphalists. That the best, the most noble, the wise, the old, the young, the lovely and beloved of our species often die ridiculous, hilarious, ignoble and untimely deaths while the worst of us sometimes get the best of ends unsettles some religious accounts.[76]

Like *American Beauty, Six Feet Under* undermines an American Dream so predicated on success and achievement that death, loss, grief, and failure are denied entrance. Ball insists, on the contrary, that death is not only necessary but also essential—a *sine qua non*—for meaningful living. The subtitle of his book—*Better Living Through Death*—captures precisely this counterintuitive notion that facing squarely one's mortality can enable one to live more fully and vibrantly.[77] Dylan's "All Along the Watchtower"—playing in the background during an argument between Lester and Carolyn—has a lyric that suggests life's temporality is the reason for meaningful engagement: "So let us not talk falsely now, the hour is getting late."

The film's interplay of death and beauty suggests that in denying death, American culture simultaneously banishes aspects of beauty that can only be experienced in embracing mortality. Ball maintains that death is imperative for experiencing beauty:

We live in a culture that goes out of its way to deny mortality. And I think you have to have a deep and fundamental acceptance of mortality to really be able to see what's beautiful in life—because beauty and truth are inextricably connected.[78]

THE ROSY ILLUSION OF THE AMERICAN DREAM

Beauty, the film proposes, resides not in Angela nor in Carolyn's façades, but in Jane, a plastic bag, and death. By locating beauty in these unexpected places the film subverts classic *American* aesthetic notions of beauty and meaning. The title alone—*American Beauty*—explicitly draws attention to American culture. Other allusions in the film evoke classic American tropes such as the painter Norman Rockwell (the film takes place in the town of Rockwell, and Jane, Ricky, and Angela attend Rockwell High). Allusions to—and similarities with—Arthur Miller's play *Death of a Salesman* reinforce these classic American associations.[79]

By repeatedly linking roses to distorted masks, the film suggests that there is a seductive masquerade about the American Dream. Ball describes the rose Carolyn holds at the beginning of the film as an "American Beauty Rose,"[80] and this flower (*Rosa American Beauty*) is prone to rot underneath at the roots and branches of the plant. Such internal decay has obvious symbolism for the film's argument about what is deemed beautiful and meaningful in the American Dream. God and beauty are not found in financial or career success, roses, or blond cheerleaders. They are experienced in death, the epitome of failure. A reflection on Nabokov's *Lolita* is pertinent to the American Dream:

> [I]t's ruinous not to look squarely, clearly, consciously at our created dream-worlds, their erasures of reality, the consequences of . . . letting those erasures get out of hand. In an empire of images, I would add, we need to apply that crucial consciousness to our collective fantasies, too.[81]

As Lester eventually does with Angela, the film invites viewers to recognize the American Dream as a lustful fantasy offering an unattainable image after which people perennially yearn, and onto which they project their desires. Like Lester's fantasies, the American Dream is capable of catalyzing or fueling an awakening (even a religious one), but in the end it remains a figment. The very term "American *Dream*" connotes an imaginary and elusive state, possibly only attainable during sleep. Certain fixtures in the American Dream (house, car, family, career, paycheck) are obtainable for some, but the dogma that these components guarantee meaning and fulfillment is another matter.

Chief among the illusions of the American Dream is the elevation of success as the ultimate value and the corresponding erasure of any kind of failure. As the archetypal failure, death has no place in the American Dream, nor does the American Dream offer any productive or healthy means of coping with it. As Lester's journey involves an increasing embrace of honesty, so too does the film propose that an essential component of religious development is confronting death in a culture that represses its existence.

American Beauty implores viewers not only to "look closer" at the film and American culture, but also at their own lives. At three points, while the camera pans over his street, Lester's voiceover reflects on his life (or lack thereof). The film concludes with the image of the plastic bag as Lester narrates these final lines:

> I guess I could be pretty pissed off about what happened to me. But it's hard to stay mad when there's so much beauty in the world. Sometimes I feel like I'm seeing it all at once, and it's too much. My heart fills up like a balloon that's about to burst.[82]
>
> And then I remember to relax and stop trying to hold onto it. And then it flows through me like rain. And I can't feel anything but gratitude for every single moment of my stupid little life. *You* have no idea what I'm talking about, I'm sure. But don't worry [screen fades to black]. *You* will some day.

With his shift to the second-person address, Lester's general reflection becomes a direct speech to the film's audience: "*You* have no idea . . . *You* will some day."[83] Speaking from beyond the grave, Lester informs viewers that they will eventually experience beauty flowing through them and have gratitude for *every* moment of their "stupid little life." Here the film embraces tremendous gratitude for a life that is replete with meaninglessness and absurdity. Lester advocates letting go of the need to control; beauty flows through him when he relinquishes control. Lester achieves these insights at death, and he intimates that viewers will have the same experience. The film (like the funeral procession moving directly toward the viewers) thus concludes with a forceful reminder of the common fate awaiting everyone, and an invitation to allow this destiny of death to engender and fuel a life well lived.

✳ 4 ✳

ABOUT SCHMIDT
An American Rich Fool

Life's but a walking shadow, a poor player
That struts and frets his hour upon the stage
And then is heard no more. It is a tale
Told by an idiot, full of sound and fury,
Signifying nothing.

—*Macbeth* V.v.24-28

From 1999 to 2010, the suicide rate among Americans ages 35 to 64
rose by nearly 30 percent, to 17.6 deaths per 100,000 people, up from
13.7. Although suicide rates are growing among both middle-aged men
and women, far more men take their own lives. . . . The most pronounced
increases were seen among men in their 50s, a group in which suicide
rates jumped by nearly 50 percent.

—*New York Times*, May 2, 2013[1]

Like *Fight Club* and *American Beauty*, Alexander Payne's 2002 film *About Schmidt* launches an offensive against the American Dream.[2] The titular character Warren Schmidt has inherited central components of the American Dream (suburban house, family, steady career, and stable income), yet like Lester Burnham and *Fight Club's* narrator, he finds his life bereft of meaning. As in these two other films, the primary lens used to examine the American Dream is the religious and existential journey of the main character.

Although *About Schmidt* did not elicit the kind of outcry that met *Fight Club* and *American Beauty*, this film's criticisms of the American Dream are—in certain ways—far more trenchant and provocative.

Based (loosely) on Louis Begley's 1996 novel of the same name and (somewhat more closely) on a previous screenplay of Payne's (*The Coward*), the film begins on the final day of Schmidt's lengthy career, and proceeds to chronicle his quest for purpose within the context of his retirement.[3] As a sixty-six year old, married for forty-two years, Schmidt offers a different generational experience from the thirty-something narrator in *Fight Club* or forty-two-year-old Lester in *American Beauty*. Together these films point to a profound cross-generational disappointment with the American Dream.

The film opens with ten consecutive images of grey, drab buildings in a grey, drab downtown Omaha, surrounded by grey, drab weather. Each successive shot brings us closer to a tall, grey building with the word "WOODMEN" in plain, square, grey letters across the top. Hinting at what will occupy the target in the film's crosshairs, the sole use of color is an American flag waving against the building. A quick cut to an interior office shows Warren Schmidt (Jack Nicholson, in a role unlike any before).

4.1 Warren Waiting

These opening colorless images—like Lester Burnham's office—symbolize the internal deadness of Warren Schmidt, a parallel suggested by the sudden transition from these shots to the first image of lifeless Warren. He sits in a grey suit, silent and immobile, staring at a clock on his office wall. Eyeing the slow advance of the second hand, he gapes at it for a full twenty seconds. When it reaches the 12 (at 5:00 p.m.), Warren rises unceremoniously, picks up his briefcase, looks around the empty office, collects his raincoat, and casts one final look at his office before turning off the light and exiting. This introduction captures Schmidt's general orientation to life: while the world moves on, he passively waits in silence.

Questions about meaningful living pervade the film and are raised explicitly at Warren's retirement party. A toast by Ray (Len Cariou), Warren's coworker and close friend of many decades, constitutes a kind of thesis for the film:

> I know something about retirement. And what I want to say to you out loud, Warren, so all these young hot shots can hear, is that all of those gifts over there don't mean a goddamn thing. And this dinner doesn't mean a goddamn thing. And the social security and pension don't mean a goddamn thing. None of these superficialities mean a goddamn thing. What means something, what really means something, Warren, is the knowledge that you devoted your life to something meaningful: to being productive, and working for a fine company—hell, one of the top rated insurance carriers in the nation—to raising a fine family, to building a fine home, to being respected by your community, to having wonderful, lasting friendships. At the end of his career, if a man can look back and say, "I did it, I did my job," then he can retire in glory and enjoy riches far beyond the monetary kind. So, all of you young people here: Take a good look at a very rich man.[4]

Ray's twofold argument rejects economic and material items as worthless, insisting instead that true value is found in family, friendships, and a career at a worthwhile company. By endorsing vocation and specific relationships as the principal sources of fulfillment, Ray upholds quintessential elements of the American Dream. His speech defends a classic American myth. The virtues Ray extols lie at the heart of the American Dream and have been etched into the American psyche through their celebratory promotion in iconic heroes from George Bailey (*It's a Wonderful Life*, 1946) to Rocky Balboa (*Rocky*, 1976), Jerry Maguire (*Jerry Maguire*, 1996), and Chris Gardner (*The Pursuit of Happyness*, 2006).

SUBVERTING THE AMERICAN DREAM

The film, however, is far more dubious about Ray's claim. The remaining hour and fifty-nine minutes relentlessly interrogate and dissect his Capraesque thesis. Wasting no time in upending the myth Ray espouses, the film takes successive aim at three pillars of assumed significance: work, family, and friends.

When Warren returns to his former office he finds that, contrary to his replacement's previous invitation, neither he nor his opinions are welcome. Schmidt's multiple attempts to offer help are civilly brushed aside; his willingness to answer questions regarding various products is dismissed. His younger replacement is polite but clear: Schmidt is unnecessary, perhaps even a bother; the company has moved on (and is doing quite fine) without him.[5] Bubbling to the surface in Warren's psyche—spurred on by his retirement—is a growing recognition of his obsolescence.

Warren's sense of being discarded is more than confirmed when, leaving the building, he notices scores of boxes containing his old files crammed into and beside a trash dumpster. Dumbfounded, he slowly approaches and stares at the boxes labeled "Schmidt Active Files" or "Schmidt Files Archive." A melancholic piece hovers over the depressing scene as he contemplates his life's work become refuse.[6] The abrupt cut to the repeated slamming of a heavy knife on a bloody chicken carcass—as his wife Helen severs meat from a bone—reflects Warren's internal battering. His difficulty coping with his vocational erasure is evident when he arrives home that day:

> HELEN: Hi, how did it go at the office?
> WARREN: Oh, Fine. Good thing I stopped by. Turns out he needed my help with a couple of loose ends.
> HELEN: That's wonderful.

After eviscerating the value of Schmidt's vocation, the film quickly turns its sights upon family and friendship. With his career behind him, Schmidt's relationship with his wife Helen (June Squibb) looms as the principal area of his future time and energy. She views their future together as pregnant with promise and potential. On the morning after his retirement party Helen ushers him aboard their brand new RV and offers a toast to their new post-retirement life: "We're gonna have a lot of good times in here, Warren." But her enthusiasm is not of the contagious variety; Warren does not muster a single ounce of energy to match her, merely muttering, "Yeah." His lack of interest is a stark contrast to her beaming smile and optimism: "Isn't this fun?! . . . Here's to a whole new chapter." This is the *second* toast that will prove to be empty.

Their whole new chapter never materializes, for Helen dies unexpectedly from a blood clot in her brain. Coming home from running errands, Warren finds her collapsed on the kitchen floor. By highlighting life's fragility and ephemerality, her death relativizes the potential value of relationships. Her death does not, however, pose the greatest threat to the value of family for Warren. Shortly afterwards he finds a cache of love letters, all addressed to Helen. Astonished, he opens one and finds that it is signed at the bottom by none other than Ray, his "best" friend.

Helen's infidelity and Ray's betrayal are the first of many efforts to undermine friends and family as sources of fulfillment. Warren confronts Ray, telling him, *"You were my friend."* Ray's betrayal is especially painful given how special his friendship with Warren appeared to be. Ray was the last to leave Warren's house after the funeral service for Helen, and he was genuinely moved by her death. *"You're a good friend, Ray,"* Warren had unknowingly told him before they embraced.

Warren's one remaining hope is his only child Jeannie (Hope Davis). She is the first person to elicit any emotional response in Warren. When he arrives home from the retirement party and hears she is on the phone for him, his whole demeanor changes. He adjusts his suit and hair while walking to the phone, as though he is on the cusp of a momentous occasion. Delighted to speak with her, he smiles and exhibits warmth for the first time in the film. The illumination of four different lights while he talks with her symbolizes her radiant presence. Within only four seconds on the phone with her, he speaks more words than he does in the first seven minutes and forty-nine seconds of the film. Warren's deep fondness for Jeannie is reflected in his tender memories (shampooing her hair while she was a baby, watching her play violin at a middle school concert). His line, "She'll always be my little girl," says it all; she is the apple of his eye. Corroborating his paternal affection is the soft use of strings when he describes her, a distinct shift from the harsh staccato playing during his description of Helen.

Unfortunately, Warren's relationship with Jeannie is fraught with conflict about her upcoming marriage. He is opposed to the union because he fears it will decrease her already infrequent visits, and he holds an unfavorable view of her fiancée, Randall Hertzel (Dermot Mulroney). Warren encourages her to abandon her nuptial plans, but his efforts come to naught. He reexperiences with Jeannie what he found at his workplace: his opinions are not welcome. Nor is his presence. He leaves two weeks early to spend time with Jeannie before her wedding, and phones her on the road to notify her of his plans:

> Jeannie, I've been thinking about things and how much you mean to me and how little time you and I have spent together these last few years. And all of a sudden I realized: What the heck am I doing in Omaha when you're out there and I can be with you? We should be together.

Jeannie rejects his overture, insisting that he arrive no earlier than a day or two before the wedding. What might have been (in another film) a moment of relational restoration becomes yet another nail in Warren's coffin. His primary hope for happiness resides in Jeannie, and her (perceived) rejection thus poses an immense existential threat.

Within minutes, the film undercuts Ray's myth about family, friends, and vocation as sources of vitality.[7] Warren begins to experience the realization of Louis Begley, the novel's author, who is "always conscious of what seems the fundamental futility of work, efforts, successes, and failures."[8] In rejecting Ray's claim, the film subverts fundamental premises about the ability of the American Dream to enhance one's life. The destabilizing effects of this critique work most effectively if viewers initially resonate with Ray's argument that worth is found in family, friends, and worthwhile employment. Agreement with his proposal is a helpful prelude and setup for the film's thorough dismantling of his worldview.

SCHMIDT'S ADVENTURE TO FIND MEANING

Determined to discover and experience meaning, Warren embarks on a literal journey (a road trip) in a literal Adventure (the name of his RV). As in his subsequent films *Sideways* (2004) and *Nebraska* (2013), Payne utilizes the road trip as a metaphorical vehicle for an existential quest. Driving from Omaha to Denver, Warren makes a series of calculated stops, hoping that each one will provide some type of fulfillment.

The results, as in Payne's other films, are utterly disappointing. Warren's first stop is at his childhood home in Holdrege, Nebraska. "I've often wondered what our old house would look like today." He is left to wonder, because his old home is now a tire store. His efforts to inform the employee inside about his childhood home fall on apathetic ears. A second stop, at his alma mater Kansas University and former fraternity (BΣE), is also dissatisfying. After sharing a story with two current frat members about his former company, the camera pans out to show his two listeners who are bored out of their minds. Unlike *American Beauty* (but in line with Woody Allen's *Midnight in Paris*), nostalgia is futile.

Warren fails to find one significant personal connection on his journey. Such an opportunity presents itself during a dinner aboard another couple's RV. Left alone on a sofa with Vicki, Warren has an uncharacteristically frank conversation:

> VICKI: Well, you put a pretty good face on things considering everything you've been through lately . . . The feeling that I get from you is that, despite your good attitude and your positive outlook, I think inside you're a *sad* man.
>
> WARREN: Well, it does take quite an adjustment there, when you lose a spouse.
>
> VICKI: It's something more than that. I see something more than grief and loss in you. Something deeper.
>
> WARREN: Well, like what?
>
> VICKI: Well, I've just met you, but—my guess is anger. Yeah, anger, and, I don't know, maybe fear. Loneliness.
>
> WARREN: Well, I am kind of lonely . . . I've only known you for an hour or so, and yet I feel like you understand me better than my wife Helen ever did. Even after forty-two years of marriage. Forty-two years. Maybe if I had met someone like you earlier.

Vicki's continued empathy engenders in Warren an awkward vulnerability and an even more humiliating attempt to kiss her. She is repulsed, instantly pushes him away, stands, and orders him to leave.

Warren's inept misreading of Vicki's kind interest for interest of another kind ends a potentially emotionally enriching encounter. Schmidt is forbidden that quintessential American cinematic source of ecstasy, a romantic escapade. Denying this intimate connection to Warren is notable, for it departs from the novel in which he finds joy in a series of erotic trysts with a much younger waitress. Unlike the novel, the film insists on stripping almost every conceivable source of significance away from Schmidt.

Schmidt's efforts to find fulfillment through relationships prove futile. Calling Ray from a pay phone, he leaves this message:

> Ray, it's Warren. I know we separated on a bit of a sour note. But I just thought I should call you and tell you that I've been doing some thinking and some soul searching. Well, I just wanted to tell you that I'm willing to talk about this because of all the things . . .

Warren, however, is abruptly interrupted by an automated message: "If you are satisfied with your message, press '1.' To listen to your message press '2.' To erase and rerecord press '3.'" He tries to comply, but apparently pushes the wrong button, for he hears: "Message erased. At the tone please rerecord your message. At the end of your message press 1." Frustrated, he hangs up the receiver. Despite his best-laid plans, Warren is denied a moment of potential reconciliation with his best friend.

The closest Warren comes to a genuine human connection is with a dead person. After constructing a makeshift altar (of Hummel figurines and candles) to Helen on his RV roof, he addresses the heavens:

> Helen? What did you really think of me? Deep in your heart? Was I really the man you wanted to be with? Was I? Or were you disappointed, and too nice to show it? I forgive you for Ray. I forgive you. It was a long time ago, and I know I wasn't always the "king of kings." I let you down. I'm sorry, Helen. Can you forgive me? Can you forgive me?

A shooting star seems to answer Warren; he looks stunned, and crosses himself. And yet.

Conforming to a pattern throughout the film, this poignant moment does not linger. In the subsequent scene, a befuddled Warren wakes on the RV roof the following morning, and drives out of the park. Drifting unsteadily on the roof of the RV are the four Hummel figurines and candles; as the RV winds its way out, they all scatter and fall to the ground. The whimsical music playing over the scene strikes a comedic note and under*scores* an equipoise the film continuously straddles between drama and comedy. A similar tone is struck by the music playing when Warren collects and dumps out Helen's belongings; it provides a comic texture that downplays the scene's potential sadness. Tension between these dramatic and comedic poles surfaced in the 2003 Golden Globes ceremony: when Nicholson received the award for Best Actor in a Motion Picture, Drama, he quipped, "I'm a little surprised. I thought we had made a comedy." Quick cutting from scenes of gravity to moments of levity destabilizes viewers used to dwelling in one genre at a time. It also under-cuts—or at least relativizes—the emotional poignancy and moral seriousness of these scenes. The film resists earnestness. A comedic U-turn immediately follows every veer toward the serious or moral.

Warren's final hope of finding some semblance of purpose on his journey is his effort to convince Jeannie not to marry Randall. Despite his increasingly desperate pleas, she refuses to comply and halt the wedding. Her response signals the relational distance between father and daughter:

> All of a sudden, you're taking an interest in what I do?! You have an opinion about my life, now?! OK, you listen to me. I am getting married, the day after tomorrow. And you are going to come to my wedding. And you are going to sit there and enjoy it and support me, or else you can just turn right around right now and go back to Omaha.

Accompanied by another whimsical musical piece, Jeannie departs with Randall, ignoring her father's rejoinder. Warren is useless not only in his old job but also in the one relationship that matters most.

Warren returns home broken and thoroughly depressed. His repeated failures to find meaning demonstrate the folly of Ray's speech, and expose the existential impotency of family, friends, and work. The film thus unsettles an American myth of what constitutes a jubilant life. Unlike George Bailey, Warren is not enlightened about the true worth of friendships, family, and his own life. His final voiceover conveys his dismal state:

> I know we're all pretty small in the big scheme of things, and I suppose the most you can hope for is to make some kind of difference. But what kind of difference have I made? What in the world is better because of me?
>
> When I was out in Denver I tried to do the right thing, tried to convince Jeannie that she was making a big mistake. But, I failed. Now she's married to the nincompoop, and there's nothing I can do about it. I am weak, and I'm a failure. There's just no getting around it.
>
> Relatively soon I will die. Maybe in twenty years, maybe tomorrow. It doesn't matter. Once I am dead and everyone who knew me dies too it will be as though I never even existed. What difference has my life made to anyone? None that I can think of, none at all.

With this morose and melancholic (non)resolution, *About Schmidt* subverts the typical trajectory in the road trip genre, which would have found Warren experiencing at least one enriching encounter, perhaps even discovering his passion for living, and returning renewed. His journey undermines these expectations of the road trip film; he finds no spark that enlivens him.

Conformity to such an arc might have seen Helen, Jeannie, Roberta, or Randall help him in this regard. But such a path is not for Schmidt. He departs on his trip depressed and returns even more miserable and bereft of hope than when he left. His is not the Odyssean journey of the hero figure. He *descends*. The grey skies, a regular feature throughout his trip, match his internal state upon returning. Unlike *Fight Club*'s narrator and Lester Burnham, Warren's every attempt to find fulfillment founders. His journey is not one of deepening substance or vitality, but a recognition that such a possibility does not exist, at least not for him.

Casting Jack Nicholson as Schmidt accentuates his despondency, since the character deviates from the flamboyant and forceful roles for which Nicholson is so well known. Schmidt bears zero resemblance to Nicholson's iconic performances in *Easy Rider, Chinatown, One Flew over the Cuckoo's Nest, The Shining, Batman, A Few Good Men, Hoffa*, or *As Good as it Gets*. Schmidt does what Nicholson's characters never do: give up, quit, resign, fold. His most rebellious act is defying Helen's edict by urinating in the bathroom standing up. Warren's persona is summed up in the earlier title of Payne's screenplay: *The Coward*.

A deleted scene cleverly alludes to the contrast between Schmidt's sheepish nature and Nicholson's previous roles. In a memorable scene from *Five Easy Pieces* (d. Rafelson, 1970), Nicholson's character Bobby Dupea and a waitress engage in an escalating battle of wills that begins with Bobby's innocuous order: "I'd like a plain omelet, no potatoes, tomatoes instead, a cup of coffee and wheat toast." When the waitress tells him, "No substitutions," Bobby offers a litany of options to accommodate his desire for wheat toast. Furious at the waitress' inflexibility, he eventually swipes all the glasses and other items off the table. Schmidt's response is a bit different:

> WAITRESS: Can I take your order?
> SCHMIDT: Um, I'd like a plain omelet, no potatoes, tomatoes instead, a cup of coffee, and wheat toast.
> WAITRESS: No substitutions.
> SCHMIDT: Oh, fine. I'll just have the potatoes.

Payne's reconfiguration of the classic *Five Easy Pieces* scene underscores Schmidt's submission. His capitulation is even more pathetic given that this deleted scene originally followed on the heels of his resolution: "I feel clear. I know what I want. I know what I've got to do. And nothing's going to stop me ever again." As in every other area of his life, however, Warren caves. "Wood-men" aptly describes Schmidt, a man who is void of passion, energy, and life. He embodies the underlying French origin of the English word "retire" (*retirer*); he has withdrawn not only from his career but also life itself. Warren's life is full of neither sound nor fury, and it still signifies nothing. Payne's commentary is instructive:

> Since that famous scene so perfectly and succinctly distills the feeling of the times in which it was made, Jim Taylor and I thought revisiting it with the same iconic actor would provide a commentary on how much we've lost since then and how conformist our current times are, a conformism that, among its many insidious effects, *helps produce empty, lost lives like Schmidt's.*[9]

SCHMIDT AND JESUS' PARABLE OF A "RICH FOOL"

Ray describes Warren in his speech as a *"very rich* man." Warren resembles in various ways another rich man featured in one of Jesus' parables:

> The land of a certain rich person produced fruitfully. And he began to converse with himself, saying, "What shall I do, for I do not have [a place] where I will gather together my crops?" And he said, "This I will do: I will pull down my barns, and I will build larger ones, and I will gather together there all my grain and goods. And I will say to myself, 'Self, you have many goods laid up for many years; rest, eat, drink, enjoy.'" But God said to him, "Fool! On this night they are demanding your life from you; and the things you prepared, whose will they be?"[10]

(Luke 12:16-20)

Similarities between the film and this parable make a comparison of the two beneficial. They both feature a rich main character on the brink of transitioning from a life of labor to one of rest. A sudden death, however, interrupts and ends both men's plans. Schmidt finds his wife dead on the kitchen floor, and God warns Luke's rich man about his imminent death. The specter of death confronts each character with the futility of planning for an uncertain or unrealized future. Each man is also relationally isolated, a prominent feature in Rembrandt's 1627 painting of this parable.

In the parable, God's labeling of the rich man as a "fool" is puzzling since storing one's goods for the future can be prudent preparation. A case can even be made that the rich man models his plans after various biblical stories and precepts.[11] The man's stated intention—to "eat, drink, and be merry"—is actually a citation of Ecclesiastes 8:15.[12]

Understanding the nature of the rich man's folly requires situating Luke's parable in a broader conversation in the ancient world regarding the interplay of death and possessions. Many ancient texts wrestle with whether and how a person can use possessions meaningfully given death's inevitability and uncertain timing.[13] In light of death, several ancient Egyptian texts advocate enjoying possessions and sharing them generously with others.[14] In his *Dialogues of the Dead*, the Greek satirist Lucian (ca. 120–180) depicts numerous postmortem scenarios that portray greed and the hoarding of wealth as pointless enterprises. Lucian argues that living well requires a willingness to contemplate death and confront one's own mortality.[15] Neglecting one's demise results in becoming possessed by one's possessions,[16] but facing one's death can free a person from slavery to wealth.

Several of the *Moral Epistles* by the Roman author Seneca (4 BCE–65 CE) link unhealthy views of death with harmful attitudes toward (and uses of) possessions. Both, he argues, are accompanying bedfellows that inhibit living well. A love of luxury and a fear of death feed off one other, apparent in greedy people who foolishly seek to prolong their lives. An insatiable craving for possessions prevents reflection upon one's own mortality and, therefore, cultivates concern with the trivial.[17] For Seneca, death is a lifelong process beginning at birth, which in some people accelerates at a much faster pace.[18] Those who live in luxury exemplify the living dead.

Ecclesiastes is more obsessed with the interplay of death and possessions than any other biblical book. The sole use of possessions it champions, in light of death, is enjoyment. On seven occasions the author insists that enjoying food and drink is the ideal human activity, often maintaining that there is "nothing better" a person can do.[19] Each of the seven recommendations to enjoy food and drink is a direct consequence of reflecting on uncontrollable aspects of death (its inevitability; its destruction of knowledge, memory, and emotions; and the impossibility of determining the recipient of one's inheritance, of taking goods beyond death, and of being remembered after death).[20] Death is omnipotent, and Ecclesiastes recommends enjoyment in the immediate present because of the varied ways death rips control out of people's hands.

Other Jewish texts make different recommendations for handling one's possessions given death's inevitability and life's fragility. Ben Sira, a 3rd century BCE text in the Septuagint (Greek translation of the Hebrew Bible), downplays the potential enjoyment one might experience in light of death, instead recommending sharing possessions with others, providing an inheritance, giving goods to God as offerings, and giving to the poor.[21] The Testament of Abraham advocates hospitality (and completing a last will and testament) given death's unavoidability.[22]

Luke's parable appropriates and reconfigures this contentious conversation on death and possessions. The rich man is foolish because he fails to adopt any of the beneficial uses of possessions proposed in light of death's inevitability and uncertain timing (enjoyment, inheritance, generosity, giving to God, giving alms, hospitality). His only plan—saving for the future—is the one option for using possessions that these ancient texts *never* endorse. Every other recommended use of possessions is potentially valuable because it enhances the life of the giver or receiver. Saving for the future helps no one. God's question to the rich man at the parable's conclusion addresses this failure to use his possessions to enrich someone's life: "The things you have prepared, *whose* will they be?"

Shattering his illusions of exercising control, the announcement of the man's imminent death highlights life's tenuousness and the futility of saving for an unrealized future. The parable does not, however, provide an explicit counterproposal for how one might experience well-being. Such proposals are implicit in the ancient conversation on death and possessions, and explicit in Jesus' subsequent discourse on anxiety (where he advocates giving to the poor, 12:33), but this proposal is not present within the actual parable. Like most parables, this one ends with more questions (a literal one in this instance) than answers.

FINDING MEANING *OUTSIDE* THE AMERICAN DREAM

As with the rich man in the parable, death shatters Schmidt's presumption that his life will follow a certain trajectory. Unlike Luke's isolated rich man, Schmidt does seek significance in various relationships. He is thwarted, however, at almost every turn. Whereas the parable holds out the possibility that relationships may have enlivened the rich fool, the film highlights the impossibility of guaranteeing that relationships will be life-giving.

About Schmidt differs from the parable in that it provides an alternative proposal for where meaning might reside. Before Helen dies, Warren views a commercial for an organization working with poor children in the two-thirds world. A voiceover by Angela Lansbury plays over images of poor African children:

> For just $22 a month, just 72 cents a day, you can become a Childreach sponsor and not only personally touch the life of a needy boy or girl overseas, but also help the child's family and community. Think of it: just $22 a month, and a little girl like this will never feel the agony of dysentery from dirty water. A child like this will be able to go to school to learn and grow. I'm so glad that you've watched. But now that you have, what are you going to do?

Warren reaches for the phone, and—in what becomes his most pivotal decision—chooses to sponsor a child.

The five letters Warren writes (each accompanied by voiceover) to six-year-old Ndugu Umbo in Tanzania are a crucial narrative device and window into Schmidt's character.[23] Like the interior monologue of Luke's "rich fool," these letters disclose Warren's thoughts and feelings. He is uncharacteristically emotionally expressive, revealing things to Ndugu that he shares with no one else. The letters are Schmidt's confessions, Ndugu his confessor. In his first letter, Schmidt vents:

> I am sixty-six years old and recently retired as assistant vice-president and actuary at Woodmen of the World Insurance Company . . . And *goddammit* if they didn't replace me with some kid who, alright, so maybe he's got a little theory under his belt and can plug a few numbers into a computer. But I could tell right off that he doesn't know a *damn thing* about genuine real world risk assessment, or managing a department for that matter, little cocky bastard.

Warren reveals regrets to Ndugu he has carried for a lifetime. Against a backdrop of photos of a younger Warren, he recounts:

> When I was a kid I used to think that maybe I was special, that somehow destiny had tapped me to be a great man. Not like Henry Ford or Walt Disney or somebody like that, but somebody, you know, semi-important. I got a degree in business and statistics and was planning to start my own business some day—build it up into a big corporation; watch it go public, you know? Maybe make the Fortune 500.

A shot of stock price listings in the newspaper shows "SchmidtIntl" at 178.83/ share, having increased by 9.01 percent. A happy and confident Schmidt graces the cover of *Fortune* magazine, with the congratulatory bylines "Warren Schmidt raises the stakes—and some eyebrows" and "Schmidt Int'l blows the bell curve with its out-of-this-world performance." Warren's sorrow is evident: "I was going to be one of those guys you read about. But somehow it just didn't work out that way." The imagined *Fortune* cover fades to a realistic black-and-white newsletter with a brief headline in the lower right-hand corner: "Schmidt Makes Assistant VP." The headline's trivial nature is signaled by the revelation that we are viewing a one-page edition of the "Woodmen Weekly Bugle" pinned to a nondescript corkboard. Occupying central space in the newsletter is a menu ("What's for Lunch?") listing the food items for each day of the week. The demoralizing contrast with the *Fortune* cover could not be more stark. Warren explains and complains:

> You gotta remember, I had a top notch job at Woodmen and a family to support. I couldn't exactly put their security at risk. Helen, that's my wife, she wouldn't have allowed it.

Casting Helen as responsible for the dashing of his dreams is a prelude to an onslaught of domestic frustrations. He inquires:

> But what about my family you might ask? What about my wife and daughter— don't they give me all the pride and satisfaction I could ever want?

If Warren replied in the spirit of Ray's speech, he would give a resounding "Yes." His answer is anything but. He instead itemizes his profound dissatisfaction with Helen, each complaint illustrated by an unflattering visual flashback:

> Why is it that every little thing she does irritates me? Like the way she gets the keys out of her purse long before we reach the car? And how she throws our money away on her ridiculous little collections. And tossing out perfectly good food just because the expiration date is passed. And her obsession, her *obsession*, with trying new restaurants. And the way she cuts me off when I try to speak. And I hate the way she sits. And the way she smells. For years now she has insisted that I sit when I urinate. My promise to lift the seat and wipe the rim and put the seat back down wasn't good enough for her. No!

Far from flourishing, Warren's marriage is primarily a source of annoyance, a gradual emasculation of his manhood.

With this first letter Schmidt eviscerates two of the three areas Ray identifies as ultimately valuable—vocation and family. Doing so with a six-year-old is touching, pathetic, and comical. This confessional tone becomes a regular fixture in his letters. Payne refers to Ndugu as "the distant, unseen confessor," pointing to the significant religious and psychological function that writing to Ndugu plays in Schmidt's journey.[24] Ndugu is a Rogerian therapist of sorts, offering Schmidt a listening and—because he is invisible—nonjudgmental ear.

Confession marks a significant development for Schmidt since honesty is so foreign to him. Befitting his Midwestern cultural values, he regularly masks his true feelings behind a veneer that everything is all right. In a deleted scene, Warren returns home after discovering Helen's affair and confronting Ray, and is greeted by a neighbor who asks how he is doing. "Oh, fine. Just fine," he lies.[25] When he tries to dissuade Jeannie from marrying Randall he falsely attributes his disapproval to Helen, insinuating that she did not approve of him.

Even with his confessor Warren engages in subterfuge. Although they channel vulnerability, his letters reflect his habitual presentation of an image at odds with his reality.[26] In his fourth letter, immediately after Jeannie *refuses* to allow him to visit early before the wedding, Schmidt writes, "Jeannie begged me to come out early and help her with the arrangements, but I told her I needed some time to myself." His fabrication conceals his inability to cope with her rejection. Like *American Beauty*, this film also unveils the impotency of the American Dream to help people cope with failure of any sort.

The juxtaposition of his words (in voiceover) with visual images accentuates Warren's deceit. Lounging in a chair, he reflects at the end of his second letter to Ndugu: "All I know is—I've got to make the best of whatever time is left. Life is short, Ndugu, and I can't afford to waste another minute." The motivational impulse of this final line is belied, however, by the stark contrast in the following scene, two weeks later: a disheveled, unkempt Warren sleeps in the same recliner, wearing the same pajamas, and wakes out of a deep and almost drunken fog to stilted dialogue emanating from a TV soap opera. This and the following scenes undercut Warren's motivational plea. He has wasted not minutes, but weeks, and—more likely—an entire lifetime.

Threaded throughout Warren's third letter to Ndugu is a series of jarring contrasts between his spoken words and visual images. The column on the left contains his voiceover, the one on the right lists the corresponding visual images on the screen:

Now I don't want to kid you. Adjusting to life without Helen has been quite a challenge. But I think you'd be proud of me.	*The dining room table is littered with dirty cups and plates, an empty ice cream container, condiments, a syrup bottle, and other plastic containers.*
Yep, this house is under new management, but you'd never know the difference.	*The kitchen is even worse. Overflowing trash bags are strewn on the floor. Dirty dishes are piled high in the sink. There is not a shred of space on the counters. In the refrigerator are mostly empty shelves.*
Oh, sure, sometimes I can be a tad forgetful, and miss a meal or two, but I guess that's hardly worth mentioning to someone in your situation.	*He opens a cupboard to find only a container of salt, box of taco shells, and coffee filters. Flies buzz around inside. He removes a taco shell and starts chewing on it.*
Helen wouldn't want me sitting around wallowing in self-pity. No siree, Bob. Why, she'd tell me to shape up or ship out. So I try to get out as much as I can—try to stay active, stick to my routine. That's very important in the face of big changes in life.	*He exits the house in pajamas and trench coat, hair disheveled, shuffling in slippers for a dozen or so paces . . . and steps up into the RV.*
Oh, sure, I'm not quite the cook Helen was, but I remember a trick or two from my bachelor days.	*He parks the RV at a supermarket. Inside, he feverishly grabs, dumps, and throws scores of frozen foods into his shopping cart.*
It's a lot of work, keeping a household . . . But for now I'm getting by just fine.	*He unloads scores of grocery bags into the RV.*

The recurring incongruity between Warren's words and behavior produces an unsettling comedic effect. His thoughtful reflections in letters to Ndugu are regularly (and usually immediately) followed by humorous elements. His claim to "make the best of whatever time is left . . . I can't afford to waste another minute" is followed by two weeks of *wasting* life. The same device is employed in his fifth letter to Ndugu, which concludes:

> And so, Ndugu, I must say it's been a very rewarding trip. And this morning I awoke from my night in the wilderness completely transformed. I'm like a new

man. For the first time in years I feel clear. I know what I want. I know what I've got to do. And nothing's going to stop me ever again.

Instantly following this inspiring moment is the deleted scene in which Warren capitulates to the waitress who refuses to grant him his dietary request. Warren's newfound courage is never actualized. His failure to convince Jeannie to cancel the wedding is yet another example of his inability to follow through on his promise that "nothing's going to stop me ever again."

This interplay of poignancy and comedy also occurs during Warren's grief over Helen's death. He reveals in a letter to Ndugu his affection, regret, and mourning over Helen:

> I'm not going to lie to you, Ndugu—it's been a rough few weeks. And I've been pretty, you know, broken up from time to time. I miss her. I miss my Helen. I guess I just didn't know how lucky I was to have a wife like Helen until she was gone.[27]

He ends the letter with his typical exhortative coda: "Remember that, young man: you've got to appreciate what you have, while you still have it." Yet this tender moment has the briefest half-life. For Warren's sentimental encouragement is immediately followed (and undercut) by finding the stockpile of Ray's love letters to Helen. His discovery of her infidelity (and frantic exorcism of all her items from the house) subverts his grief-inspired wisdom of "appreciating what you have."

Payne's consistent comedic disruption undercuts—and highlights the tenuous nature of—cultural wisdom. He also presents a compelling vision of comedy as an intrinsically constructive experience and valuable way of understanding (and coping) with the futility that pervades and is guaranteed in the world. The worldview in Payne's films differs from Woody Allen's quip ("comedy is tragedy plus time"); for Payne tragedy and comedy are interlinked *all* the time, whether in the warring factions over abortion and Ruth's body in *Citizen Ruth* (1996), the flailing schemes of Jim McAllister in *Election* (1999), the lascivious antics of Jack in *Sideways* (2004), or the bumbling Sid in *The Descendants* (2011).[28]

DEATH: THE NECESSARY CONTEXT FOR MEANING

As with Jesus' parable, *About Schmidt* positions death as the principal frame for understanding how to live meaningfully. Both texts explore the possibility of such a meaningful existence given the unseen shadow of death that, hovering over us, might intrude at any moment. Helen's death is a reminder, like God's announcement to the rich man, of life's transience and the potential imminence of our mortal collapse. Her death is a shock, appearing to Warren and viewers with no hint or anticipation. Warren's astonishment at finding her lying face down on the kitchen floor, the vacuum still running, is no doubt due to seeing her alive only hours before. Situating her death in the midst of her mundane chore and Warren's quotidian errands evokes death's potentially unexpected and intrusive nature. As in *No Country for Old Men* (d. Joel and Ethan Coen, 2007), death keeps its own schedule and arrives, unbidden, on its own terms.

Helen's death catalyzes Warren's quest for purpose by leading him to ponder his own ultimate end. Unable to sleep the night after her funeral, he sits alone and eats in his pajamas while writing to Ndugu:

> I believe I mentioned in my previous letter that I am an actuary at Woodmen of the World Insurance Company. If I am given a man's age, race, profession, place of residence, marital status, and medical history, I can calculate with great probability how long that man will live.
>
> In my own case, now that my wife has died, there is a 73% chance that I will die within nine years, provided that I do not remarry. All I know is—I've got to make the best of whatever time is left. Life is short, Ndugu, and I can't afford to waste another minute.

Even before this point Warren has (perhaps unconscious) awareness of his mortality, indicated by his dissatisfaction with his old age. In his first letter, before Helen dies, he remarks, "Anyway, sixty-six must sound pretty old to a young fellow like yourself." He then itemizes a list of complaints: "wrinkles around my eyes, sagging skin on my neck, hair in my ears, veins on my ankles."

Allusions to Schmidt's death, explicit and tacit, pervade the film. Even animals are put in service of symbolically representing his demise. His retirement party opens with a series of four successive pictures of cows on the restaurant wall that culminate in a picture of Warren. This progression draws a parallel between the future destiny of the cows (the slaughterhouse) and Warren (the grave), anticipating the latter's death. The images draw attention to how Warren has been led over several decades to his own kind of psychic and spiritual slaughter.[29] Cows are later connected to death when, during Helen's funeral, a cattle truck is washed down in the background. On his road trip, a cattle truck passes Warren, and he can hear some of them mooing and even see them between the grates. For fifteen seconds the camera lingers on the truck and (mostly) the eyes of some of the cows.[30] It is as though Warren peers into the eyes of his own future end.

Another foreshadowing of Warren's future death is the brief shot of him in the bathtub that closely resembles Jacques-Louis David's 1793 painting "Death of Marat." Reconfiguring the image of Marat's assassination, this shot of Warren evokes the specter of his own (somatic and internal) death.

4.2 Death of Warren

In the conclusion to his final letter to Ndugu, Warren explicitly frames his quest for a worthwhile life within the contours of his death:

> Relatively soon I will die. Maybe in twenty years, maybe tomorrow. It doesn't matter. Once I am dead and everyone who knew me dies too it will be as though I never even existed. What difference has my life made to anyone? None that I can think of, none at all. Hope things are fine with you.
>
> Yours truly,
> Warren Schmidt

Warren's malaise is rooted in his fear that death will eventually erase him. Departing from his usual practice, he ends this final missive without his typical moral or relational exhortation. This absence matches Warren's despair and perhaps his realization that the pursuit of fulfillment, given death's erasure of his existence, is indeed vain. Having failed to find what he so desperately sought for himself, he also gives up imparting any advice to Ndugu. He learns that there *is* nothing to learn.

The film opts, however, not to end on such an entirely dismal note. Entering his study during his final line to Ndugu, Warren dumps loads of mail on his desk, and one letter (addressed via airmail from Tanzania) catches his attention. He picks it up, sits, opens it, and reads while we hear a woman's voiceover:

Dear Mr. Warren Schmidt,

My name is Sister Nadine Gautier of the order of the Sisters of the Sacred Heart. I work in a small village near the town of Embeya in Tanzania. One of the children I care for is little Ndugu Umbo, the boy you sponsor. Ndugu is a very intelligent boy and very loving. He is an orphan. Recently he needed medical attention for an infection of the eye, but he is better now. He loves to eat melon, and he loves to paint. Ndugu and I want you to know that he receives all your letters. He hopes that you are happy in your life and healthy. He thinks of you every day and he wants very much your happiness. Ndugu is only six years old, and cannot read or write. But he has made for you a painting. He hopes that you will like his painting.

Yours Sincerely,
Sister Nadine Gautier

Warren removes a single sheet of paper which contains the following drawing:

4.3 Ndugu's Painting

As he stares at and absorbs the image, tears come to his eyes and roll down his cheeks. He has a difficult time stopping them. The camera cuts to a close-up on the two faces in the drawing. Ever so slowly Schmidt begins to smile. His eyes look up from the drawing, and the film ends. If this chapter were a parable, it would end here as well.

AN AMERICAN PARABLE

About Schmidt endorses Ray's critique of the economic and material aspects of the American Dream as hollow. The film also rejects his subsequent claim that meaning is found in family, friendships, and career. These aspects of the American Dream fail Warren. So also do the Protestant Midwestern values of "an old-fashioned work ethic, a stolid stoicism, and a social conservatism."[31] The film insists that what is of true value or "ultimate concern" is found not in family, friends, or career, but is rooted in an entirely different concern— knowing that one has improved the world. *"But what kind of difference have I made? What in the world is better because of me?"*

Schmidt's need to make such a difference is compounded by the realization that, as in Ecclesiastes, death forever erases one's body, and even one's life from the memory of others.[32] The haunting specter of death deepens Schmidt's despondency. "Once I am dead," he reflects, "and everyone who knew me dies too it will be as though I never even existed." "What difference has my life made to anyone? None that I can think of, none at all." Like Luke's parable of the "Rich Fool," the film reevaluates the relative importance of life choices by framing them within an acute awareness of life's fragility and transience.[33]

In the discourse on anxiety following Luke's parable, Jesus proposes selling one's goods and giving alms to the poor as the optimal use of possessions given death's inevitability and uncertain timing (Luke 12:33). *About Schmidt* resonates with this proposal in championing the sharing of economic resources with the socially and economically vulnerable. Both texts propose an *ethical* solution to the dilemma of living meaningfully given death's inevitability, potential imminence, and possible erasure among the memory of others.

The film's ethical impulse was originally featured more prominently. A scene that showed more extensive footage of hungry children during the Childreach commercial cut immediately to a shot of a tray of four plates stacked high with food, carried by a waitress to a table where Warren and Helen sit with Ray and his wife. The camera zooms in on Ray's face as he stuffs a large forkful of food in his mouth and begins chewing; Ray's wife and Helen do the same. Warren, visibly uncomfortable, is unable to take a bite. All around him dissolves to black. The mouth of Ray's wife fills the entire screen as she chews her food, its sound deafening. Tight close-ups of Ray and Helen repeat the pattern. No longer able to bear the unseemly sight, Warren covers his eyes with his hand. Having witnessed the hungry children, he is unable to engage in the communal gorging. Removing this scene shifts the focus from the *issue* of poverty to a *person* in poverty, and Schmidt's relationship with him. *About Schdmidt's* ethical proposal is present, but it is fundamentally relational.

Payne contributed this relational emphasis to the film; neither Ndugu nor Warren's letters are in Begley's novel. Schmidt writes diary entries in the latter, and Payne could have kept this device if he merely wanted access to Schmidt's honesty and the humor produced by the dissonance between Schmidt's claims and reality. But the correspondence with Ndugu provides an element the diary lacks: a relationship with a child in poverty, one that has a profound effect on both Ndugu and Warren.[34]

The film maintains an ethical texture, and is one of many relatively recent films that addresses issues of social (in)justice.[35] *About Schmidt* functions as an ethical text in inviting viewers to act, not only to dignify the humanity of those in poverty but also to experience the transformation that such action can produce in themselves. Such an invitation is relevant in a world in which the numbers of children who die daily from hunger and related diseases is nine times greater than the number of people killed in the attacks on September 11, 2001. Those who respond to such an invitation (such as the film's production crew who established through Childreach a lifetime scholarship for the child Abdallah Mtulu) enable the film to have an ongoing ethical and existential afterlife.[36]

Warren longs to make a difference. And he does so—in almost complete ignorance—in the life of Ndugu. In some small way he addresses, and perhaps assuages his guilt about, the gross disparity between the worlds of the "stuffed and starved."[37] Sister Nadine informs Warren that Ndugu receives all his letters, and it is possible that the medical care for Ndugu's eye is made possible by Schmidt's sponsorship.[38] Sister Nadine is explicit regarding Warren's influence: *"He thinks of you every day and he wants very much your happiness."* It is the drawing, however, that conveys most profoundly and poignantly the difference Warren has made in the young child's life. Ndugu appears happy and his happiness seems rooted in the relational connection he feels with Warren, the man whose hand he presumably holds. As with the use of video in *American Beauty,* it is the image—not the word—that facilitates a sacred epiphany.

Obliquely foreshadowing the difference Warren makes is the first sentence of a letter Childreach sends Warren after he decides to sponsor a child: "Dear Mr. Schmidt, You're about to change the world for little Ndugu Umbo."

Warren anticipated neither the degree to which this would be true nor the extent to which Ndugu would be a source of genuine joy for him. Suggestive, however, of the potential fragility of this moment is the melody playing when the final scene cuts to the credits. Because it is the same music that plays in comedic episodes, Payne might hint here that even this incident—like the other "poignant" scenes that are undercut or balanced with humor—must not be granted too much gravity. On the other hand, Warren's tears and beginning of a smile seem to be a genuine sign of the profound influence of Ndugu's painting.

The renewing power of Schmidt's relationship with Ndugu is absent not only in the novel but also in Luke's parable of the "Rich Fool." Jesus does, following the parable, advocate selling one's goods and giving them to the poor. But even here there is silence about forming relational bonds between the privileged and vulnerable. In the gospels, Jesus repeatedly stresses caring for the poor. The film illustrates the transformation that such care can produce.

About Schmidt invites people to consider how they might form relational bonds with actual people living in poverty. Doing so would enable them to answer the challenge of Peruvian theologian Gustavo Gutierrez: "So you say you love the poor. Name them." Such relationships, the film illustrates, have the potential to enhance the life and humanity of the giver and the receiver. By the film's end—and to a certain degree throughout—these roles are reversed: Ndugu becomes the giver, Schmidt the receiver.

This argument—that meaning is to be found in entering into relationship with a person in poverty—marks the film as more subversive than Jesus' parable of the "Rich Fool." The film rejects emphatically the fundamental claims of the American Dream that fulfillment is to be found in family, friends, and work. Jesus' critique of the rich man's folly is rooted in the man's failure to adopt certain expectations regarding the beneficial use of goods in light of death's uncertain timing. The parable upsets certain practices (e.g., saving for the future), but to do so it draws upon other (Jewish, Greco-Roman, Egyptian) established and recognizable cultural values.

About Schmidt more thoroughly rejects core tenets of American cultural values; its proposal that fulfillment can be found in providing for and entering some kind of relationship with a poor child in the two-thirds world does not even dwell on the periphery of American culture. What the film deems most meaningful is not even an option within the framework of the American Dream. Its absence underscores the film's indictment of the American Dream as a bankrupt enterprise—ethically, existentially, and relationally. In this case, the film out-parables the biblical parable.[39]

For the same reason, *About Schmidt* is more culturally subversive than *Fight Club* or *American Beauty*. Notwithstanding their respective rejections of American cultural elements, both *Fight Club* and *American Beauty* conclude by conforming to certain cultural scripts. The narrator in *Fight Club* manages to connect (ever so briefly) with Marla, a potential romantic partner. Immediately before he is killed, Lester Burnham finds gratitude for his nuclear family. These typical American tropes (romance, family) are denied to Schmidt.[40] Unlike the novel, the film does not conform to a cultural expectation that finds value in romance, even depriving Schmidt of his sole effort to find satisfaction in his botched pass at Vicki. The film's vision is more expansive (and enriching) than the myopic fixation of the American Dream on family, friends, and career as vessels of meaning.

✳ 5 ✳

FILMS AS PARABLES OF DISORIENTATION

You have built a lovely home, myth assures us: but, whispers parable,
you are right above an earthquake fault.

—John Dominic Crossan[1]

*F*ight Club, American Beauty, and About Schmidt undermine American cultural values, depicting these cherished myths as meaningless.
In their searing critique of the sacrosanct wisdom of the American
Dream, these films function like Jesus' parables. For like these films, Jesus' stories subvert conventional myths of his culture.

Jesus was a storyteller. This perhaps obvious remark is necessary since
Jesus' ability as a raconteur is neglected, often overlooked in light of other
(more "lofty") perceptions of him as Christ/Messiah, Lord, Son of God, etc.
But in the beginning were stories. Before all the claims about Jesus, and even
before the stories *about* him, were the stories *he* told. His storytelling is—in
addition to being Jewish and crucified—one of the relatively few things about
which there is scholarly consensus.[2] The Synoptic Gospels (Mark, Matthew,
and Luke) attribute about forty-nine different stories to Jesus.[3] Parables were
a prominent part of his repertoire. In Luke's Gospel, roughly one-third of
Jesus' teaching is in the form of parables. A comment in Mark's Gospel, while

exaggerated, captures Jesus' proclivity for storytelling: *"without a parable* he did not speak to them" (4:34).

Parables, however, do far more than "speak." They illustrate, paint, and perform. Communicating information or making "points" is not their primary purpose.[4] Parables are first and foremost stories. Jesus' parables reveal meaning, but they do so—like film—through narrative devices of character, action, and plot. The parables are narrative, not propositional discourse, and thus belong to the realm of the artistic.[5] Jesus' stories reveal a distinct artistry, and chief among the many legitimate titles for Jesus should be artist.

JESUS' SACRILEGIOUS STORIES

A common perception of Jesus' parables is that they communicate a moral or a "heavenly truth."[6] The opposite is true. Far from inculcating morals, Jesus' parables undermine them. His stories provoke rather than comfort, disturb instead of console. In the words of one classic definition, a parable "arrest[s] the hearer by its vividness or *strangeness,* and leav[es] the mind in sufficient doubt about its precise application to tease it into active thought."[7] Jesus' parables do far more than even this; they shatter orthodox perceptions.[8]

Jesus' parables demolish cultural myths by turning them on their head.[9] The parable of the Samaritan—one of Jesus' most well known—upends basic religious expectations.[10] Found only in Luke's Gospel (10:25-37), the parable is situated within this crucial dialogue:

> LAWYER: Teacher, what can I do so that I will inherit eternal life?[11]
> JESUS: What is written in the law? How do you read it?
> LAWYER: You shall love the Lord your God from all your heart and with all yourself and with all your strength and with all your mind; and your neighbor as yourself.
> JESUS: You answered correctly. Do this, and you shall live.
> LAWYER: And who is my neighbor?
> JESUS: A certain person was going down from Jerusalem to Jericho, and fell among bandits who—even after they stripped him and beat him—departed, leaving him half-dead. And by chance a certain priest was going down that road, and when he saw him, he passed by on the other side. And similarly, a Levite also came by the place, and when he saw him, he passed by on the other side. But a certain Samaritan, while traveling,

came by, and when he saw him he was filled with compassion. And after he came near, he bandaged his wounds by pouring oil and wine, and after he put him on his own animal he led him to an inn and he took care of him. And the next day he took out and gave two denarii to the innkeeper and said, "Take care of him, and whatever more you spend, I—when I return—will repay you."

JESUS: Which of these three—does it seem to you—was a neighbor to the one who fell among the bandits?

LAWYER: The one who showed him mercy.

JESUS: Go and *you*, you do likewise.

Two treasured myths are subverted in this dialogue, and both relate to the Samaritan. Samaritans were ethnic and religious outcasts to many first-century Jews. Descended from intermarriage between Israelites and foreigners, Samaritans were part Jewish; they were "Mudbloods" (to use J. K. Rowling's phrase). Religious differences between Samaritans and Jews were also (perhaps more) significant. Samaritans regarded only the first five books of the Hebrew Bible as canonical, and they had their own version of these texts (the Samaritan Pentateuch). Finally, and in explicit violation of Deuteronomy 12, Samaritans worshipped God in their own temple at Mount Gerizim rather than at the Jerusalem temple. There was also violence between Jews and Samaritans; John Hyrcanus and a group of Jews destroyed the Samaritan temple in 129/8 BCE.[12]

In light of the preceding dialogue between Jesus and the lawyer, the parable undercuts the belief that eternal life is the exclusive privilege of one's own religious (or ethnic) community. The character who inherits eternal life (because he loves the needy man) is the ethnic/religious outsider and enemy. Potentially disconcerting as well is the tacit claim that the priest and Levite would *not* inherit eternal life due to their failure to love the man in need.

All the more troubling, Jesus presents the Samaritan not as someone to love, but as a person to imitate. Referring to the Samaritan, Jesus says, "Go and you, you *do likewise*." The ethnic and religious enemy is not only the story's hero; he is the moral exemplar—the model of behavior and of how to inherit eternal life.[13] One is not to pity him, but to become *like* him. Such a message—part of Luke's broader interest in using social outcasts as models of behavior—is far more provocative than imploring his audience to love or be kind to Samaritans.[14]

The threat of the Samaritan is evident if we consider that the twenty-first-century parallel of the Samaritan for Christians in America would be a member of *al-Qaeda*. Like the Samaritan, a Muslim terrorist is an ethnic (usually) and religious outsider and enemy. It is difficult to imagine American Christians believing that such a person could inherit eternal life as a result of loving his neighbor. It would be even more astonishing if Christians were willing to learn from such a person, regarding him as a model to emulate.

For Christian (ancient and contemporary) readers the parable retains an additional unsettling element. In directing the lawyer to the law, and affirming his response, Jesus indicates that the answer to inheriting eternal life is to be found not in him (or anywhere in the New Testament!), but in obeying the Torah's commands to love God and neighbor (Deut 6:5; Lev 19:18). Christians who locate eternal life in Jesus ironically depart from Jesus' own emphasis.[15]

Jesus' dialogue with the lawyer represents a parabolic pedagogy. Throughout the conversation Jesus employs a Socratic technique by mirroring the lawyer: he responds to the lawyer's two questions not with answers, but with questions of his own. Jesus never replies to a question with an answer, and he only gives answers in response to the lawyer's answers. Jesus thereby invites the lawyer to participate actively in discovering the answers to his own questions. Parables employ a rhetorical strategy similar to this dialogic mirroring, one that invites and empowers people to engage more fully in creating and constructing meaning for themselves.

Jesus' parable of Lazarus and the Rich Man also upsets a number of religious myths:

> And there was a certain rich person, and he would wear purple and fine linen, enjoying himself joyously every day. And a certain poor man named Lazarus lay at his gate, covered in sores, and longing to be filled from what fell from the rich man's table. But even the dogs would come and lick his sores. And the poor man died, and he was carried away by the angels into Abraham's bosom. And the rich man also died and was buried. And in Hades, while being tortured, he raised his eyes, and sees Abraham from afar and Lazarus in his bosom. And calling out, he said, "Father Abraham, show me mercy and send Lazarus so that he might dip the tip of his finger in water and cool my tongue; for I am in torment in this blaze." But Abraham said, "Child, remember that you received your good things in your life, and Lazarus likewise evil things. But now he is comforted here, and you are suffering. And in any case, between you and us a great chasm has been

firmly set so that those who want to cross over from here to you are unable, nor to pass through from there to us." And he said, "Then I ask you, father, that you send him to my father's house, for I have five brothers, so that he might warn them, lest they also come into this place of torture." And Abraham says, "They have Moses and the Prophets—let them listen to them." But he said, "No, father Abraham! But if someone from the dead should go to them they will repent." But he said to him, "If they are not listening to Moses and the Prophets, they will not be persuaded even if someone rises from the dead."

(Luke 16:19-31)

This story shatters expectations regarding the criteria used to determine one's eternal destination. For what people may consider to be most crucial (faith, belief, attitudes, motives, etc.) is of zero concern. No attention is given to the internal state of Lazarus or the rich man. Readers of this parable have been so distraught over this lacuna that they often supply it themselves. Several interpreters amplify the rich man's wickedness by attributing to him an extensive range of moral deficiencies.[16] Another common strategy is to magnify the noble stature of Lazarus.[17] The Protestant reformer Martin Luther claims that the poor man was so satisfied with God's blessings that he "would have heartily and willingly suffered *even more misery*, if the will of his gracious God had so determined."[18] Lazarus had, Luther claims, a "soul inside more precious than any gold."[19] It is likely, however, that the actual element would have held more appeal for Lazarus. Perhaps *mis*interpretation is the opiate of the people.

Such misreadings reveal how easily the subversive edge of parables can be dulled.[20] This domesticating effort—of forcing parables to conform to a conventional mentality—demonstrates how threatening parables can be. Attempts to tame the text's disturbing implications contradict Abraham's remark that the rich man is in agony *because* he received "good things" in life, and that Lazarus is comforted *because* his life was one of "agony" (16:25). Unlike the Egyptian tale upon which this parable might be based—and to the dismay of many readers—Luke's story shows no interest in the internal moral state of Lazarus or the rich man.[21] The only reason given for Lazarus' comfort and the rich man's punishment is their socio-economic status.[22] Luther's adamant opposition to this plain sense of the parable points to the pervasive (yet largely unconscious) power of myth.[23] Its maintenance requires a relentless rejection or radical reshaping of contrary perspectives.

Jesus' most perplexing parable is the Dishonest Manager:

> There was a certain rich person who had a manager, and this one was accused
> before him of squandering his property. And after he summoned him, he said to
> him, "What is this I hear about you? Give the account of your management, for
> you are no longer able to be a manager." And the manager said to himself, "What
> shall I do, for my master is taking away the management from me? I am not
> strong enough to dig; I am ashamed to beg. I know what I will do, so that when I
> am removed from management they will receive me into their homes." And after
> he summoned every one of his master's debtors he said to the first, "How much
> do you owe my master?" And he said, "One hundred measures of oil." And he said
> to him, "Take your bill and sit down. Quickly, write fifty!" Then to another he
> said, "And you, how much do you owe?" And he said, "One hundred measures of
> wheat." He says to him, "Take your bill and write eighty." And the master praised
> the unjust manager for he acted shrewdly.
>
> (Luke 16:1-8a)

The shock of this parable comes in its concluding line when the master *praises*
the manager's criminality.[24] With his commendation, the parable seems to
extol theft, even for a selfish motive! For the master applauds the manager's act
of reducing debts—money owed to the master—in order to secure for himself
future employment/housing. Efforts to reduce or eliminate the tension provoked by the praising of this vice are as unconvincing as they are legion.[25]

Despite its innocuous appearance, Jesus' briefest parable of the Leaven/
Yeast is also provocative:

> The kingdom of heaven is like yeast that a woman took and hid in three measures
> of flour until it was all leavened.
>
> (Matt 13:33; cf. Luke 13:21)

The parable's controversial edge is clearer when one realizes that throughout
the Bible leaven (yeast) is consistently used as a symbol of *im*purity. Of the
myriad references to leaven in the Bible, zero are positive. Instructions for the
Jewish Passover insist on banishing leaven from the home; anyone who eats
leavened bread is to be "cut off" from the community of Israel (Exod 12:14-20).
Offerings to God must not include leaven (Lev 2:11), and leaven is used as a
metaphor for adultery (Hos 7:4). This pejorative use of leaven continues in the
New Testament. It is a symbol of the Pharisees' "hypocrisy" (Luke 12:1). The

apostle Paul twice uses the phrase "a little leaven leavens all the dough" (Gal 5:9; 1 Cor 5:6) to convey the idea that "a rotten apple spoils the whole barrel." When Paul uses leaven as a symbol of sexual immorality, he insists on getting rid of "old leaven" and replacing it, not with "*new* leaven" as one might expect, but with "*un*leavened bread" (1 Cor 5:7-8). The ancient process of making leaven/yeast helps explain its function as a symbol for corruption: a piece of bread was stored "in a damp, dark place until mold forms. The bread rots and decays," and leaven is produced.[26]

Jesus' parable thus likens the kingdom of heaven to a woman (also potentially provocative!) who takes a symbol of decay and rot, and *hides* it in flour until it is all blended together.[27] The kingdom of heaven, contrary to popular perceptions, is *im*pure. It is infused with corruption, rot, and decay, and so thoroughly that it is not possible to distinguish—as many are wont to do—the pure from the impure.[28]

Jesus' parable of the Mustard Seed offers a similar subversive message, despite its apparent banality:

> The kingdom of heaven is like a mustard seed that a person sowed in his field. It is the smallest of all seeds, but when it grows it is greater than the garden vegetables, and it becomes a tree so that the birds of the air come and rest in its branches.
>
> (Matt 13:31-32)

The mustard plant was regarded in Jesus' time as invasive and contaminating. The ancient Roman historian Pliny describes it as growing "entirely wild, though it is improved by being transplanted: but on the other hand, when it has once been sown it is scarcely possible to get the place free of it, as the seed when it falls germinates at once."[29] It is likely for this reason that the Mishnah (a Jewish commentary on the Torah, ca. 200 CE) forbids planting mustard seeds by a field of grain or in a garden bed.[30] The kingdom of heaven in this parable is thus likened to a wild, uncontrollable plant whose proclivity to contaminate must be carefully curbed.

Even stranger is what this plant becomes. The tree that the mustard seed grows into ("the birds of the air came and dwelt in its branches") is not only hyperbolic (mustard seeds become shrubs not trees), but also significant given its similarity to these two descriptions of trees in the Hebrew Bible:

Its leaves were fair and its fruit abundant, and in it was food for all. The beasts of the field found shade under it, *and the birds of the air dwelt in its branches,* and all flesh was fed from it.

(Dan 4:12, NRSV)

So it towered high above all the trees of the field; its boughs grew large and its branches long, from abundant water in its shoots. *All the birds of the air made their nests in its boughs;* under its branches all the animals of the field gave birth to their young; and in its shade all great nations lived.

(Ezek 31:5-6, NRSV)

Both trees described above are symbols for infamous enemies of Israel. The tree in Daniel represents Nebuchadnezzar, the Babylonian king who in 587/86 BCE destroyed Jerusalem, razed the Jewish temple, and kidnapped and exiled many Jews to Babylon. The tree in Ezekiel symbolizes Pharaoh, the Egyptian ruler who enslaved the Israelites. These two figures—Nebuchadnezzar and Pharaoh—are the two most notorious nemeses of the Jewish people in the Hebrew Bible. The kingdom of heaven, Jesus thereby claims, is like a contaminating plant whose uncontrollable growth culminates in a destructive adversary.

Two other parables in Matthew 13 controvert the myth that the kingdom of heaven is pure. The parable of the Net compares the kingdom to a net that catches fish "of every kind" (Matt 13:47). This comprehensive catch would include fish whose consumption the Torah (and kosher dietary practice) forbids (cf. Lev 11:9-12; Deut 14:9-10). The tainted nature of the catch is made explicit: the "good" fish are kept, but the "rotten" are thrown out (Matt 13:48). The parable of the Wheat and the Weeds, like that of the net, is more straightforward about the impurity of the kingdom of heaven (Matt 13:24-30). The kingdom is likened to a field of good (wheat) seeds which is infiltrated by an enemy who sows weeds among the wheat.

These four kingdom parables also undermine the myth that people can discern between the pure and impure. In the parable of the wheat and weeds, a servant proposes cutting down all the weeds in order to protect the wheat. The master vetoes this idea, arguing that doing so would undoubtedly harm the wheat. The wheat and weeds will instead be separated at the harvest by reapers. In this allegorical interpretation, the harvest represents the "end of the age," and the reapers symbolize angels who cast the "weeds" into "the furnace of fire" (Matt 13:38-42). Similarly, in the parable of the net, judgment occurs at the "end of the age" when angels will separate the wicked from the just (Matt 13:49-50). Coupled with these disturbing images of future torture is the implicit warning that humans are neither fit nor capable of exercising such judgment.

The parable of the Workers in the Vineyard (Matt 20:1-15) controverts certain economic myths:

> For the kingdom of heaven is like a housemaster who went out first thing in the morning to hire workers for his vineyard. After agreeing with the workers on a denarius for the day, he sent them into his vineyard. And after he went out about the third hour he saw others standing, unemployed, in the marketplace. And to those he said, "You also go into the vineyard, and whatever is just I will give you." And they departed. And again after he went out about the sixth and ninth hour he did similarly. And about the eleventh hour after he went out he found others standing and he says to them, "Why are you standing here the whole day unemployed?" They say to him, "Because no one hired us." He says to them: "You also go into the vineyard." And when it was early evening the lord of the vineyard says to his steward, "Call the workers and give to them the wage that is due, beginning with the last up to the first." When the ones hired about the eleventh hour came they each received one denarius. And when the first ones hired came they thought that they would receive more. And they each also received a denarius. And when they received [it] they grumbled against the housemaster, saying, "These last worked one hour, and you made them equal to us who bore the misery of the day and the burning heat." And he answered one of them and said, "Friend, I am not unjust to you. Did you not agree with me for a denarius? Take yours and go. And I want to give to this last one as also to you. Am I not allowed to do what I want with what is mine? Or are you jealous because I am good?"

Expectation of a correlation between labor and payment is upended when the master pays the final workers without regard for how long they have toiled. The sharp edge of this parable is dulled when the explicit economic exchange is interpreted allegorically to refer to a kind of salvation schema. The parable's distinctive character is more evident when compared to these two ancient rabbinic parables:

They parable a parable. Unto what is the matter like? It is like a king who hired many laborers. And along with them was one laborer that had worked for him many days. All the laborers went to receive their pay for the day, and this one special laborer went also. He said to this one special laborer: "I will have regard for you. The others, who have worked for me only a little, to them I will give small pay. You, however, will receive a large recompense."[31]

Unto what was Rabbi bar Hiya like? He was like unto a king who hired many laborers of whom one was more industrious than the others. What did the king do? He called him out and walked up and down with him. In the evening the workmen came to be paid. He gave also a full day's pay to the man he had walked with. When the other workers saw this they complained and said: "We have been working hard all day, and this one who only labored two hours receives as much wages as we do?" The king answered: "It is because this one has done more in two hours than you in a whole day."[32]

Both these parables uphold customary notions, either that one should be compensated for working longer hours or that the quality of one's work should merit a reward. Jesus' parable accents generosity over merit; it counters a "pull yourself up by your bootstraps" mentality.

The parable of the Sheep and Goats (Matt 25:31-46) undercuts several common expectations regarding the criteria for eternal salvation:

And when the Son of Man comes in his glory and all the angels with him, then he will sit upon his throne of glory. And all the nations will be gathered before him, and he will separate them from one another, just as the shepherd separates the sheep from the goats. And he will stand the sheep on his right, but the goats on the left. Then the king will say to those on his right, "Come, Blessed of my father, inherit the kingdom prepared for you from the foundation of the world. For I was hungry and you gave me food, I was thirsty and you gave drink to me, I was a foreigner and you welcomed me, naked and you clothed me, I was sick and you visited me, I was in prison and you came to me." Then the righteous ones will answer him, saying, "Lord, when did we see you hungry and feed you, or thirsty and give you drink? And when did we see you a foreigner and welcome you, or naked and clothe you? And when did we see you sick or in prison and come to you?" And the king will answer and say to them, "Amen, I say to you, whatever you did to one of these least of my brothers/sisters, you did to me." Then he will say also to those on the left, "Go from me, cursed into the eternal fire prepared for the devil and his angels. For I was hungry and you did not give me food, I was thirsty and you did not give me drink, I was a foreigner and you did not welcome me, naked and you did not clothe me, sick and in prison and you did not visit me." Then they will answer and say, "Lord, when did we see you hungry or thirsty or a foreigner or naked or sick or in prison and not serve you?" Then he will answer them, saying, "Amen, I say to you, whatever you did not do to one of these least, you did not do to me." And these will depart into eternal punishment, but the righteous into eternal life.

The sole criterion determining one's eternal destiny is whether a person provides for the basic needs of the most vulnerable (hungry, thirsty, sick, imprisoned, naked, foreigners). Caring for those who dwell on the bottom rungs of Maslow's hierarchy of needs results in eternal life.[33] Failing to meet those needs brings eternal punishment. As in "Lazarus and the Rich Man," there is no concern with a person's faith or belief, either what kind they have or whether they have any at all. No consideration is given to whether a person participates in religious activities (prayer, worship, circumcision, baptism, Eucharist). Sexual morality is not mentioned. The motives of people who help or do not help are of no interest. Nor does a person's religious/ethnic identity (as a Jew or Christian) matter. The only standard for judgment is an ethical one. There is also nothing a person can *do* that results in eternal punishment. The only failure is a failure to act.

SUBVERTING MYTHS THAT SUSTAIN OUR WORLD

Jesus' parables disrupt and destabilize.[34] Myths are the chief target of this parabolic dismantling. Whether true or false (often a mix of both), a myth is a story or narrative that provides a community with meaning.[35] A myth may explain where we come from, where we are going, or what our purpose is. Inscribing and enshrining a community's core values, myths confer security and stability.[36] Cultures and communities—nations, religions, churches, and families— subsist on a steady albeit largely unconscious diet of myths.

Parables dislodge myths from their throne of assumed inerrancy and omnipotence. To reconfigure Picasso's dictum ("art is a lie that makes us realize truth"), parables are fictions that devastate the lies of myth. Parables function as narratives of disorientation, or stories of subversion, destabilizing audiences by assaulting long cherished myths.[37] "The threat of the parable," one scholar notes, "is that it subverts the myths that sustain our world."[38] Parables are to myths what the underground British artist Banksy is to Norman Rockwell. Banksy's graffiti excoriates myths that society embraces uncritically. Whether it is a long string of British flags culminating with a child slave stitching these flags on a sewing machine, a picture of Joseph and pregnant Mary blocked on their journey to Bethlehem by the Israeli/Palestinian wall, or a crucified Jesus holding shopping bags crammed with gifts in his outstretched hands, Banksy's art compels viewers to reexamine basic cultural assumptions.

A helpful framework for understanding parables comes from Jesus scholar John Dominic Crossan. He outlines five types of narrative (Myth/Apologue/ Action/Satire/Parable), explaining, "Story establishes world in *myth*, defends such established world in *apologue*, discusses and describes world in *action*, attacks world in *satire*, and subverts world in *parable*."[39] Parables—those of Jesus, Banksy, and the three films we examined—leave people groundless by ripping out the mythical rug on which they have stood securely for so long. Acknowledging the bankruptcy of a myth in which one has participated is to confront the possibility that the source of one's security is empty, and that one's existence is (potentially) meaningless. By catalyzing a process of *un*learning, parables have the potential to plunge audiences into a religious vacuum or existential crisis.[40]

CINEMATIC MYTHS AND PARABLES

Myths are frequently transmitted through images, and in America a primary graphic vehicle for conveying myths is cinema.[41] Films about Native Americans illustrate a range of conflicting narratives regarding American myths.[42] For decades, scores of Westerns portrayed Caucasian cowboys as noble heroes and Native Americans as bloodthirsty savages. Many of John Ford's films (e.g., *Stagecoach*, 1939; *The Searchers*, 1956) exemplify this strategy and conform to a fairly predictable script: Native Americans instigate violent aggression, and their violence is unprovoked with no (logical) motive. Europeans, by contrast, are the innocent victims of unwarranted aggression, and when they do use violence it is to defend themselves (usually their women and children) and/or to avenge a previous attack. Native American family life is absent in these films; this cinematic erasure echoes their historical elimination. Such films function as apologues in supporting American myths. The ironic butchering of the historical record serves as a coping mechanism for a dominant culture unable to face its ancestral violence.

A second wave of Native American films are apologues of a contrary myth: that Native Americans were nonviolent, wise sages who spent all their time communing with nature. In this myth, violence was a foreign commodity imported by invading European hordes. *Dances with Wolves* (d. Costner, 1990) and its reincarnated doppelgängers, *Pocahontas* (d. Gabriel and Goldberg,

1995) and *Avatar* (d. Cameron, 2009) typify this approach. Films in the first wave demonize native peoples; films in this second wave romanticize them, often literally, by coupling the leading white male with an indigenous woman. The white savior defends the native peoples against his own ethnic tribe, and it is through his eyes that viewers romanticize the native peoples. It was not until *Smoke Signals* (d. Eyre, 1998) that First Nations persons were portrayed on their own terms and in their own voice.[43]

Two 1980s films, both starring Tom Cruise, illustrate contrasting functions of narratives vis-à-vis American myths. *Top Gun* (d. Scott, 1986) unabashedly and uncritically celebrates a myth of American military supremacy. The film justifies—without argument or exploration of ethical or moral complexities—America's militaristic violence against its enemies. Assumed throughout is the moral prerogative (and duty) of the United States to unleash violence in order to kill its adversaries. It is taken for granted that America's military violence is used to defend and protect. Moreover, scoring the jet fighting sequences to rock and roll music gives them a kind of video game aesthetic. In these ways, *Top Gun* functions as an apologue in its defense and support of American myths of military and moral supremacy.

Based on the life story of Ron Kovic, *Born on the Fourth of July* (d. Stone, 1989) is a scathing attack of many of the myths extolled in *Top Gun*. Kovic returns from the Vietnam War as a paraplegic and undergoes a lengthy transition to his later role as a prominent war critic. The erosion of his glorification of cultural myths is depicted when he returns to his parent's house after a long night of drinking. His mom reprimands him for removing a crucifix off the wall, instigating a fierce conflict:

RON: This is what you believe in, isn't it Mom? But I don't. I don't believe in him anymore, because he only spent three days up there. Me, I gotta spend the rest of my life. I wish I were dead like him. . . . I believed in everything they told us—"Go fight!" "Go kill!" . . . It's all a lie. The whole thing is a bunch of lies!

MOM: What did they do to you in that war? What happened to you? You need help, Ronnie. You need help.

RON: No, you need help! With all your God and your bullshit dreams about me. You are ashamed of me! You're embarrassed by me. . . . You tell them all, tell them all what they did

> to me. What they did to this whole block, this whole country. We went to Vietnam to stop communism. We shot women and children.
>
> MOM: You didn't shoot women and children. What are you saying?
>
> RON: Communism—the "insidious evil." They told us to go.... Thou shalt not kill, mom. Thou shall not kill women and children. Thou shall not kill, remember? Isn't that what you taught us? Isn't that what they taught us?

Kovic highlights the moral vacuity of the main argument ("stop communism") proffered to defend America's war in Vietnam. He also identifies a religious hypocrisy inherent in any war in which Christians participate: the impossibility of reconciling obedience to the Ten Commandments with killing others. His poignant confession and lament of killing women and children shows that his physical paralysis is part of a broader psychic and spiritual wounding—a moral injury. In its dismantling of American myths, *Born on the Fourth of July* enacts a parable.

PARABLES: A SACRED SECULARITY

Jesus' parables offer a framework for identifying and understanding other modes of parabolic discourse.[44] In eviscerating a sacred cultural myth, *Fight Club*, *American Beauty*, and *About Schmidt* function like Jesus' parables. They provoke rather than comfort, disorient rather than stabilize; they too demolish fundamental tenets of a cultural credo. Understanding these films as parables illuminates their specific religious texture. For these films undermine a collective American mythology that is a source of "ultimate concern" for many. Through its zealous exaltation of success, the American Dream inoculates people against their fear of death, and thereby becomes a medium of immortality. These three films insist, to the contrary, that death is not only inevitable, but that facing it is an essential step toward meaningful living.

Some might hesitate to call such films religious, worrying that doing so vitiates the term "religious" and renders it vapid or insipid. Others might view the use of religious terminology with such films as a foreign imposition, an unwarranted "baptism" of an unwilling secular medium. Jesus' own parables, however, are noteworthy for lacking explicit "religious" or "theological" elements. This absence of overtly religious ornamentation is striking. God appears as a character in only *one* of Jesus' fifty or so parables.[45] The parables display no overt interest in the abstract, the philosophical, or the systematic.[46] Populating the parables are instead the everyday, ordinary materials of first-century Jewish (and, occasionally, Greco-Roman) life: sheep, fish, seeds, dough, coins, houses, brothers, feasts, farms, roads, robberies, managers, masters, debt, manual labor.[47] Employment and economic predicaments are paramount. Jesus' parables bear a secular stamp.[48]

This secularity does not, however, preclude the presence of the sacred. Parables embrace the concrete materials of everyday life as the locus of sacred activity. In doing so, they reveal and illustrate a sacramental imagination.[49] Like films, Jesus' stories are vehicles of profane revelation, or sacred secularity.[50] In the parables, as one scholar observes, the "deeper dimensions" of humanity and divinity "are married to such ordinariness and secularity."[51] The parables reveal a "Jewish mind and heart . . . where *religion becomes secular without loss*."[52] Like the biblical texts Song of Songs and Esther (neither of which mention God), the human element in Jesus' parables is foremost.[53] Human concerns take center stage.

Existential interests—questions about meaningful living—pervade many of Jesus' parables.[54] This human quest for meaning does not preclude ethical, religious, or even theological concerns. Indeed, it can at times be inextricably bound up with them.[55] Most of Luke's unique parables, for example, focus on wealth and possessions,[56] and explore how—especially in light of death—possessions can be used meaningfully.[57] Similar existential and ethical concerns also surface in *Fight Club, American Beauty,* and *About Schmidt.*

The existential disposition of many parables is not surprising given that parables hold much in common with wisdom (sapiential) texts. Parables can be understood as a type of wisdom literature.[58] Of all the possible titles for Jesus, the third century biblical interpreter Origen preferred "Wisdom" as the most appropriate.[59] Common to many wisdom texts is an interest in negotiating where meaning is, and is not, located.[60] Jesus' parables are similarly concerned with meaning and questions related to meaningful living.[61] Because they subvert common myths, Jesus' parables perform as narratives of alternative wisdom.[62] As Ecclesiastes and Job repudiate strands of prevailing wisdom in other Hebrew Bible texts such as Proverbs, so too do Jesus' parables reject many claims of conventional wisdom. This critique of established and esteemed worldviews is a point of overlap between Ecclesiastes, laments, and Jesus' parables. All three have the potential to destabilize audiences in their subversion of orthodox values. The parables are distinct in that they place such subversion into narrative form.

Parables and films do more than subvert. In addition to deconstructing certain myths—revealing them as impotent sources of meaning—they also construct worlds of possibility and invite audiences to consider alternative (and more meaningful) ways of living.[63] They often can and do function, in other words, as narratives of *dis*orientation and *re*orientation.[64] *Fight Club*, *American Beauty*, and *About Schmidt* do precisely this, identifying alternative sources of meaning apart from the American Dream.

Biblical and cinematic parables construct imaginative worlds and invite audiences to dwell and live within them.[65] Viewers and hearers are summoned to participate in a drama that can continue to unfold in their own lives.[66] Like Jesus' parables, these films are most effective if viewers imagine themselves into the living fabric of the story, and animate this living narrative so that it becomes interlaced with the drama of their own lives.

CONCLUSION

Such are the new questions we are beginning to ask beyond the death
of the sacred. Are we not on the verge of a renaissance of the sacred,
at least if humankind itself is not to die?

—Paul Ricoeur[1]

When you have the intuition that there is something which is there, but
out of the reach of your physical world, art and religion are
the only means to get to it.

—Guillermo del Toro, film director[2]

I believe cinema is now the most powerful secular religion and people gather in cinemas to experience things collectively the way they
once did in church. The cinema storytellers have become the new
priests. They're doing a lot of the work of our religious institutions,
which have so concretized the metaphors in their stories, taken so much
of the poetry, mystery and mysticism out of religious belief, that people
look for other places to question their spirituality.

—George Miller, film director/producer[3]

The development of Christianity coincided with an abandonment of
the use of parable as a dominant form of discourse. Christianity generated its own sets of myths (anti-parables) as it sought to provide the

111

kind of security required in the transition from an incipient faction to an established religion. The radical ethnic shift in the early stages of Christianity (from entirely Jewish to entirely Gentile) was accompanied by a fundamental paradigmatic and perspectival shift: from deconstructing myths to propagating them. Christianity is rooted in the destabilization of myths. For the past two thousand years it has been in the myth-making business.[4] Perhaps it is time to return to the art of parable as a fundamental discourse. In the meantime, the primary task of creating parables belongs to artists—poets, novelists, painters, musicians, and filmmakers.

Cinema is a primary locus of the sacred in contemporary American culture. Those who mourn the death of the sacred in the twenty-first century overlook its vibrant and flourishing presence in the theater. Many continue to flock to this hallowed darkness where they experience film as "profane revelation." Many find the sacred in the secular.

One manifestation of this blasphemous unveiling are parables of disorientation, narratives that undermine prevailing wisdom and threaten consecrated values. *Fight Club, American Beauty,* and *About Schmidt* are parables that subvert the cherished American Dream. These films are *cinematic* parables, and in this specific medium lies much of their rhetorical force. The parabolic power of these films is directly tied to their specific form. For cinema communicates in ways that other types of art do not.

American Beauty creatively promotes the power of film as a medium of sacred encounter. The entire film is framed between a bracketing—an inclusio—of Ricky's video camera. The first sound in the film is of his camera turning on, and the first visual shot is his camera's recording of Jane. Similarly, the film's final image (before fading to black) is the plastic bag Ricky films. Viewers enter and leave the film through his camera lens. His video camera plays a significant role beyond this, for it is Ricky's main vehicle for encountering beauty and the divine. Film is also the means by which he conveys his religious experiences.[5] Although he apologizes for the medium ("Video's a poor excuse, I know"), he recognizes its power. His video "helps him to remember" that a benevolent life force wants him to never fear, a salutary and perhaps salvific reminder given his father's torrential abuse. His video also catalyzes genuine intimacy between him and Jane, facilitating their first kiss. Contrary to Freud, beauty—captured and conveyed through film—is a sufficient distraction from the misery in Ricky's life.[6] Film is also, however, the same instrument Ricky uses to record child abuse, revealing the savage realities lingering under the veneer of domestic bliss. Both Carolyn's abuse of Jane and the Colonel's pummeling of Ricky are caught on his camera.

American Beauty thus offers video—film—as a metaphor for the cinematic experience itself, illuminating cinema's power to function as a vehicle of sacred beauty and abusive terror, of the sublime and grotesque.[7] The film promotes *film itself* as profane revelation, a medium which unveils truth in all its glory and horror. Film is, *American Beauty* illustrates and argues, the chief means of authentic religious experience. As Ricky encounters death, beauty, and God through his camera, so too can viewers find in his filming, in *American Beauty*, and in cinema more broadly, an aesthetic encounter with the sacred.

Other, less explicit, examples of the power of the visual image as a sacred instrument are noteworthy. In *American Beauty*, it is the family photograph that nudges Lester toward his moment of genuine gratitude. Another visual image—Ndugu's painting—is the main catalyst for Warren Schmidt's epiphany that he has indeed made the world better for another person. Warren's letters—an instrument of storytelling unto themselves—also reveal valuable insights, but they do not match the narrative and emotional power of Ndugu's drawing. In *Fight Club*, director David Fincher employs multiple tools—shaking the camera, using grainy filters, splicing split-second frames into the picture—that visually enhance the film's disorienting content. By inserting the split-second frames (especially the final one), Fincher adopts and enacts Tyler Durden's role in the film, as one who uses film to unsettle and unnerve. All these images illustrate a crucial and fundamental part of cinema's powerful fabric; in these films they serve parabolic ends.

In their assault of a revered American ethos, these films are somewhat of a cultural anomaly. They depart from the traditional and more typical support that cinema—and other media—lends to the American Dream. Explaining why these films were made or appeared when they did is beyond the scope of this work. It is, however, potentially revealing that these films—like *The Great Gatsby*—appeared during an economic zenith in American history.[8] At the apex of this economic success (1999), a number of films emerge that target the American Dream. There is a correlation (and possible causal link) between rabid economic success and profound dissatisfaction with the national ethos. Like the prophets of the Hebrew Bible whose messages of judgment were often delivered during times of peace and prosperity, these films condemn a system during its peak of accomplishment; and like the main characters they feature, these films reflect the acute disenchantment of people who have experienced the American Dream's benefits, but find them wanting and perhaps even spiritually toxic.

What remains under the "Red, White, and Blue" are three cinematic parables whose vilification of a sacrosanct myth exemplifies Edward Norton's description of art:

> My feeling is that it is film, the responsibility of people making film, and people making all art, to specifically address dysfunctions in the culture. I think that any culture where the art is not reflecting a really dysfunctional component of the culture, is a culture in denial.[9]

In *Fight Club, American Beauty,* and *About Schmidt,* America's collective dysfunction, its denial of death, comes under attack. This cultural neurosis beckons consumers who are desperate to avoid death (the ultimate failure) and its related existential threats of collapse and termination. The counterintuitive and sacrilegious proposal of these films is that this same unspeakable object of scorn somehow holds the key to meaningful living and religious vitality.

NOTES

INTRODUCTION

1   Glen Duncan, *The Last Werewolf* (New York: Alfred A. Knopf, 2011), 30.

2   John Steinbeck, letter to Peter Benchley, 1958, in *Steinbeck: A Life in Letters* (ed. Elaine Steinbeck and Robert Wallstern; New York: Viking Press, 1975), 523.

3   William Carlos Williams, "An Approach to the Poem," in *English Institute Essays 1947* (New York: Columbia University Press, 1948), 60.

4   As Gary Laderman notes, "The history of film is a religious history" (*Sacred Matters: Celebrity Worship, Sexual Ecstasies, The Living Dead, and Other Signs of Religious Life in the United States* [New York: The New Press, 2009], 1).

5   Jean Epstein, "De quelques conditions de la photogénie," *Cinéa-Ciné-pour-tous* 19 (1924): 6–8. Translation by Tom Milne in *Afterimage* 10 (1981): 20–23.

6   Antonin Artaud, "Sorcery and Cinema," in *The Shadow and Its Shadow* (ed. Paul Hammond; City Lights, 2000), 103–5.

7   André Bazin, "Le journal d'un Curé de Campagne and the Stylistics of Robert Bresson," in *What is Cinema?* (vol. 1; ed. and trans. Hugh Gray; Berkeley/Los Angeles: University of California Press, 1967), 125–43, here 136; orig. pub. as "Le Journal d'un curé de campagne et le stylistique de Robert Bresson," *Cahiers du Cinéma* 3 (June 1951): 7–21.

8   See John R. May and Michael Bird, eds., *Religion in Film* (Knoxville: University of Tennessee Press, 1982); Robert K. Johnston, ed., *Reframing Theology and Film* (Grand Rapids: Baker Academic, 2007); Margaret Miles, *Seeing and Believing: Religion and Values in the Movies* (Boston: Beacon Press, 1996); Clive Marsh and Gaye Ortiz, eds., *Explorations in Theology and Film* (Oxford: Wiley-Blackwell, 1997);

S. Brent Plate, *Representing Religion in World Cinema: Filmmaking, Mythmaking, Culture Making* (New York: Palgrave Macmillan, 2003); Eric S. Christianson, Peter Francis, and William R. Telford, *Cinéma Divinité: Religion, Theology, and the Bible in Film* (London: SCM Press, 2005); Melanie J. Wright, *Religion and Film: An Introduction* (London: I.B. Tauris, 2007); Paul V. M. Flesher and Robert Torry, *Film and Religion: An Introduction* (Nashville: Abingdon, 2007); Christopher Deacy and Gaye Williams Ortiz, *Theology and Film: Challenging the Sacred/Secular Divide* (Malden, Mass.: Blackwell, 2008); Mary Lea Bandy and Antonio Mondo, eds., *The Hidden God: Film and Faith* (New York: Museum of Modern Art, 2003); Jolyon Mitchell and S. Brent Plate, *The Religion and Film Reader* (New York: Routledge, 2007).

9   Herbert Jump, "The Religious Possibilities of the Motion Picture" (New Britain, Ct.: South Congregational Church, 1911).

10 See, e.g., John R. May, "Visual Story and the Religious Interpretation of Film," in *Religion and Film* (ed. John R. May and Michael Bird; Knoxville: University of Tennessee Press, 1982), 23–43; Christopher Deacy, "Integration and Rebirth through Confrontation: *Fight Club* and *American Beauty* as Contemporary Religious Parables," *Journal of Contemporary Religion* 17, no. 1 (2002): 61–73; Paul Nathanson, "Between Time and Eternity: Theological Notes on *Shadows and Fog*," in *The Films of Woody Allen: Critical Essays* (ed. Charles L. P. Silet; Lanham, Md.: Scarecrow Press, 2006), 284–98; Edward N. McNulty, *Faith and Film: A Guidebook for Leaders* (Louisville, Ky.: Westminster John Knox, 2007); Greg Friedman, "Parables on Screen: John Sayles and *Men with Guns*," in *Through a Catholic Lens: Religious Perspectives of Nineteen Film Directors from around the World* (ed. Peter Malone; Lanham, Md: Rowman & Littlefield, 2007), 57–70; James Hogan, *Reel Parables: Life Lessons from Popular Films* (Mahwah, N.J.: Paulist Press, 2008); Larson Powell, "Mama, ich lebe: Konrad Wolf's Intermedial Parable of Antifascism," in *Contested Legacies: Constructions of Cultural Heritage in the GDR* (eds. Matthew Philpotts and Sabine Rolle; Edinburgh German Yearbook 3; Rochester, N.Y.: Camden House, 2009), 63–75; Robert K. Johnston, "Film as 'Parable': What Might This Mean?," in *Doing Theology for the Church: Essays in Honor of Klyne Snodgrass* (eds. Rebekah A. Eklund and John E. Phelan Jr.; Eugene, Ore.: Wipf & Stock; Chicago: Covenant Press, 2014), 19–32.

11 See Matthew S. Rindge, "Teaching the Bible *and* Film: Pedagogical Promises, Pitfalls, and Proposals," *Teaching Theology and Religion* 13, no. 2 (2010): 140–55.

12 One limitation of these films is their focus upon the experiences of a white male protagonist. There is ample room for work on cinematic parables that foreground the experiences of women, people of color, and LGBTQ persons in America.

13 Paul Tillich, *Theology of Culture* (Oxford: Oxford University Press, 1959), 7–8.

14 Vítězslav Gardavský, *God Is Not Yet Dead* (trans. Vivienne Menkes; Harmondsworth, UK: Penguin, 1973), 214.

15 On the Bible and film, see Robert Jewett, *Saint Paul at the Movies: The Apostle's Dialogue with American Culture* (Louisville, Ky.: Westminster John Knox, 1993); idem, *Saint Paul Returns to the Movies: Triumph over Shame* (Grand Rapids: Eerdmans, 1999); Larry J. Kreitzer, *Gospel Images in Fiction and Film: On Reversing the Hermeneutical Flow* (The Biblical Seminar 84; London: Sheffield Academic Press, 2002); George Aichele and Richard Walsh, *Screening Scripture: Intertextual Connections*

between Scripture and Film (Harrisburg: Trinity International, 2002); Richard Walsh, *Reading the Gospels in the Dark: Portrayals of Jesus in Film* (Harrisburg: Trinity International, 2003); Jeffrey L. Staley and Richard Walsh, *Jesus, the Gospels, and Cinematic Imagination: A Handbook to Jesus on DVD* (Louisville, Ky.: Westminster John Knox, 2007); Adele Reinhartz, *Scripture on the Silver Screen* (Louisville, Ky.: Westminster John Knox, 2003); idem, ed., *Bible and Cinema: Fifty Key Films* (New York: Routledge, 2012); idem, *Bible and Cinema: An Introduction* (New York: Routledge, 2013).

16   Joel W. Martin and Conrad E. Ostwalt Jr., eds., *Screening the Sacred: Religion, Myth, and Ideology in Popular American Film* (Boulder, Colo.: Westview Press, 1995); John Lyden, *Film as Religion: Myths, Morals, and Rituals* (New York: New York University Press, 2003).

17   For films as windows into American myths and cultural conflicts, see Bernard Brendan Scott, *Hollywood Dreams and Biblical Stories* (Minneapolis: Fortress, 1994). Three of his chapters focus on the "cowboy figure." In his discussion of the film *Witness* (d. Weir, 1985), Scott argues that the parables of the "Good Samaritan" and "Prodigal Son" offer an "antihero" who upsets conventional expectations, but he does not utilize parable as a frame for understanding how films might function as stories of subversion.

18   As does Craig Detweiler, *Into the Dark: Seeing the Sacred in the Top Films of the 21st Century* (Grand Rapids: Baker Academic, 2008).

1: THE AMERICAN DREAM

1   Honoré de Balzac, *The Jealousies of a Country Town* (Philadelphia: Avil Publishing, 1901), 145.

2   Ernest Becker, *The Denial of Death* (New York: Free Press, 1997; orig. pub. 1973), 180.

3   Alexander Irwin, *Saints of the Impossible: Bataille, Weil, and the Politics of the Sacred* (Minneapolis: University of Minnesota Press, 2002), 119.

4   The National, "Fake Empire," from the album *Boxer*, Beggars Banquet Records, 2007.

5   Robert N. Bellah, "Civil Religion in America," in his *Beyond Belief: Essays on Religion in a Post-Traditional World* (Berkeley: University of California Press, 1970), 168–89. "What we have, then, from the earliest years of the republic is a collection of beliefs, symbols, and rituals with respect to sacred things and institutionalized in a collectivity. This religion—there seems no other word for it—while not antithetical to and indeed sharing much in common with Christianity, was neither sectarian nor in any specific sense Christian" (175).

6   Bellah claims, "While some have argued that Christianity is the national faith ... few have realized that there actually exists alongside of and rather clearly differentiated from the churches an elaborate and well-institutionalized civil religion in America.... [T]his religion ... [h]as its own seriousness and integrity and requires the same care in understanding that any other religion does" ("Civil Religion in America," 168). Bellah maintains that this "American civil religion" is codified in a "set of beliefs, symbols and rituals" (186). He notes that—with the exception of Washington's second—every presidential inaugural mentions or refers to God (187, n. 3). He contends that "the average American saw no conflict between" American

civil religion and Christianity. "The civil religion was able to build up without any bitter struggle with the church powerful symbols of national solidarity and to mobilize deep levels of personal motivation for the attainment of national goals" (181).

7 Michael E. Bailey and Kristin Lindholm, "Tocqueville and the Rhetoric of Civil Religion in the Presidential Inaugural Addresses," *Christian Scholar's Review* 32, no. 3 (2003): 259–79, here 269.

8 Bailey and Lindholm, "Tocqueville and the Rhetoric of Civil Religion," 272; emphasis added.

9 Bailey and Lindholm, "Tocqueville and the Rhetoric of Civil Religion," 275.

10 Martin E. Marty, "Addressing the Nation," *Sightings*, July 26, 2004.

11 Bellah, who claims that "the American civil religion is *not* the worship of the American nation," seems to have underestimated the potential for America to worship itself ("Civil Religion in America," 186; emphasis added).

12 Bellah acknowledges some of these elements, noting that America's civil religion has "its own prophets and its own martyrs, its own sacred events and sacred places, its own solemn rituals and symbols," but he does not explore these in depth ("Civil Religion in America," 186). I thank Rabbi Elizabeth Goldstein, Jocelyn Hendrickson, and Shannon Dunn for help with the Judaism and Islam portions of this chart.

13 So Bellah ("Civil Religion in America," 176) who notes they were "sacred scriptures." See Pauline Maier, *American Scripture: Making the Declaration of Independence* (New York: Alfred A. Knopf, 1997).

14 McNaughton presents Jesus as a founding father of sorts. Of the Constitution McNaughton writes, "Inspired of God and created by God fearing, patriotic Americans." http://jonmcnaughton.com/content/ZoomDetailPages/OneNationUnder God.html

15 On Memorial Day, 1990, a bill passed the Louisiana state House legislature (54–39) that would reduce the punishment (typically $200–$500 and six months in jail) for assaulting a flag burner to $25. The sponsor of the bill, Democrat James David Cain, explained: "The people who love the flag ought to have rights just like the marijuana-smoking, yuppie hippies that are burning it." Cited in Tanya Barrientos, "La. Bill: Punch A Flag Burner, Pay $25," *The Philadelphia Inquirer*, June 16, 1990, http://articles.philly.com/1990-06-16/news/25913080_1_flag-burners-flag-burner-address-flag-desecration. In the following month in Romeoville, Ill. a city resolution was unanimously passed that reduced the fine of assaulting a flag burner to $1. Mayor John Strobbe explained that when he was growing up, "If someone burned the flag, you beat the hell out of them." Cited in Martin Zabell, "Flag-burning Retaliation May Come Cheap," *Chicago Tribune*, June 22, 1990, http://articles.chicagotribune.com/1990-06-22/news/9002200728_1_flag-burner-assaulting-resolution. See Michael Welch and Jennifer L. Bryan, "Reactions to Flag Desecration in American Society: Exploring the Contours of Formal and Informal Social Control," *American Journal of Criminal Justice* 22, no. 2 (1998): 151–68.

16 Montana had the most severe penalties for those convicted of "mutilating, defiling or showing contempt for the U.S. flag or the Montana state flag" (a fine of up to $50,000 and up to ten years in jail). In Florida, Louisiana, Mississippi, and South Carolina these laws also applied to the Confederate flag. Wisconsin, Wyoming,

and Alaska are the only states without specific penalties for flag desecration, http://www.firstamendmentcenter.org/state-flag-protection-laws.

17 Former presidential candidate Steve Forbes was the guest host that evening, and band members suspect the show was anxious not to offend him. The use of an upside down flag as the *House of Cards* (Netflix, 2013–) logo has not elicited this kind of antipathy.

18 Democratic primary, Philadelphia, Pennsylvania (ABC, aired April 16, 2008). For a transcript of the debate, see http://www.nytimes.com/2008/04/16/us/politics/16text-debate.html?pagewanted=print.

19 Emphasis added.

20 Emphasis added.

21 In 1924 "*my* Flag" was changed to "*the* Flag," perhaps indicating unease with a subjective understanding of what the flag represents.

22 In 1940 the U.S. Supreme Court ruled (*Minersville School District v. Gobitis*) that a group of Jehovah's Witnesses who refused to salute the flag (on the grounds that it was idolatrous) could be compelled to do so. The Court reversed its decision three years later, allowing students to opt out of saying the Pledge (*West Virginia State Board of Education v. Barnette*).

23 On sports as a sacred activity, see Laderman, *Sacred Matters*, 43–62.

24 36 US Code §301, http://www.gpo.gov/fdsys/granule/USCODE-2011-title36/USCODE-2011-title36-subtitleI-partA-chap3-sec301/content-detail.html.

25 http://www.utsandiego.com/news/2006/jul/02/oh-say-can-you-sing-versions-of-the-national/.

26 See Bellah, "Civil Religion in America," 174.

27 Bellah argues that the function of this holiday is "to integrate the family into the civil religion" ("Civil Religion in America," 179). James W. Loewen describes Thanksgiving as a ritual that fits all the characteristics Mircea Eliade applies to ritual observances of origin myths. Thanksgiving constitutes the history of the acts of the founders; it is considered to be true; it explains how the institution came to be; while performing the ritual associated with the myth one "experiences knowledge of the origin"; and one can thus "live" the myth, as a religion (*Lies My Teacher Told Me: Everything Your American History Textbook Got Wrong* [New York: The New Press, 2007], 88–89).

28 On Memorial Day, see W. Lloyd Warner, *American Life* (Chicago: University of Chicago Press, 1962), 8–9. Bellah contends that Memorial Day "has acted to integrate the local community into the national cult" ("Civil Religion in America," 179).

29 Celestine Bohlen, "In New War on Terrorism, Words are Weapons, Too," *New York Times*, September 29, 2001, http://www.nytimes.com/2001/09/29/arts/think-tank-in-new-war-on-terrorism-words-are-weapons-too.html.

30 See James P. Byrd, *Sacred Scripture, Sacred War: The Bible and the American Revolution* (New York: Oxford University Press, 2013).

31 George W. Bush, speech to Congress, September 20, 2001. For a transcript, see http://www.washingtonpost.com/wp-srv/nation/specials/attacked/transcripts/bushaddress_092001.html.

32　Gary Laderman refers to violence as the "sacred sacrament" of American civil religion (*American Civil Religion* [Minneapolis: Augsburg Fortress, 2012, e-book]); cf. Peter Gardella, *American Civil Religion: What Americans Hold Sacred* (New York: Oxford University Press, 2014).

33　See Raymond Haberski Jr., *God and War: American Civil Religion since 1945* (New Brunswick, N.J.: Rutgers University Press, 2012).

34　*Shut Up & Sing* (d. Kopple and Peck, 2006).

35　George Orwell, "Notes on Nationalism," in *As I Please: The Collected Essays, Journalism, and Letters of George Orwell* (vol. 3; New York/London: Harcourt Brace Jovanovich, 1968), 370; orig. pub. 1945.

36　Amanda Paulson, "Who Decides What's Patriotic? Colorado Students Walk Out over History Plan," *Christian Science Monitor*, September 24, 2014, www.csmonitor .com/USA/Education/2014/0924/Who-decides-what-s-patriotic-Colorado -students-walk-out-over-history-plan-video .

37　*60 Minutes* (CBS, aired May 12, 1996).

38　Jim Cullen, *The American Dream: A Short History of an Idea That Shaped a Nation* (Oxford/New York: Oxford University Press, 2003), 5.

39　On the power of myths such as the American Dream, see W. R. Fisher, "Reaffirmation and Subversion of the American Dream," *Quarterly Journal of Speech* 59 (1973): 160–67, here 161.

40　So Peter Freese, who contends that any effort to propose "something even faintly resembling a definition of the 'Dream' is doomed to failure" (*"America": Dream or Nightmare? Reflections on a composite image* [3rd ed. rev.; Arbeiten zur Amerikanistik; Essen: Verlag Die Blaue Eule, 1994], 94); cf. Cullen, *American Dream*, 7. Fisher identifies two myths in the American Dream: one materialistic, the second an "egalitarian moralistic myth of brotherhood" ("Reaffirmation and Subversion," 161).

41　J. Emmett Winn identifies "mobility" as "the most basic aspect of the American Dream of success" (*The American Dream and Contemporary Hollywood Cinema* [New York: Continuum, 2007], 1; cf. 13). On the centrality of mobility, cf. Cullen, *American Dream*, 8; N. Birdsall and C. Graham, eds., *New Markets, New Opportunities? Economic and Social Mobility in a Changing World* (Washington, D.C.: Brookings Institute Press, 2000), 195. On the central role of optimism in the American Dream, see C. Kleinhans, "Working Class Film Heroes: Junior Johnson, Evel Knievel, and the Film Audience," in *Jump Cut: Hollywood, Politics and Counter-Cinema* (ed. Peter Steven; Toronto: Between the Lines, 1985), 64–82, here 66.

42　James Truslow Adams, *The Epic of America* (Boston: Little Brown, 1931), 404; emphasis added. In the preface, Adams refers to the "American dream of a better, richer, and happier life" (viii).

43　Nitin Nohria, "Envy and the American Dream," *Harvard Business Review* (January–February 2013), https://hbr.org/2013/01/envy-and-the-american-dream.

44　Emphasis added.

45　Much of the essay argues for maintaining the American Dream by embracing an "ambition" economy rather than an "envy" economy. "In the meantime, instead of envying the good fortune of others, let's focus on what we can do to stoke and further individual ambition."

46   Frederick Douglass, "What to the Slave is the 4th of July?" (speech, Rochester, N.Y., July 5, 1852) in *Frederick Douglass: Selected Speeches and Writings*, ed. Philip S. Foner (Chicago: Lawrence Hill, 1999), 188–206.

47   Martin Luther King Jr., "I Have a Dream" (speech, Washington D.C., August 28, 1963), in *A Call to Conscience: The Landmark Speeches of Dr. Martin Luther King, Jr.* (ed. Clayborne Carson and Kris Shepard; New York: IPM, 2001), 85, 82.

48   Martin Luther King Jr., "I've Been to the Mountaintop" (speech, Memphis, Tennessee, April 3, 1968) in *A Call to Conscience*, 221.

49   James H. Cone notes that the "idea of the American Dream dominated King's perspective during most of his career as a civil rights activist" (*Martin & Malcolm & America: A Dream or a Nightmare* [Maryknoll, N.Y.: Orbis, 1991], 214).

50   King summoned America to "realize this dream" since "the price that America must pay for the continued oppression of the Negro and other minority groups is the price of its own destruction" (Martin Luther King Jr., "The American Dream" speech, Drew University, Madison, New Jersey, February 5, 1964), http://depts.drew.edu/lib/archives/online_exhibits/King/speech/TheAmericanDream.pdf.

51   He was born as Malcolm Little (1925), and died as El-Hajj Malik El-Shabazz (1965).

52   Malcolm X, "The Ballot or the Bullet" (speech, Cleveland, Ohio, April 3, 1964), in *Malcolm X Speaks* (ed. George Breitman; New York: Grove Press, 1966), 23–44. On Malcolm's life, see Malcolm X and Alex Haley, *The Autobiography of Malcolm X* (New York: Ballantine Books, 1973; orig. pub. 1965); Cone, *Martin & Malcolm*; Manning Marable, *Malcolm X: A Life of Reinvention* (New York: Viking, 2011).

53   Malcolm made this comment less than one year before his death, and about three weeks after his official break from Elijah Muhammad and the Nation of Islam.

54   James Cone makes this point about the views of both Martin and Malcolm in general (*Martin & Malcolm*, 212–43).

55   Malcolm once remarked, "That's why Martin Luther King would lose a debate with me. Why King? Because integration is a ridiculous dream. I am not interested in dreams, but in the nightmare" (cited in Cone, *Martin & Malcolm*, 255, n. 19).

56   Martin Luther King Jr. (speech, Atlanta, Georgia, December 24, 1967), quoted in Cone, *Martin & Malcolm*, 213.

57   On at least one occasion (in a March 19, 1968 speech in Clarksdale, Mississippi), King mentions Langston Hughes (and another Black poet, Countee Cullen), in emphasizing the need for young Blacks to learn about Black artists and philosophers. Cone interprets King's movement from integrationism toward a kind of Black separatism as a contradiction in King's "deep faith in the American dream" (*Martin & Malcolm*, 226).

58   Langston Hughes, "Let America Be America Again," in *The Collected Poems of Langston Hughes* (ed. Arnold Rampersad and David Roessel; New York: Vintage Books, 1994; orig. pub. 1936 in *Esquire*), 189–91.

59   These minority reports of lament issue not only from the "Negro bearing slavery's scars," but also from a broad spectrum of oppressed groups: the "poor white," the "red man driven from the land," "the immigrant," "the farmer, bondsman to the soil," "the worker sold to the machine," and "the Negro, servant to you all" ("Let America Be America Again," 190).

60   *The Collected Poems of Langston Hughes*, 426. Dream imagery suffused Hughes' poetry, and he often returned to the motif of failed dreams. See, e.g., "Dreams," "The Dream Keeper," and "As I Grew Older" (*The Collected Poems of Langston Hughes*, 32, 45, 93).

61   The same attitude greeted King, and he argued that great disappointment (with America) could only spring from great love (King, "Why I Am Opposed to the War in Vietnam," [sermon, Riverside Baptist Church, New York, April 30, 1967], http://www.lib.berkeley.edu/MRC/pacificaviet/riversidetranscript.html). Gibson also asked Obama: "If you knew he got rough in sermons, why did it take you so long to publicly disassociate yourself from him?"

62   Cone, *Martin & Malcolm*, 31; emphasis added.

63   Sigmund Freud, *Civilization and Its Discontents* (trans. James Strachey; New York: W. W. Norton, 1962; orig. pub. 1930), 11. It is unclear if Freud has America in mind here. Later in the book he writes of the "psychological poverty of groups," and notes: "The present cultural state of America would give us a good opportunity for studying the damage to civilization which is thus to be feared. But I shall avoid the temptation of entering upon a critique of American civilization; I do not wish to give an impression of wanting myself to employ American methods" (67).

64   Freud, *Civilization and Its Discontents*, 91. "[M]ay we not be justified in reaching the diagnosis that, under the influence of cultural urges, some civilizations, or some epochs of civilization—possibly the whole of mankind—have become 'neurotic'?" (91).

65   Erich Fromm, *The Sane Society* (Greenwich, Conn.: Fawcett Premier, 1955). Anticipating a subsequent emphasis on "systems" thinking, Fromm not only shifts the attention of psychological health from the individual to the society, but also insists on framing a person's health within the relative health of the broader society. "Whether or not an individual is healthy, is primarily not an individual matter, but depends on the structure of his society" (71).

66   Fromm, *The Sane Society*, 19. WHO stands for the World Health Organization.

67   Society, Fromm avers, must conform to the needs of people, not vice-versa (*Sane Society*, 71). A healthy society "furthers man's capacity to love his fellow men, to work creatively, to develop his reason and objectivity, to have a sense of self which is based on the experience of his own productive powers. An unhealthy society is one which creates mutual hostility, distrust, which transforms man into an instrument of use and exploitation for others, which deprives him of a sense of self, except inasmuch as he submits to others or becomes an automaton" (71).

68   Fromm, *Sane Society*, 103. Alienation is when a person "does not experience himself as the active bearer of his own powers and richness, but as an impoverished thing, dependent on powers outside of himself, unto whom he has projected his living substance" (114).

69   Fromm, *Sane Society*, 122, 124; cf. 288, 302. "The world is one great object for our appetite, a big apple, a big bottle, a big breast; we are the sucklers, the eternally expectant ones, the hopeful ones—and the eternally disappointed ones" (149).

70   Fromm, *Sane Society*, 149.

71   People see themselves "as the embodiment of a quantitative exchange value" (Fromm, *Sane Society*, 108). "Everybody is to everybody else a commodity" (126). Gauging their personal worth in economic terms, people in this "marketing orientation" lose their sense of self and must sell themselves "successfully on the market" (129–30). Lacking the freedom "to be [themselves], to be productive, to be fully awake," people direct their energies toward "the domination of nature and ever-increasing material comfort" (308–9).

72   "Man himself became a part of the machine, rather than its master. He experienced himself as a commodity, as an investment; his aim became to be a success, that is, to sell himself as profitably as possible on the market. His value as a person lies in his salability, not in his human qualities of love, reason, or in his artistic capacities" (Fromm, *Sane Society*, 309).

73   Fromm, *Sane Society*, 32; cf. 241.

74   Fromm, *Sane Society*, 313, 19; cf. 30.

75   Emphasis original. Fromm continues: "The danger of the past was that men became slaves. The danger of the future is that men may become robots. True enough, robots do not rebel. But given man's nature, robots cannot live and remain sane" (*Sane Society*, 312–13).

76   "[O]ne might expect that ministers, priests and rabbis would form the spearhead of criticism of modern Capitalism" (Fromm, *Sane Society*, 158).

77   Fromm, *Sane Society*, 158.

78   Fromm, *Sane Society*, 60. "[L]ove for one's country which is not part of one's love for humanity is not love, but idolatrous worship." Citing the Pauline and subsequent Christian community as an example, Freud argues that any community that focuses on loving those within its ranks will inevitably proceed to harming outsiders (*Civilization and Its Discontents*, 61–62). Fromm cites Albert Schweitzer's contention that "national civilization is to-day worshipped as an idol, and the notion of a humanity with a common civilization lies broken to fragments" (*Sane Society*, 202; cf. Albert Schweitzer, *The Philosophy of Civilization* [New York: Macmillan, 1949]).

79   Fromm does not use the term "American Dream" here, but he does refer to the "American Way of Life" (*Sane Society*, 184).

80   Fromm, *Sane Society*, 314. Fromm dates the rise of nationalism to the period after the seventeenth and eighteenth century revolutions in which "nationalism and state worship became the symptoms of a regression to incestuous fixation" (61). The leader and the state "become idols when the individual projects all his powers into them and worships them, hoping to regain some of his powers by submission and worship" (113).

81   He continues, "Not quite as drastic, but nevertheless qualitatively the same would be the reaction to a man who says, 'I do not love my country,' or in the case of war, 'I do not care for my country's victory.' Such a sentence is a real sacrilege, and a man saying it becomes a monster, an outlaw in the feelings of his fellow men" (Fromm, *Sane Society*, 60–61).

82   Fromm, *Sane Society*, 61; emphasis original.

83　"[A]ll cultures are religious and every neurosis is a private form of religion, provided we mean by religion an attempt to answer the problem of human existence" (Fromm, *Sane Society*, 34–35).

84　"Among all my patients in the second half of life—that is to say, over thirty-five—there has not been one whose problem in the last resort was not that of finding a religious outlook on life. . . . [A]nd none of them has been really healed who did not regain his religious outlook. This of course has nothing whatever to do with a particular creed or membership in a church" (Carl Jung, *Modern Man in Search of a Soul* [trans. W. S. Dell and Cary F. Baynes; San Diego: Harvest/HBJ, 1933], 229).

85　Jung, *Modern Man in Search of a Soul*, 231; emphasis added.

86　"But all creativeness in the realm of the spirit as well as every psychic advance of man arises from a state of mental suffering, and it is *spiritual stagnation, psychic sterility*, which causes this state" (Jung, *Modern Man in Search of a Soul*, 225; emphasis added). The tragedy for Jung is the person who "has failed to read the meaning of his own existence" (225). Freud and Adler, Jung avers, failed to attend to this existential facet; they offered "psychology without the psyche." Their overly "rational" methods "actually hinder the realization of meaningful experience" since their patients are "alienated from a spiritual standpoint" (226).

87　Viktor Frankl, *Man's Search for Meaning* (New York: Washington Square Press, 1985; orig. pub. 1946 as *Ein Psycholog erlebt das Konzentrationslager*). He argues that a person's primary concern is "to see a meaning in his life" (*Man's Search for Meaning*, 136).

88　Fromm, *Sane Society*, 157.

89　Fromm, *Sane Society*, 157–58; emphasis added.

90　Matthew J. Bruccoli, "Explanatory Notes," in *The Great Gatsby*, by F. Scott Fitzgerald (New York: Collier Books, 1992; orig. pub. 1925), 207.

91　F. Scott Fitzgerald, *The Great Gatsby* (New York: Collier Books, 1992; orig. pub. 1925), 101; emphasis added. Daisy's elusive and illusive nature at times overwhelms Gatsby. "I think that voice held him most with its fluctuating, feverish warmth *because it couldn't be over-dreamed*—that voice was a deathless song" (101; emphasis added).

92　Fitzgerald, *Great Gatsby*, 105; emphasis added.

93　Literary scholar Matthew J. Bruccoli notes about Gatsby, "He believes in the American Dream of success ('the orgastic future'); he fulfills it; he confuses it with Daisy; he is betrayed by it" (preface to *The Great Gatsby*, by F. Scott Fitzgerald, xi). For an analysis of the novel that focuses on the American Dream, see W. R. Fisher and R. A. Fillory, "Argument in Drama and Literature: An Exploration," in *Advances in Argumentation Theory and Research* (ed. R. Cox and C. A. Willard; Carbondale: Southern Illinois Press, 1982), 343–62.

94　Fitzgerald, *Great Gatsby*, 189; emphasis added.

95　Fitzgerald, *Great Gatsby*, 189; emphasis added.

96　Fitzgerald, *Great Gatsby*, 116.

97　Fitzgerald, *Great Gatsby*, 189; emphasis added.

98　Cited by Bruccoli, Preface, xv; emphasis added.

99 Émile Durkheim's diagnosis of modern civilization ("a disorganized dust of indi-
    viduals") aptly describes Gatsby's world. It is "a restless movement, a planless
    self-development, an aim of living which has no criterion of value and in which hap-
    piness lies always in the future, and never in any present achievement" (Durkheim,
    Le Suicide [Paris: Felix Alcan, 1897], 449; cited in Fromm, *Sane Society*, 191). Gatsby
    loses himself in an illusive *past*.

100 Becker, *Denial of Death*, 11.

101 Becker, *Denial of Death*, 15. Becker outlines his thesis: "this whole book is a network
    of arguments based on the universality of the fear of death, or 'terror' as I prefer to
    call it, in order to convey how all-consuming it is when we look it full in the face" (15).
    "I don't believe," he writes, "that the complex symbol of death is ever absent" (22).

102 Becker, *Denial of Death*, 57. Becker was not the first to focus so intently on the driv-
    ing power of the fear of death, and he refers to likeminded predecessors. Freud
    remarked: "Is it not for us to confess that in our civilized attitude towards death
    we are once more living psychologically beyond our means, and must reform and
    give truth its due? Would it not be better to give death the place in actuality and
    in our thoughts which properly belongs to it, and to yield a little more prominence
    to that unconscious attitude towards death which we have hitherto so carefully
    suppressed?" ("Thoughts for the Times on War and Death," in *Collected Papers* 4
    [New York: Basic Books, 1959], 316–17; orig. pub. 1915). Thirty years before Becker,
    Gregory Zilboorg wrote, "For behind the sense of insecurity in the face of danger,
    behind the sense of discouragement and depression, there always lurks the basic fear
    of death, a fear which undergoes most complex elaborations and manifests itself in
    many indirect ways. . . . No one is free of the fear of death. . . . We may take for granted
    that the fear of death is always present in our mental functioning" ("Fear of Death,"
    Pschoanalytic Quarterly 12 [1943]: 465–75, here 465–67; cited in Becker, *Denial of
    Death*, 16). Zilboorg argued that constantly expending "psychological energy on
    the business of preserving life would be impossible if the fear of death were not as
    constant. The very term 'self-preservation' implies an effort against some force of
    disintegration; the affective aspect of this is fear, fear of death" ("Fear of Death,"
    467; cited in Becker, *Denial of Death*, 16; cf. 288, n. 21). Becker clarifies this as fear
    of "annihilation." Repressing this fear of death, necessary for people to function
    properly, requires "a constant psychological effort to keep the lid on and inwardly
    never relax our watchfulness" ("Fear of Death," 467). Becker agrees and in so doing
    rejects Freud: "*Consciousness of death*," he maintains, "is the primary repression, not
    sexuality" (*Denial of Death*, 96; emphasis original). What remains, asserts Becker,
    is "an impossible paradox: the ever-present fear of death in the normal biological
    functioning of our instinct of self-preservation, as well as our utter obliviousness to
    this fear in our conscious life" (17).

103 "Death, so omnipresent in the past that it was familiar, would be effaced, would dis-
    appear. It would become shameful and forbidden" (Philippe Ariès, *Western Attitudes
    toward Death: from the Middle Ages to the Present* [trans. Patricia M. Ranum; Bal-
    timore: Johns Hopkins University Press, 1974], 85). Cf. Philippe Ariès, "La mort
    inverse," *Archives europénnes de sociologie* 8 (1967): 169–95.

104 On death in the American context, see Jessica Mitford, *The American Way of Death Revisited* (New York: Alfred A. Knopf, 1998); Herman Feifel, ed., *The Meaning of Death* (New York: McGraw-Hill, 1959); Gary Laderman, *The Sacred Remains: American Attitudes Toward Death, 1799–1883* (New Haven: Yale University Press, 1996); idem, *Rest in Peace: A Cultural History of Death and the Funeral Home in Twentieth-Century America* (New York: Oxford University Press, 2003).

105 Ariès, *Death*, 87–88.

106 The antithesis of the acceptable death was "the embarrassingly graceless dying, which embarrasses the survivors because it causes too strong an emotion to burst forth; and emotions must be avoided both in the hospital and everywhere in society. One does not have the right to become emotional other than in private, that is to say, secretly" (Ariès, *Death*, 89).

107 Ariès, *Death*, 90. Michel Foucault discusses the "disqualification of death which marks the recent wane of the rituals that accompanied it," and he attributes this evasion of death not to "a new anxiety which makes death unbearable for our societies," but to "the fact that the procedures of power have not ceased to turn away from death" (*The History of Sexuality, Volume 1: An Introduction* (New York: Vintage Books, 1990), 138. He writes, "[T]he ancient right to *take* life or *let* live was replaced by a power to *foster* life or *disallow* it to the point of death" (138; emphasis original).

108 Ariès, *Death*, 91.

109 Embalming represents "a certain refusal to accept death" (Ariès, *Death*, 98–99). Ariès observes another tendency at work: "Americans are very willing to transform death, to put make-up on it, to sublimate it, but they do not want to make it disappear" (100). "Thus during the wakes or farewell 'visitations' which have been preserved, the visitors come without shame or repugnance. This is because in reality they are not visiting a dead person, as they traditionally have, but an almost-living one who, thanks to embalming, is still present, as if he were awaiting you to greet you or to take you off on a walk. The definitive nature of the rupture has been blurred. Sadness and mourning have been banished from this calming reunion" (101–2).

110 As Ariès notes, "one must avoid—no longer for the sake of the dying person, but for society's sake, for the sake of those close to the dying person—the disturbance caused by the ugliness of dying and by the very presence of death in the midst of a happy life, for it is henceforth given *that life is always happy or should always seem to be so*" (*Death*, 87; emphasis added). He cites Tolstoy's stories about death as examples of this shift toward emptying death rituals of their "dramatic impact."

111 Ariès, *Death*, 94: "The cause of the interdict is at once apparent: the need for happiness—the moral duty and the social obligation to contribute to the collective happiness by avoiding any cause for sadness or boredom, by appearing to be always happy, even if in the depths of despair. By showing the least sign of sadness, one sins against happiness, threatens it, and society then risks losing its *raison d'être*."

112 Ariès, *Death*, 90.

113 Becker claims that cultural vehicles enable people to enact their need to be heroic. Heroism is "our central calling, our main task on this planet," and society is "a symbolic action system, a structure of statuses and roles, customs and rules for behavior, designed to serve as a vehicle for earthly heroism" (*Denial of Death*, 1, 4).

114   Becker claims that history is a "succession of immortality ideologies" (*Denial of Death*, 190; cf. 120, 133).

115   Becker, *Denial of Death*, 105.

116   The American Dream meets Becker's criterion of being "rooted in the emotions, in an inner feeling that one is secure in something stronger, larger, more important than one's own strength and life" (Becker, *Denial of Death*, 120).

117   See J. Emmett Winn, *The American Dream and Contemporary Hollywood Cinema* (New York: Continuum, 2007). For "hardworking protagonists who achieve upward mobility" (thus conforming to the "Cinderella formula" that celebrates the "materialistic myth of the American Dream") he singles out *Working Girl* (d. Nichols, 1988), *An Officer and a Gentleman* (d. Hackford, 1982), *Flashdance* (d. Lyne, 1983), and *Saturday Night Fever* (d. Badham, 1977) (41). Films that reinforce moral elements of the American Dream (by urging "viewers to accept their working-class status as the moral high ground") include *Wall Street* (d. Stone, 1987), *The Firm* (d. Pollack, 1993), *Someone to Watch over Me* (d. Scott, 1987), *The Flamingo Kid* (d. Marshall, 1984), *Breaking Away* (d. Yates, 1979), *Maid in Manhattan* (d. Wang, 2002), and *Good Will Hunting* (d. Van Sant, 1997) (85). Films focusing on "cross-class relationships" that maintain an illusion of a "classless society" and offer a "reassuring, calming, and egalitarian view of America" include *Pretty Woman* (d. Marshall, 1990), *Titanic* (d. Cameron, 1997), *Mrs. Winterbourne* (d. Benjamin, 1996), *White Palace* (d. Mandocki, 1990), *Passion Fish* (d. Sayles, 1992), and *The Fisher King* (d. Gilliam, 1991) (123–24). On film as a chief conduit of American mythologies, see E. C. Hirschman, *Heroes, Monsters, & Messiahs: Movies and Television Shows as the Mythology of American Culture* (Kansas City: Andrews McMeel Publishing, 2000). W. J. McMullen argues that the American Dream (in various ways) is promoted in films such as *Kramer v. Kramer* ("Gender and the American Dream in *Kramer vs. Kramer*," *Women's Studies in Communication* 19 [1996]: 29–54).

118   Winn, *American Dream*, 6.

119   Becker, *Denial of Death*, 7; emphasis added.

120   "Death has become *unnamable*. Everything henceforth goes on as if neither I nor those who are dear to me are any longer mortal. Technically, we admit that we might die; we take out insurance on our lives to protect our families from poverty. But really, at heart we feel we are non-mortals. *And surprise! Our life is not as a result gladdened!*" (Ariès, *Death*, 106; emphasis added).

121   Becker follows the suggestion of Eliot Jacques who wrote of the need for "self-mourning" (*Denial of Death*, 215–16). Cf. Eliot Jacques, "Death and the Mid-Life Crisis," *International Journal of Psychoanalysis* 46 (1965): 502–14.

2: FIGHT CLUB

1   *Side by Side: The Science, Art, and Impact of Digital Cinema* (d. Chris Kenneally; narrated by Keanu Reeves; PBS, August 22, 2012).

2   David Fincher, cited in *Empire Magazine* 80 (February 1996).

3   Chuck Palahniuk, *Non-Fiction* (London: Vintage, 2005), xv.

4   Roger Ebert, "Fight Club," *Chicago Sun-Times*, October 15, 1999, http://rogerebert.suntimes.com/apps/pbcs.dll/article?AID=/19991015/REVIEWS/910150302.

5   Kenneth Turan, "The Roundhouse Miss," *Los Angeles Times*, October 15, 1999, http://articles.latimes.com/1999/oct/15/entertainment/ca-22382.

6   Rex Reed, *The New York Observer*, October 1999, http://www.nytimes.com/2009/11/08/movies/homevideo/08lim.html.

7   *The Rosie O'Donnell Show* (NBC, aired October 15, 1999).

8   http://www.imdb.com/chart/top?s=ir.

9   http://www.imdb.com/chart/top?s=nv.

10   "The 500 Greatest Movies of all Time," *Empire Magazine*, http://www.empire online.com/500/94.asp; in 2014, they ranked *Fight Club* as the fourteenth best film of all time (http://www.empireonline.com/301/list.asp?page=28). "Ten Greatest Films of the Past Decade," *Total Film* 98 (April 2007).

11   Peter Travers, "Fight Club," *Rolling Stone*, October 15, 1999, http://www.rolling stone.com/movies/reviews/fight-club-19991015

12   Michael McCarthy, "Illegal, Violent Teen Fight Clubs Face Police Crackdown," *USA Today*, July 31, 2006, http://usatoday30.usatoday.com/life/2006–07–31 -violent-fight-clubs_x.htm

13   Palahniuk, *Non-Fiction*, 228.

14   Douglas Quenqua, "Fight Club Generation," *New York Times*, March 15, 2012, http://www.nytimes.com/2012/03/15/fashion/mixed-martial-arts-catches-on -with-the-internet-generation.html?pagewanted=all.

15   Ginia Bellafonte, "In Milan, a 'Fight Club' Mood, But Real Men Suit Up," *New York Times* Review/Fashion, January 11, 2000, http://www.nytimes.com/2000/01/11/ style/review-fashion-in-milan-a-fight-club-mood-but-real-men-suit-up.html.

16   Chuck Palahniuk, *Fight Club 2* (illustrated by David Mack and Cameron Stewart; Dark Horse Comics, 2015).

17   On the enduring polarization of the film, see Dennis Lim, " 'Fight Club' Fight Goes On," *New York Times*, November 6, 2009, http://www.nytimes.com/2009/11/08/ movies/homevideo/08lim.html?_r=0. James Christopher notes that the film "touched a nerve in the male psyche that was debated in newspapers across the world" ("How Was It for You?" *The Times*, September 13, 2001).

18   So Deacy, "*Fight Club* and *American Beauty* as Contemporary Religious Parables."

19   He is the type of zombie Erich Fromm describes as "half asleep when awake, and half awake when asleep" (*The Art of Loving* [New York: Harper Perennial, 1989], 128). All *Fight Club* quotes, unless otherwise indicated, are from the DVD version of the film (Los Angeles: Twentieth Century Fox Home Entertainment, 1999).

20   Gardavský, *God Is Not Yet Dead*, 214.

21   The Roman moralist Seneca, who—like Gardavský—warned of a living death, links certain cases of premature death to a person's obsessive commitment to luxury (*Moral Epistles* 24.20–21; 71.15; 82.3–4; 93.3–5; 122.3–4, 10; cf. 120.18). For more on Seneca's attitude toward death and possessions, see Rindge, *Jesus' Parable of the Rich Fool: Luke 12:13-34 among Ancient Conversations on Death and Possessions* (*Early Christianity and Its Literature* 6; Atlanta: Society of Biblical Literature, 2011).

22   Jim Uhls, *Fight Club: The Original Screenplay* (ScreenPress, 2000), 11.

23   To borrow the title from Neil Postman, *Amusing Ourselves to Death: Public Discourse in the Age of Show Business* (New York: Penguin, 1986).

24   Jeffrey Sconce cites *Fight Club* (along with *Being John Malkovich* [d. Jonze, 1999] and *Ghost World* [d. Zwigoff, 2001]) as a film that "wrestles quite explicitly with the 'politics' of constructing one's identity from the resources of consumer capitalism" ("Irony, Nihilism and the new American Smart Film," *Screen* 43, no. 4 [2002]: 349–69, here 366).

25   Palahniuk, *Non-Fiction*, xviii-xix; emphasis added. He adds, "In these places I found the truest stories. In support groups. In hospitals. Anywhere people had nothing left to lose, that's where they told the most truth" (xix).

26   So Claus Westermann, *Praise and Lament in the Psalms* (trans. Keith R. Crim and Richard N. Soulen; Atlanta: John Knox, 1981), 261–62, 264, 266.

27   Westermann, *Praise and Lament*, 264.

28   Westermann, *Praise and Lament*, 272: "The lament is the language of suffering; in it suffering is given the dignity of language. It will not stay silent!" Cf. Walter Brueggemann, "The Costly Loss of Lament," in *The Psalms and the Life of Faith* (ed. Patrick Miller; Minneapolis: Augsburg Fortress, 1995), 98–111; idem, *The Message of the Psalms: A Theological Commentary* (Minneapolis: Augsburg Fortress, 1984), 52–53.

29   So Brueggemann, "Costly Loss of Lament," 106–7.

30   Patrick Miller, *Interpreting the Psalms* (Philadelphia: Fortress, 1986), 101.

31   Mark cites the Aramaic (*elōi elōi lema sabachthani*) which he translates into Greek (*ho theos mou ho theos mou, eis ti egkatelipes me?*).

32   Other lament psalms include Psalms 39, 59, 70, 102, 120, and 143.

33   For a defense of Jesus' cry—and the entire Gospel of Mark—as a lament of divine abandonment, see Matthew S. Rindge, "Reconfiguring the Akedah and Recasting God: Lament and Divine Abandonment in Mark," *Journal of Biblical Literature* 131, no. 4 (2012): 755–74.

34   Most scholars think that the authors of Matthew and Luke used Mark's Gospel as a source. John's Gospel—not considered by most scholars to be literarily dependent on the Synoptics—portrays a triumphant Jesus who dies declaring, "It is finished" (John 19:30).

35   Dietrich Bonhoeffer, *Letters and Papers From Prison* (trans. Reginald H. Fuller; ed. Eberhard Bethge; New York: Collier, 1972), 360.

36   A similar rhetoric of empowerment may inform the absence of references to God in the biblical book of Esther. Facing a potential genocide by Haman, God's absence is in striking juxtaposition to Esther's actions of saving her people from annihilation. Implicit in Esther is an argument that (in this case Jewish) survival depends on people whose personal intervention incarnates a divine justice.

37   See Brueggemann, "Costly Loss of Lament."

38   Mary Doria Russell, *The Sparrow* (New York: Ballantine, 1996). Shusaku Endo's *Silence* (trans. William Johnston; New York: Taplinger, 1980)—under production as a film and directed by Martin Scorsese—is another narrativized lament. On cinematic laments, see Matthew S. Rindge, "Lament in Film and Film as Lament," in *The Bible in Motion: Biblical Reception in Film* (ed. Rhonda Burnette-Bletsch; 2 vols.; Berlin: De Gruyter, 2016), 1:379–90. On biblical and contemporary laments, see Nancy C. Lee, *Lyrics of Lament: From Tragedy to Transformation* (Minneapolis: Augsburg Fortress, 2010).

39   *The West Wing,* "The Two Cathedrals" (d. Thomas Schlamme; written by Aaron Sorkin; NBC, May 16, 2001).

40   Bartlet had planned—while a student at the University of Notre Dame—to become a priest. Screenwriter Aaron Sorkin was raised as a Catholic, and his interest in the interplay of Christian faith and politics is evident in many episodes (in seasons one–four) of the show (Sorkin left the show after season four).

41   See Martha W. Kleder, "FCC Says Cursing God 'OK'" (May 2, 2002), http://www .westwingepguide.com/S2/Episodes/44_TC.html.

42   Aaron Sorkin, forum at "Television Without Pity" (formerly Mighty Big TV; May 29, 2001), http://mightybigtv.com. Commenting on this scene, Sorkin remarks, "No, there was nothing that standards and practices found objectionable in the Latin. As for the clergy, there were many of them on the set while we shot the scene (some of them were used on camera.) I was introduced to a minister and said, 'You know he's about to renounce God, right?' The minister said, 'Yeah, I saw rehearsal, it's gonna be great.' I said, 'That's fine, but am I going straight to hell?' He said, 'Maybe for other stuff, but not for this.' Then he gave me a pretty good talking-to about how true people of faith are supposed to question God."

43   Sorkin, Mighty Big TV forum (May 29, 2001). The episodes Sorkin cites include "the meeting with Karl Malden in Sabbath Day, dressing down Jenna Jacobs in The Midterms, his meeting with [the] Chinese refugee in Shibboleth, his friendship with Al Caldwell."

44   So Brueggemann, "Costly Loss of Lament," 101.

45   Fatherlessness is an important motif in the film. The narrator mentions that he belongs to a generation "raised by women."

46   Brueggemann, "Costly Loss of Lament," 102–4.

47   Brueggemann, "Costly Loss of Lament," 103.

48   Fromm, *Art of Loving,* 85.

49   On different stages of faith development, see M. Scott Peck, *The Different Drum: Community Making and Peace* (New York: Touchstone, 1987), 86–106; James W. Fowler, *Stages of Faith: The Psychology of Human Development and the Quest for Meaning* (San Francisco: Harper & Row, 1982); James W. Fowler and Sam Keen, *LifeMaps: Conversations on the Journey of Faith* (ed. Jerome Berryman; Waco, Tex.: Word Books, 1978).

50   Brueggemann, "Costly Loss of Lament," 102. Cf. idem, "Lament as Wake-Up Call (Class Analysis and Historical Possibility)," in *Lamentations in Ancient and Contemporary Cultural Contexts* (eds. Nancy C. Lee and Carleen Mandolfo; Atlanta: Society of Biblical Literature, 2008), 221–36.

51   Brueggemann, "Costly Loss of Lament," 102.

52   Brueggemann, "Costly Loss of Lament," 102.

53   Brueggemann, "Costly Loss of Lament," 106.

54   "Mona Lisa" (Internet advertising spot), supplemental *Fight Club* DVD, Two-Disc Collector's Edition (Twentieth Century Fox, 2000).

55   Chuck Palahniuk, *Fight Club* (New York: W. W. Norton, 1996), 141.

56   Chuck Palahniuk makes the American attempt to avoid and escape death a recurring motif in his novel *Damned* (New York: Anchor Books, 2011).

57   Palahniuk volunteered for a local hospital where he drove terminally ill patients to support groups (*Non-Fiction*, xviii).

58   The practice among young women in America of cutting and self-mutilation provides a contemporary parallel to the self-mutilation in the film.

59   The screenplay adds here, "Deal with it the way a living person does."

60   The screenplay reads, "First, you have to know that someday, you are going to die. Until you know that, you will be useless."

61   Quoted in *Fight Club* DVD booklet.

62   See Matthew S. Rindge, "Mortality and Enjoyment: The Interplay of Death and Possessions in Qoheleth," *Catholic Biblical Quarterly* 73 (2011): 265–80; cf. Rindge, *Jesus' Parable of the Rich Fool*, 43–65.

63   Palahniuk, *Fight Club*, 70.

64   Palahniuk, *Non-Fiction*, xv; emphasis added.

65   Palahniuk, *Non-Fiction.*, xv–xvi.

66   Tyler's previous flashes in the film seem to be outside the narrator's conscious control. Only one or two of these appearances is obvious to viewers: when Tyler and the narrator sit by each other on an airplane, and when Tyler is on a walkway in an airport (during the latter scene the narrator states in voiceover: "If I could wake up in a different place, at a different time, could I wake up as a different person?"). Five additional appearances of Tyler are in the beginning of the film, but each lasts only $1/24$ of a second (representing Tyler's faint existence in the narrator's subconscious).

67   Palahniuk, *Fight Club*, 207.

68   Chuch Palahniuk, "This Much I Know," *The Guardian*, Novmber 1, 2014, http://www.theguardian.com/books/2014/nov/01/chuck-palahniuk-this-much-i-know?CMP=fb_gu.

69   The film's critique of advertisement resonates with Fincher's comments: "I'm totally anti-commercialism. . . . Anybody looking outside themselves to make themselves whole is delusional and probably sick." Actor Edward Norton remarked, "I feel that *Fight Club* . . . probed into the despair and paralysis that people feel in the face of having inherited this value system out of advertising" (quoted in Stephen Schaefer, "Two of Hollywood's hottest thirtysomethings embrace mayhem and millennial meltdown in Fight Club," [1999], http://www.edward-norton.org/fc/articles/mrshowbiz1099.html).

70   Palahniuk, *Fight Club*, 142–43.

71   Palahniuk, *Non-Fiction*, 231.

3: *AMERICAN BEAUTY*

1   Heather Havrilesky, "An Alan Ball Postmortem," *Salon*, August 20, 2005, http://www.salon.com/2005/08/20/alan_ball/.

2   W. H. Auden, *The Age of Anxiety: A Baroque Ecologue* (Princeton: Princeton University Press, 201; orig. pub. 1947), 105.

3   Jon Foreman, "Learning How to Die," from the album *Limbs and Branches*, Lowercase People Records, 2008.

4   Film reviewer Andrew O'Hehir notes, "It's remarkable that any movie that's so ambitious and angry—and that treats ordinary American life so seriously—made

it through the mainstream production channels in the first place. Plenty of 'independent' films aren't half this daring" ("American Beauty," *Salon*, September 15, 1999, http://www.salon.com/1999/09/15/beauty/). For Robert K. Johnston, the film "portrays the hollowness of suburbia's chase after the American dream—after money, status, youth, and, of course, beauty" (*Reel Spirituality: Theology and Film in Dialogue* [updated version; Grand Rapids: Baker Academic, 2006], 101). He cites the film as one of several that critique the American Dream (*Useless Beauty: Ecclesiastes through the Lens of Contemporary Film* [Grand Rapids: Baker Academic, 2004], 60).

Unlike *Fight Club, American Beauty* met with early critical acclaim, receiving five of eight Oscar nominations (Best Picture, Director, Actor, Screenplay, and Cinematography) and several other awards: DGA award for Outstanding Directorial Achievement, three Golden Globes (Best Director, Motion Picture, and Screenplay), three SAG awards (Best Cast, Male Actor, and Female Actor), and the WGA award for Best Screenplay. *American Beauty* was the thirteenth highest grossing film of 1999, making over $350 million globally (with only a $15 million budget) (http://www.imdb.com/title/tt0169547/?ref_=fn_al_tt_1, and http://boxoffice mojo.com/movies/?id=americanbeauty.htm).

Not all critics were impressed. See, e.g., J. Hoberman, "Boomer Bust," *The Village Voice*, September 14, 1999, http://www.villagevoice.com/1999–09–14/film/boomer-bust/. Others gave the film mixed reviews. See, e.g., O'Hehir, "American Beauty."

5   All quotes are from the DVD version of *American Beauty* (Universal City, Calif.: DreamWorks, 2000). This is the opening sequence in Ball's screenplay, but during postproduction Mendes added a Prologue featuring Jane speaking directly to the camera.

6   Ball notes that Carolyn is "contemptuous but also bored, as if she gave up expecting anything more long ago" (*American Beauty Shooting Script* [New York: Newmarket Press, 1999], 5).

7   Mendes calls Lester's voiceovers "the ultimate spiritual extension of the loneliness that is present in much of the movie" (DVD audio commentary).

8   Oscar Wilde, "The Soul of Man under Socialism," in *The Works of Oscar Wilde* (New York: Lamb Publishing, 1909; orig. pub. 1891), 8:133–34.

9   Ball remarks, "It's startling how happy they look" (*Shooting Script*, 11). Accentuating the photo's revelation is the nine seconds spent lingering on it, and Thomas Newman's accompanying musical shift to a slow melancholic piano piece. A shot of the photo recurs (with the same piano music) at the end of the film, and this inclusio is in the screenplay as well (*Shooting Script*, 11, 96).

10   Roger Ebert, "American Beauty," *Chicago Sun-Times*, September 24, 1999, http://rogerebert.suntimes.com/apps/pbcs.dll/article?AID=/19990924/REVIEWS/909240301/1023

11   Mendes, DVD audio commentary. He notes that Lester "is constantly seen early on in the movie—I think Alan wrote this almost subconsciously in a series of jail cells—in the shower cubicle and the cubicle at work and cars—a series of images of

Lester trapped behind glass, and the kids trapped behind glass, and within frames, and this was something I wanted to bring out in the film" (DVD audio commentary).

12   My student Michael Orr pointed this out to me. Mendes changed the horizontal bars (in the original storyboards) to vertical so that they would "look more like a cell" (DVD storyboard featurette). The wide shot of the cubicles was influenced by *The Apartment* (d. Wilder, 1960); Spacey has stated that his portrayal of Lester was influenced by Jack Lemmon's character C. C. Baxter in this same film.

13   Mendes returns to the theme of the hollowness of the American Dream in *Revolutionary Road* (2008).

14   Other films that identify the workplace as a locus of existential angst and moral vacuity include *Glengarry Glen Ross* (d. Foley, 1992), *Office Space* (d. Judge, 1999), *Horrible Bosses* (d. Gordon, 2011), and *The Insider* (d. Mann, 1999). Mike White and Laura Dern's HBO show *Enlightened* (2011–2013) offers a complex attitude toward the immorality of the American workplace.

15   The use of photos to give a sense of history and background are an homage to Terrence Malick's *Badlands* (DVD audio commentary).

16   Mendes searched for a table that would "put enough distance between the characters to make them . . . alienated from each other" (DVD audio commentary).

17   Cinematographer Conrad Hall lit the windows with what Mendes describes as an "almost ethereal light," and he beat steam around the room to produce an "emptiness, almost like a church" (DVD storyboard featurette).

18   Ball, *Shooting Script*, 41.

19   Mendes, DVD audio commentary. Emphasis added. He reiterates that he had the set built in such a way that it would convey a "religious sense" (DVD storyboard featurette).

20   Mendes calls the scene "crucial . . . the biggest turning point for him . . . he's finally breaking free" (DVD audio commentary).

21   As Mendes points out, Hall lit this second dinner shot differently to make the walls look closer together, and (therefore) more like a jail cell (DVD audio commentary).

22   He does so literally while smoking pot and unabashedly rocking out to "American Woman," a song whose lyrics capture his individuation and differentiation from Carolyn:

> American woman, stay away from me / American woman, mama let me be
> Don't come knockin' around my door / I don't wanna see your face no more
> I got more important things to do / Than spend my time growin' old with you
> Now woman, I said stay away / American woman, listen what I say

23   Michel Foucault, *Surveiller et punir: Naissance de la Prison* (Paris: Gallimard, 1975), 34.

24   Ball notes that Lester is "reveling in the sheer physical pleasure of his body" (*Shooting Script*, 73). Mendes acknowledges that this shot is an homage to *Marathon Man* (d. Schlesinger, 1976) (DVD audio commentary).

25   Mendes remarks, "The movie if anything is about imprisonment and escape from imprisonment—it's a rites of passage story" (DVD audio commentary). Mendes and Hall used 35mm film (in the beginning office sequence) so that "you get a sense

of the epic within the domestic . . . to try to get a feeling of the scale . . . the epic journey that he's going on—a huge rites of passage story" (DVD storyboard featurette).
Mendes shot Lester "from above for the first 20–25 minutes of the movie" since "it's
all about status. This is the story of a small man who grows big" (DVD storyboard
featurette).

26   These include the Colonel in the rear view window of his Ford Explorer; Barbara
Fitts' face in the top of her dining room table; Jane's reflections in her mirror (eval-
uating herself before school, sitting on her bed, and looking at herself after Carolyn
slaps her); Ricky looking in his mirror (wiping blood off his face and later getting
ready for school); the Colonel in Ricky's mirror; and Lester's face lying on a table
of blood.

27   If examining one's reflection is symbolic then Jane, Lester, and Ricky—unlike Carolyn and the Colonel—are willing to scrutinize themselves.

28   She carries a basket of roses when she confronts him in the garage; roses are on the
living room coffee table when she and Lester fail to connect romantically.

29   Ball, *Shooting Script*, 52.

30   Purchasing the car may of course be due to Lester's nostalgia for joyful moments in
his youth.

31   So Kathleen Rowe Karlyn, "Too Close for Comfort: *American Beauty* and the
Incest Motif," *Cinema Journal* 44 [2004]: 69–93, here 72. Louis-Paul Willis notes
that the rose petals "simultaneously represent eroticism and femininity. As such,
they connote what they 'purport to conceal': Angela's budding sexuality" ("From
Jocasta to Lolita: The Oedipal Fantasy Inverted," *International Journal of Žižek Studies* 6, no. 2 [2012]: 1–19, here 16, http://zizekstudies.org/index.php/ijzs/article/
view/375/435).

32   This concealment is evident when Angela brushes her hand past Lester as she reaches
into the refrigerator. Mendes speaks of "finding the surreal within the real" so that
the audience is not clearly aware that they are "going into fantasy" (DVD storyboard
featurette). When Lester finds Angela in the tub, Mendes notes that he wants the
audience to be unsure if Lester was entering a fantasy (DVD audio commentary).

33   Fitzgerald, *The Great Gatsby*, 189.

34   "Out of each fantasy I cut to the most mundane shot—here, in the kitchen, after the
bathroom fantasy" (Mendes, DVD storyboard featurette).

35   Mendes, DVD storyboard featurette.

36   Ball, *Shooting Script*, 16, 35, 41.

37   Ball notes this dichotomy during Lester's first fantasy: "Angela's awkwardness gives
way to a fluid grace" (*Shooting Script*, 16).

38   For a more detailed discussion, see Matthew S. Rindge, "Lusting after Lester's Lolita: Perpetuating and Resisting the Male Gaze in *American Beauty*," in *Now Showing: Film Theory in Biblical Studies* (ed. Caroline Vander Stichele and Laura Copier;
Semeia Study Series; Atlanta: Society of Biblical Literature, 2016).

39   Susan Bordo finds the film's presentation of Angela's body refreshing because it does
not conform to conventional films in which images of young girls "do not jar us into
moral wakefulness; rather, they lull us into comfort with the eroticization of imma-
ture bodies" ("The Moral Content of Nabokov's *Lolita*," in *Aesthetic Subjects* [ed.

Pamela R. Matthews and David McWhirter; Minneapolis: University of Minnesota Press, 2003], 125–52, here 149). "Unlike Nabokov," she writes, "we are not much inclined to tunnel deep into the content and meaning of the images that obsess us, whether as sexual fantasies or as blueprints for girls' bodies (and souls)" (148).

40   Bordo notes, "It's very rare that popular culture exposes or interrogates (rather than simply reproduces) our fantasies about Lolita-like girls. I believe that this is one reason *American Beauty* seemed fresh and innovative" ("Nabokov's Lolita," 148). She makes a similar claim for Kubrick's presentation of Leelee Sobieski's two scenes in *Eyes Wide Shut* (1999). *American Beauty*'s critique of sexualizing young girls is critical, she remarks, for a real world "where nasty things do indeed happen to little girls" (149).

41   Accompanying their encounter is Neil Young's "Don't Let It Bring You Down." The lyric "Red lights flashing through the window in the rain" plays as rain is visible in a window behind Lester and Angela, and red roses are in a bowl on the table between them.

42   Contrary to Freud's contention, Lester demonstrates that the sexual drive is not the ultimate and "central point" of his life (Freud, *Civilization and Its Discontents*, 48).

43   Vladimir Nabokov, *Lolita* (New York: Vintage International, 1997; orig. pub. 1955 by Olympia Press). Part of Ball's inspiration for his script was the story of Amy Fisher, the "Long Island Lolita."

44   On the film's connections to *Lolita*, see Bordo, "The Moral Content of Nabokov's Lolita," and Karlyn, "*American Beauty* and the Incest Motif." Tracy Lemaster argues that *American Beauty* both reissues the "nymphet" theme from *Lolita*, and borrows specific themes (rose petals, cheerleading performance, film) directly from the novel ("The Nymphet as Consequence in Vladimir Nabokov's *Lolita* and Sam Mendes' *American Beauty*," *Trans. Internet-Zeitschrift für Kulturwissenschaften* 16 [2006], http://www.inst.at/trans/16Nr/02_2/wendt-lemaster16.htm).

45   Lemaster contends that "*American Beauty*, at its core, is trying to valorize and legitimize a pedophile" ("The Nymphet as Consequence"). Karlyn claims that Lester's sexual interest in Angela is a displaced desire for incest with his daughter ("*American Beauty* and the Incest Motif"); cf. Willis, "From Jocasta to Lolita: The Oedipal Fantasy Inverted."

46   Bordo claims that Humbert's "moral failing (a failing that many of us share, although perhaps to a lesser degree of self-abandon) consists in his trying to realize the fantasies of imagination, memory, and desire—in themselves beautiful and soul feeding—in the body of an actual human being. . . . For although finding a child achingly beautiful, being sexually shaken by that beauty, even enshrining it in words and images, is not monstrous, forgetting that she *is* a child—not a sexual equal, whatever her precocity—is" ("Nabokov's Lolita," 127).

47   For an insightful analysis of the respective film versions (Kubrick and Lyne) of *Lolita*, see Bordo, "The Moral Content of Nabokov's Lolita." On "nymphets" in cinema, see Marianne Sinclair, *Hollywood Lolita* (London: Plexus, 1988).

48   Ball notes that Angela here is "embarrassed and vulnerable. This is not the mythically carnal creature of Lester's fantasies; this is a nervous child" (*Shooting Script*, 93). Bordo finds *American Beauty* to be "more the moral descendant of Nabokov's

Lolita than" Lyne's film version of *Lolita* ("Nabokov's Lolita," 146). This claim is significant given her argument that Nabokov "wants us to remember that the power difference between adult and child is the essence of the pedophile's pleasure—and of the violence done to the child" (145). Bordo emphasizes that one view of Lolita that Nabokov gives is of the "twelve-year-old child," noting that she cries herself to sleep every night (135). "And Nabokov refuses to allow the reader to share Humbert's mythical view of Lolita's sexual power. For Nabokov—as for Lester Burnham—the sobering fact is that Lolita is a child" (147).

49   So Mendes: "Suddenly you see that this woman who you thought was knowing, is an innocent child, and she reveals herself to him as a virgin. This is a big turning point for Lester. And in these moments he becomes a father again . . . he just wants to give her a hug . . . he wraps her up, and he becomes a father again. It's the most satisfying end to his journey that there could have been. And a very moving one" (DVD audio commentary).

50   Johnston claims that Lester "discovers enjoyment and contentment within himself" once he declines to have sex with Angela. This decision, Johnston asserts, enables Lester's subsequent "recovery of love for" Jane and Carolyn (*Useless Beauty*, 70).

51   Casey McKittrick argues that Lester's fantasies do not aid his growth ("'I Laughed and Cringed at the Same Time . . .': Shaping Pedophilic Discourse Around *American Beauty* and *Happiness*," *The Velvet Light Trap* 47 [2001]).

52   Amazon.com interview with Jeff Shannon, 1999. Republished on http://www.spiritualteachers.org/alan_ball.htm.

53   "What I love about the video," Mendes remarks, "is that it's almost like going inside Ricky's head" (DVD storyboard featurette). Before we even first see Ricky, we see *what he is seeing* through his camera, as we (and he) watch Lester and Jane arguing in the kitchen.

54   Mendes, DVD audio commentary.

55   Mendes calls the scene "another one of these zooms in past Angela, past the conventional beauty, into the person that Ricky thinks is much more interesting" (DVD audio commentary).

56   Karlyn argues that Ricky's actions reveal that the film "romanticizes the stalking of women," and she accuses Ricky of seducing Jane ("*American Beauty* and the Incest Motif," 81).

57   Ball, *Shooting Script*, 15.

58   Abraham H. Maslow, *Religions, Values, and Peak-Experiences*, (New York: Viking Press, 1970), x; emphasis original. Ball sees a similar religious sensibility at work in Ricky: "There's a Buddhist notion of the miraculous within the mundane, and I think we certainly live in a culture that encourages us not to look for that" (Jeff Shannon interview, 1999).

59   For a constructive dialogue between *American Beauty* and Ecclesiastes, see Johnston, *Useless Beauty*, 57–72.

60   The Colonel is disgusted when he realizes his neighbors are a gay couple: "How come these faggots always have to rub it in your face?! How can they be so shameless?" When he sees Lester jogging with these two, he mutters, "Now what is this, the fucking gay pride parade?"

61   Ball reflects, "But the Colonel, a lot of people say, 'Oh, he's so evil.' And I so didn't see that, it was just that he was so shattered and so broken and so deeply, deeply, deeply alone" (Alan Ball interview with Susan Royal, "American Beauty Screenwriter Alan Ball Conducts Case Study at the IFP/West Screenwriters Conference" [InsideFilm, 2000], http://insidefilm.com/alan_ball.html).

62   Alan Ball interview with Susan Royal.

63   Victor Hugo, *La Préface de Cromwell* (Paris: Ambroise Dupont, 1827).

64   Ball, *Shooting Script*, 114.

65   Elizabeth Barrett Browning, "Aurora Leigh," in *Aurora Leigh and Other Poems* (ed. John Robert Glorney Bolton and Julia Bolton Holloway; London: Penguin, 1995), 232.

66   Setting the scene's somber tone is Thomas Newman's instrumental reprise of his piece from the first kitchen sequence, when the camera lingered on the family photograph. Johnston remarks that Lester discerns not "merely 'death in life,'" but also "'life in death'" (*Useless Beauty*, 68).

67   Johnston accents both elements (*Reel Spirituality*, 102). He notes that the film has, in this moment, a "fragile joy" (*Useless Beauty*, 58).

68   Mendes, DVD audio commentary.

69   This and the final image of Carolyn convey a sense of hope about her. Her laughing recalls her potential; her weeping over Lester's clothes demonstrates remorse.

70   *Contra* the (anti)sentiment in Woody Allen's *Midnight in Paris* (2011).

71   Alan Ball and Alan Poul, eds., *Six Feet Under: Better Living through Death* (New York: Pocket Books, 2003), 5.

72   Ball and Poul, *Six Feet Under*, 5.

73   Alison Rosen, "Alan Ball: The *Six Feet Under* Creator Returns to His Theatrical Roots," *Time Out*, February 1, 2007, http://www.timeout.com/newyork/theater/alan-ball.

74   Peter N. Chumo II, "*American Beauty*: An Interview with Alan Ball," *Creative Screenwriting* 71 (January–February 2000): 26–35.

75   Havrilesky, "An Alan Ball Postmortem."

76   Thomas Lynch, "Grave Affairs: HBO's 'Six Feet Under,'" *Christian Century* 121, no. 22 (November 2, 2004): 18–22, http://www.religion-online.org/showarticle.asp?title=3104.

77   Ball and Poul, *Six Feet Under*.

78   Jeff Shannon interview, 1999, http://www.spiritualteachers.org/alan_ball.htm.

79   Among the many similarities between the film and Miller's play is the name (the Lomans) given to the Burnhams' former neighbors, and the foreshadowing of—and concluding with—the main character's death. See Arthur Miller, *Death of a Salesman* (New York: Viking Press, 1973).

80   Ball, *Shooting Script*, 2.

81   Bordo, "Nabokov's Lolita," 149.

82   At this point the camera shifts to an overhead view, moving up and away from Lester's street, in the opposite direction from the beginning of the film where the camera moves from the sky toward his street.

83   A similar device is employed with the final voiceover in *Smoke Signals* (d. Eyre, 1998).

4: *ABOUT SCHMIDT*

1   Tara Parker-Pope, "Suicide Rates Rise Sharply in U.S.," *New York Times*, May 2, 2013, http://www.nytimes.com/2013/05/03/health/suicide-rate-rises-sharply-in-us.html?_r=0.

2   Payne directed the film and cowrote the screenplay with his longtime associate Jim Taylor.

3   Louis Begley, *About Schmidt* (New York: Ballantine Books, 1996).

4   All film quotes are from the DVD version of *About Schmidt* (Los Angeles: New Line Cinema, 2003).

5   In a deleted scene, Schmidt's replacement Gary tells him there actually is a way he can help. When Schmidt hopefully asks what it is, Gary says he has had trouble opening the lock on the left-hand drawer of the desk.

6   For Johnston, the Woodmen building functions "almost as a tower of Babel, a monument to human wisdom that proves to be folly" (*Useless Beauty*, 197, n. 4).

7   Warren's initial response to Ray's speech hints that he might already be aware of the emptiness of Ray's claims. He does not seem emotionally moved by the speech, nor does he appear to resonate with it. He instead rises and sloughs off to a bar where he sits, orders a vodka gimlet, and sits alone in silence.

8   Louis Begley, "A Conversation with Louis Begley," *About Schmidt*, 277.

9   Alexander Payne, introduction to Deleted Scene 161 (DVD special features). Emphasis added.

10   Translation mine. The parable also occurs in the Gospel of Thomas (63).

11   Bernard Brendan Scott suggests that the man's plan to store his goods imitates Joseph's injunction to Pharaoh to store up goods for seven years in order to prepare for a leaner future (cf. Gen 37–50) (*Hear Then the Parable: A Commentary on the Parables of Jesus* [Minneapolis: Augsburg Fortress, 1989], 133–34).

12   The three Greek verbs that Luke uses are the same as the verbs in the Greek version (LXX) of Ecclesiastes. The parable also appears to allude to this excerpt from Ben Sira:

> "One becomes rich through diligence and self-denial,
>> and the reward allotted to him is this:
> When he says, 'I have found rest, and now I shall feast on my goods!'
>> *he does not know how long it will be*
> until he leaves them to others and dies" (11:18-19, NRSV).

Facing both rich men is the dilemma of how death's unpredictable timing can forever end one's use of possessions.

13   See Rindge, *Jesus' Parable of the Rich Fool.*

14   See the Admonitions of Ipuwer; *Dispute Between a Man and his Ba*; the biographical inscription on the statue of Nebneteru; the Sixteenth Instruction of *Papyrus Insinger* 17.4–20; Inscription 127 on the tomb of Petosiris; the Song from the Tomb of King Intef; Stela of Taimhotep; Setne II; The Instruction of Ankhsheshonq 8.7–14, 12.5, 17, 18; Harwa; statue inscription of Udjahorresne; Instruction to King Merikare; the eighth petition of "The Eloquent Peasant;" and the inscription of Seti

I. See Miriam Lichtheim, *Ancient Egyptian Literature: A Book of Readings* (vols. 1–3; Berkeley: University of California Press, 1973–1980).

15   Like Qoheleth, he insists that "to live always with death before their eyes" will enable people to cease their "vain toil" (*Charon* 20). Translations of Lucian are my own.

16   *Menippus* 12.

17   "But how will a person take thought of his own end, if he craves all things without end? And yet there is nothing so essential for us to consider" (*Ep.* 70.17-18 [Grummere, LCL]).

18   A person who spends his life in idleness "has not lived; he has merely tarried awhile in life. Nor has he died late in life; he has simply been a long time dying" (*Ep.* 93.3-4). Rather than living (in this case, eighty years), such a person has merely "existed eighty years, unless perchance you mean by 'he has lived' what we mean when we say that a tree 'lives'" (93.4).

19   Eccl 2:24-26; 3:12-13, 22; 5:17-19; 7:14; 8:15; 9:7-10; 11:7–12:7.

20   Eccl 2:14-16; 3:2, 19-21; 5:15-16; 7:1-2, 4, 17, 26; 8:8; 9:2-12; 11:8. For a fuller version of this argument, see Rindge, "Mortality and Enjoyment."

21   On enjoyment (including its limitations) and giving an inheritance: 11:20-21; 14:8-16; on generosity with others: 14:8; on giving to God: 14:11; on alms: 3:30; 7:32; 12:3; 17:23.

22   On death's inevitability, see *T. Abr.* 1:4-5; 4:11; 8:9, 11; 15:1, 7; 19:7; cf. 17:1-3; 19:2-3; on hospitality, see 4:1-7; 17:7; 20:15; on making a will/testament, see 1:4-5; 4:11; 8:11; 15:1, 7. For the Greek text, see Francis Schmidt, *Le Testament grec d' Abraham: Introduction, édition critique des deux recensions grecques, traduction* (Tübingen: J.C.B. Mohr [Paul Siebeck], 1986).

      1 Enoch, unlike these other texts, offers no recommendations regarding the use of possessions, for it assumes that anyone who has possessions will be judged negatively by God (1 Enoch 94:6-11; 95:2; 97:8-10; 98:3). It critiques enjoyment and other values central to Qoheleth (1 Enoch 102:6-11; 103:3-4, 7-8). See George W. E. Nickelsburg and James C. VanderKam, trans., *1 Enoch: A New Translation* (Minneapolis: Augsburg Fortress, 2004).

23   Payne deleted several scenes in order to "get more quickly to Schmidt's next letter to Ndugu" (Introduction to [Deleted] Scenes 110–113; DVD special features).

24   Payne, introduction to (Deleted) Scenes 34–37 (DVD special features).

25   Deleted Scene 103 (DVD special features).

26   Johnston identifies "three levels of 'truth'" in Warren's letters: "what Warren has been conditioned to say and believe, what he is willing to risk questioning given his pain, and what viewers see portrayed on the screen" (*Useless Beauty*, 149).

27   In this case, there is harmony between the visual images and Warren's words; during the above voiceover he uncorks and sniffs Helen's perfume, smears his face with her makeup remover, and begins to cry.

28   Comedic elements also punctuate Warren's letters. These are often rooted in his cluelessness about poverty in the two-thirds world (he recommends that Ndugu pledge a fraternity when he attends college) or child sponsorship ("I am your new foster father," "I'll close now and get this in the mail. Here I am rambling on and on, and you probably want to hurry on down and cash that check and get yourself something

to eat.") Warren includes a pamphlet on Buffalo Bill Cody, expecting (?) that Ndugu can read it. Many details in his letters are inappropriate for a six-year-old ("cocky bastard!"). His letters exhibit a general ignorance, as when he tells Ndugu (with a genuine sense of discovery): "Later that same day I happened to meet a real Indian, or Native American, as they like to be called nowadays. We had a nice chat about the history of the area and he really opened my eyes. Those people got a raw deal, just a raw deal!"

29 Johnston refers to a "metaphor of cows/humans being led to the slaughter," which he observes in the following scenes (*Useless Beauty*, 159).

30 Meat is twice cut off the bone of an animal: by Helen early on and later at Jeannie's wedding reception.

31 Johnston, *Useless Beauty*, 148; cf. 159. Some of these values are reflected in a sign Warren observes near the film's end: "The Cowards Never Started / The Weak Died on the Way / Only the Strong Arrived / They Were the Pioneers."

32 See Eccl 8:10; 9:5-6, 10.

33 Payne's interest in the death of the loved one as a frame for searching for meaning is heightened to an even greater degree in *The Descendants* (2011), also featuring a husband whose view of his marriage is shattered after discovering his wife's infidelity.

34 Johnston writes, "A story that might have been simply a black comedy has become a journey of self-realization.... There might not be a tidy resolution, but there is a relationship" (*Useless Beauty*, 165).

35 *Dogville* (d. von Trier, 2003); *Cidade de Deus* (d. Meirelles and Lund, 2002); *The Constant Gardener* (d. Meirelles, 2005); *The Girl in the Café* (d. Yates, 2005).

36 Marc Lacey, "Via Hollywood, a Glimpse of African Poverty," *New York Times*, December 21, 2002. http://www.nytimes.com/2002/12/21/movies/via-hollywood-a-glimpse-of-african-poverty.html.

37 See Raj Patel, *Stuffed and Starved: The Hidden Battle for the World Food System* (Brooklyn: Melville House, 2012). Warren's choice to sponsor a child is a radical departure from his otherwise consistent frugality. At the funeral home, he asks if he can drive himself to limit expenses. Jeannie accuses Warren of buying the cheapest casket for Helen's burial, and he defends himself by saying he bought the *second* cheapest option. When he cites the Winnebago he bought for Helen as evidence of generosity, Jeannie reminds him that Helen had to pay for half of it, and this with money from her savings. Warren even checks for loose coins in a payphone's coin slot.

38 Johnston highlights the ways in which Warren has been able to "love another" through his letters to Ndugu (*Useless Beauty*, 165).

39 Jesus' parables of the Sheep and Goats (Matt 25:31-46) and Lazarus and the Rich Man (Luke 16:19-31) also bear similarity with the film's emphasis on Warren's relationship with Ndugu.

40 In the novel, Schmidt finds meaning in a vacation in the Amazon—where he is "overcome by intense, rather stupid happiness.... [A]ll that matters is that and his gratitude. It is so very splendid to be alive!" (Begley, *About Schmidt*, 173). He also finds meaning in his sexual escapades with the waitress Carrie. The way she calls

him "darling," e.g., "was enough to make one believe in the remission of sin and life eternal" (Begley, *About Schmidt*, 199).

5: FILMS AS PARABLES OF DISORIENTATION

1   John Dominic Crossan, *The Dark Interval: Towards a Theology of Story* (Niles, Ill.: Argus Communications, 1975), 57.

2   So C. H. Dodd, *The Parables of the Kingdom* (rev. ed.; New York: Scribners, 1961), 1.

3   Estimates of the number of parables vary (between thirty-two and fifty-three) due to the different criteria used to determine what constitutes a "parable." See Robert H. Stein, *An Introduction to the Parables of Jesus* (Philadelphia: Westminster, 1981), 22–26; Arland J. Hultgren, *The Parables of Jesus: A Commentary* (Grand Rapids: Eerdmans, 2000), 2–5. The absence of parables in John's Gospel is striking. An additional six–eight stories of Jesus appear in two extra-biblical texts (Gospel of Thomas and Apocryphon of James). Three other stories of Jesus are included in the Apocryphon of James. See William D. Stroker, "Extracanonical Parables and the Historical Jesus," in *The Historical Jesus: Critical Concepts in Religious Studies* (ed. Craig A. Evans; London: Routledge, 2004), 4:186–209.

4   So Dan O. Via (*The Parables: Their Literary and Existential Dimension* [Philadelphia: Fortress, 1967], 70), against the central claim of Adolf Jülicher who argued that each parable had one principal point (*Die Gleichnisreden Jesu* [2 vols.; Tübingen: Mohr Siebeck, 1888–1899; repr., 1910]). Cf. Robert W. Funk, *Parables and Presence: Forms of the New Testament Tradition* (Philadelphia: Fortress, 1982), 30.

5   Parables are "genuine works of art, real aesthetic objects" (Via, *The Parables*, ix). Dodd concludes his study of the parables by speaking of their "imaginative and poetical quality. They are works of art" (*Parables*, 157). Cf. G. V. Jones, *The Art and Truth of the Parables: A Study in Their Literary Form and Modern Interpretation* (London: SPCK, 1964), 113, 122, 129–31, 163–65. On poetic elements in the parables see Funk, *Parables and Presence*, 25–27.

6   So George A. Buttrick: "The old definition, 'an earthly story with a heavenly meaning,' can hardly be improved" (*The Parables of Jesus* [New York: Harper & Brothers, 1928], xv).

7   Dodd, *Parables of the Kingdom*, 5; emphasis added. Dodd recognizes that parables are not mere illustrations of "moral generalities" (13).

8   Joachim Jeremias (*The Parables of Jesus* [2nd ed.; trans. S. H. Hooke; Upper Saddle River, N.J.: Prentice Hall, 1972]) gives minimal attention to this disturbing and subversive aspect of Jesus' parables. He does note occasions where Jesus' parables would be surprising (143, 200, 204).

9   Some of the following material on Lukan parables appears in a modified form in Matthew S. Rindge, "Luke's Artistic Parables: Narratives of Subversion, Imagination, and Transformation," *Interpretation* 68, no. 4 (2014): 403–15.

10   See Matthew S. Rindge, "The 'Good' Samaritan," *Bible Odyssey* (Atlanta: Society of Biblical Literature, 2014), http://bibleodyssey/passages/main-articles/good-samaritan. Many scholars such as John Dominic Crossan remove the parable from its immediate literary frame, recognizing that such frames are the product of the gospel writers and not the historical Jesus ("Parable and Example in the Teaching of Jesus,"

Semeia 1 [1974]: 63–104). For arguments that parables should be understood within their broader literary context, see Paul Ricoeur, "The Bible and the Imagination," in *Figuring the Sacred: Religion, Narrative, and Imagination* (trans. David Pellauer; ed. Mark I. Wallace; Minneapolis: Fortress, 1995), 150. Many classify the Samaritan story as a parable: Crossan, "Parable and Example," 63–104; Funk, "How Do You Read (Luke 10:25-37)," *Interpretation* 18 (1964): 56–61; idem, "The Old Testament in Parable: A Study of Luke 10:25-37," *Encounter* 26 (1965): 251–67; idem, *Language, Hermeneutic, and Word of God* (New York: Harper & Row, 1966), 191–222; idem, "The Good Samaritan as Metaphor," *Semeia* 2 (1974): 74–81. Dan O. Via sees the "Samaritan" as an example story, and not a parable ("A Response to Crossan, Funk, and Petersen," *Semeia* 1 [1974]: 222–35).

11   Unless otherwise indicated, all biblical texts are translated by the author.

12   See Josephus, *Antiquities* 11.174; 13.254–56; 20.118–36; *Jewish Wars* 1.62–63, 2.232–46. While perhaps exaggerated, the remark in John's Gospel—"Jews don't have dealings with Samaritans"—might reflect an animosity familiar to the audience of Luke's parable (John 4:9).

13   Unlike Crossan ("Parable and Example," 74, 77), I think that the story—even its final form in Luke—retains a parabolic element of disruption and disorientation. Crossan argues that in the process of transformation from a parable (historical Jesus) to example story (Luke), the story loses its parabolic edge. He finds the provocative edge of the parable to be its forcing the hearer to join the word "good" to the word "Samaritan" (75–76). Funk finds the challenge of the parable to be imagining (as a Jew) that one is being helped by a Samaritan and that the vehicle of grace is a Samaritan (*Parables and Presence*, 33, 50, 63, 65).

14   Throughout Luke is an effort to show how women, children, the poor, physically disabled, and tax collectors are models of behavior. Six of the seven episodes in Luke 18:1–19:10 feature social outcasts, and in each case the outcast is a moral exemplar.

15   The focus on Torah obedience as the key to inheriting eternal life also appears in Luke 18:18-30 and 16:19-31. In all three texts, eternal life is also tied to using one's possessions to benefit people in desperate need.

16   John Chrysostom (ca. 347–407) claims that the rich man gives daily drinking parties, is scented with perfumes, feeds flatterers, and that his soul is "buried in wine" (*St. John Chrysostom: On Wealth and Poverty* [trans. Catharine P. Roth; Crestwood, N.Y.: St. Vladimir's Seminary, 1984], 105–6. Erasmus claims that the rich man dressed "sensually," gave a "magnificent party" every day, and was a "slave to his ambition, his extravagance, and his pleasure" (*Paraphrase on Luke 11–24* [ed. and trans. Jane E. Phillips; vol. 48 of *Collected Works of Erasmus*; Toronto: University of Toronto Press, 2003], 98–99). Most English translations describe the rich man as "feasting sumptuously" even though "rejoicing splendidly" is just as legitimate a translation of the Greek (*euphrainomenos. . . lamprōs*).

17   Chrysostom notes that Lazarus endured "inconsolable distress" as a result of suffering as a virtuous person (*On Wealth*, 30, 40). He describes Lazarus' "patient endurance of poverty," noting that he endured his evils with "courage" (23, 37). The poor man, Chrysostom notes, did not "become discouraged, blaspheme, or complain." He even "gave thanks in hunger" and glorified God! (28, 39). Erasmus applauds

Lazarus since he "patiently bears his afflictions" (*Paraphrase on Luke*, 101), and Jean Calvin commends Lazarus for his "patient endurance of the cross" (*Commentary on a Harmony of the Evangelists, Matthew, Mark, and Luke* [3 vols.; trans. William Pringle; Grand Rapids: Eerdmans, 1949], 2:190).

18   Martin Luther, *Sermons on Gospel Texts for the 1st to 12th Sundays After Trinity* (vol. 4 of *The Complete Sermons of Martin Luther*; ed. and trans. John Nicholas Lenker et al.; Grand Rapids: Baker, 1983), 13:23; emphasis added.

19   Chrysostom, *On Wealth*, 1:35.

20   As John Donahue notes, "The revelation of God in parable cannot be reduced to a series of theological platitudes or moral maxims. Here we touch on one of the major problems of preaching on the parables: the tendency to soften their shock by moralizing them, that is, turning the good news into good advice" (*The Gospel in Parable: Metaphor, Narrative and Theology in the Synoptic Gospels* [Philadelphia: Fortress, 1988], 16–17).

21   So Crossan, "Parable and Example," 80. He takes 16:19-26 as the original parable of Jesus, one "whose literal point was a strikingly *amoral* (in contrast to its source) description of situation reversal between the rich man and Lazarus" (81). The Egyptian story of Si-Osiris concludes with this overt moral: "He who has been good on earth, will be blessed in the kingdom of the dead, and he who has been evil on earth, will suffer in the kingdom of the dead." See Hugo Gressmann, *Vom reichen Mann und armen Lazarus: eine literargeschichtliche Studie* (Abhandlungen der Königlich Preussischen Akademie der Wissenschaften, Philosophisch-Historische Klasse, 1918, 7; Berlin: Königlichte Akademie der Wissenschaften, 1918), cited in Jeremias, *Parables of Jesus*, 183.

22   Rudolf Bultmann notes that "Luke 16:19-26 simply teaches the reversal of earthly fortune in the world to come as a warning to the rich and a consolation to the poor" (*The History of the Synoptic Tradition* [trans. John Marsh; Oxford: Blackwell, 1963], 204). The parable's apparent "class warfare" perspective is anticipated earlier in Luke when Jesus blesses the poor and curses the rich (6:20-24).

23   On (or against) this story, Luther argues, "poverty and suffering make no one acceptable to God" (*Sermons*, 12:22).

24   Many such as Crossan ("Structuralist Analysis and the Parables of Jesus: A Reply to D. O. Via Jr., 'Parable and Example Story: A Literary-Structuralist Approach,'" *Semeia* 1 [1974]: 192–221, here 206) regard this concluding line as an addition and not original to the parable. For arguments that the master's affirmation is original, see Wilhelm Michaelis, *Die Gleichnisse Jesu: Eine Einführung* (3rd ed.; UCB 32; Hamburg: Furche-Verlag, 1956), 227–28; Jeremias, *Parables of Jesus*, 45–46; Via, *The Parables*, 156–57, 161.

25   Jeremias eliminates the disquieting implications of the parable by removing 16:9-13, and asserting that for the historical Jesus the parable sought to encourage people to act in the face of the terrible crisis facing them (*Parables of Jesus*, 182); J. D. M. Derrett argues, unconvincingly, that the amount of the debt lowered by the manager would have been his own cut of the deal ("Fresh Light on St. Luke XVI. I. The Parable of the Unjust Steward," *NTS* 7 [1960–1961]: 198–219). Such efforts to make

sense of the parable's provocative nature begin as early as Luke's Gospel with the series of sayings (16:8b-13) appended as a form of commentary to the parable.

26   Scott, *Hear Then the Parable*, 324.

27   The Greek word translated as "hides" is *egkryptō*.

28   Given Dodd's recognition of the consistently negative use of leaven in biblical texts, it is puzzling that he concludes that in this parable "it should be used here as a symbol for a wholesome influence" (*Parables of the Kingdom*, 154–55)!

29   Pliny, *Natural History* 29.54.170 (Jones, LCL).

30   *Mishnah Kilayim* 2.8; 3.2.

31   *Sifra* on Lev 26:9. English translation appears in Robert M. Johnston and Harvey K. McArthur, *They Also Taught in Parables: Rabbinic Parables from the First Centuries of the Christian Era* (Grand Rapids: Zondervan, 1990; repr., Eugene, Ore.: Wipf & Stock, 2014), 58. Used with permission.

32   *J. Ber.* 2:8. English translation appears in Johnston and McArthur, *They Also Taught in Parables*. Used with permission.

33   See Abraham Maslow, "A Theory of Human Motivation," *Psychological Review* 50, no. 4 (1943): 370–96; idem, *Motivation and Personality* (New York: Harper, 1954).

34   Cf. Funk, *Parables and Presence*, 59–60.

35   On myth, see Claude Lévi-Strauss, "The Structural Study of Myth," in *Structural Anthropology* (Garden City, N.Y.: Doubleday, 1967), 202–28; Crossan, *Dark Interval*, 48–54.

36   Frank Kermode calls myths "the agents of stability," adding that they call for "absolute assent" (*The Sense of an Ending* [New York: Oxford University Press, 1967], 39).

37   Paul Ricoeur notes that Jesus' proverbs "reorient by disorienting" ("Love and Justice," in *Figuring the Sacred*, 329). Ricoeur does not, however, provide specific examples of such disorientation.

38   Scott, *Hear Then the Parable*, 424.

39   Crossan, *Dark Interval*, 9. See also Crossan, *In Parables: The Challenge of the Historical Jesus* (New York: Harper & Row, 1973). For critiques of Crossan's categories of myth and parable, see, e.g., Richard Walsh, *Mapping Myths of Biblical Interpretation* (Playing the Texts 4; Sheffield: Sheffield Academic, 2001), 124–28; Shawn Kelley, *Racializing Jesus: Race, Ideology and the Formation of Modern Biblical Scholarship* (New York: Routledge, 2002), 190–209.

On apologue, action, and satire, see Sheldon Sacks, *Fiction and the Shape of Belief: A Study of Henry Fielding with Glances at Swift, Johnson, and Richardson* (Berkeley: University of California Press, 1966). Satire reaches from Aristophanes to Stephen Colbert, and includes varied practitioners (Juvenal, Lucian, Thomas More, Erasmus, Jonathan Swift, Voltaire, Mark Twain). Niall Rudd identifies attack, entertainment, and preaching as the three elements of satire (*Themes in Roman Satire* [London: Duckworth, 1986], 1–39). On satire in film, see Donald W. McCaffrey, *Assault on Society: Satirical Literature to Film* (Lanham, Md.: Scarecrow, 1992).

40   As Crossan remarks, parables "shatter the deep structure of our accepted world and thereby render clear and evident to us the relativity of story itself." By doing so, they "remove our defences and make us vulnerable to God. It is only in such experiences

that God can touch us, and only in such moments does the kingdom of God arrive. My own term for this relationship is transcendence" (*Dark Interval*, 100).

41   Amos Wilder notes that "in all cultures men live by images. The meaning of things, the coherence of the world, its continuities, values and goals, all these are established for the multitudes and for societies of men by this or that world-picture or mythos, with its associated emblems, archetypes, paradigms, fables, heroes, cults" (*Early Christian Rhetoric: The Language of the Gospel* [Cambridge, Mass.: Harvard University Press, 1971], 121).

42   On Native Americans in film, see Jacquelyn Kilpatrick, *Celluloid Indians: Native Americans and Film* (Lincoln: University of Nebraska Press, 1999); Edward Buscombe, *'Injuns!': Native Americans in the Movies* (Bodmin, Cornwall: Reaktion Books, 2006).

43   So Denise K. Cummings, "'Accessible Poetry'? Cultural Intersection and Exchange in Contemporary American Indian and American Independent Film," *Studies in American Indian Literatures* 2, no. 13 (2001): 57–80.

44   Crossan, e.g., christened the short stories of Franz Kafka and Jorge Luis Borges as contemporary parables (*Dark Interval*, 77–87).

45   Via asserts that the parables "do not teach directly or focally about God" (*Parables*, 95).

46   Dodd notes that the parables express "a mind that sees truth in concrete pictures rather than conceives it in abstractions" (*Parables of the Kingdom*, 5).

47   Dodd observes that a parable is "drawn from nature or common life" (*Parables of the Kingdom*, 5). Ricoeur notes that "the whole narrative" of a parable "is told at the level of ordinary life events" ("Biblical Hermeneutics," *Semeia* 4 [1975]: 29–148, here 93). Cf. Via, *Parables*, 98–99.

48   For Wilder, the parables "are so human and realistic. . . . The persons in question, the scenes, the actions are not usually 'religious'" (*Early Christian Rhetoric*, 73).

49   On the implications of sacramental theology for constructing a dialogue between theology and film, see Johnston, *Reel Spirituality*. In light of the parables, Wilder maintains that a person's destiny "is at stake in his ordinary creaturely existence, domestic, economic and social" (*Early Christian Rhetoric*, 74). For Via, the parable's "existential understanding is that existence is gained or lost in the midst of ordinary life, that the eschatological occurs within the everyday" (*Parables*, 106).

50   Ricoeur highlights the "essential profaneness" and "profane language" of the parables ("Manifestation and Proclamation," in *Figuring the Sacred*, 57, 66). He explains that he does so because "Everything it contains is ordinary." He refers to the "extraordinary within the ordinary" as a hallmark of the parables (60).

51   Wilder, *Early Christian Rhetoric*, 76.

52   Wilder, *Early Christian Rhetoric*, 87; emphasis added.

53   The name of God is inserted numerous times in the Greek translation of Esther. Wilder comments, "The parables give us this kind of humanness and actuality. There is no romance or idealization here, no false mysticism, and no miracles, no impulse towards escape into fantasy or into sentimentality. We have stories, indeed, but they stay close to things as they are" (*Early Christian Rhetoric*, 74). "It is implicit," Wilder asserts regarding the parables, "that a man can be saved where he is. And, indeed, the

Gospel proposes not to substitute another world for this one, but to redeem and to transfigure the present world" (75); cf. Ernst Fuchs, "Das Neue Testament und das hermeneutische Problem," *ZTK* 58 (1961): 198–226, here 211. For Via, "the lack of specifically religious terminology in the parables might make them especially usable by and suggestive for a non-religious interpretation of Christianity" (*Parables*, 31); cf. Gerhard Ebeling, *Word and Faith* (trans. J. W. Leitch; Philadelphia: Fortress, 1967), 124–26.

54   Ricoeur, "Manifestation and Proclamation," 59–60.

55   As Gerhard Ebeling notes, "The art of the parable . . . is none other than that of bring-ing the hearer face to face with *what it is to be human* and thereby to make clear *what it means for God to draw near*" ("Hauptprobleme der protestantischen Theologie in der Gegenwart," *ZTK* 58 [1961]: 123–36, here 135; trans. Wilder, *Early Christian Rhetoric*, 7; emphasis added).

56   "The Samaritan" (10:30-36); "Friend at Midnight" (11:5-8); "Rich Fool" (12:16-20); "Father and Two Sons" (15:11-32); "Dishonest Manager" (16:1-8); "Lazarus and the Rich Man" (16:19-31).

57   See Rindge, *Jesus' Parable*. Luke's parables construct imaginative worlds in which the use of possessions is evaluated in light of life's fragility and death's inevitability, uncertain timing, and potential imminence. As narratives, Luke's parables illustrate sapiential concerns for meaning and provide the opportunity for literary characters and readers/hearers of Luke–Acts to evaluate their own use of possessions in light of the world constructed in the parable. In Luke, the question "What might/shall I do?" is almost always associated (in and outside parables) with the use of posses-sions (Luke 3:10, 12, 14; 10:25; 12:17; 16:3; 18:18).

58   See Rindge, *Jesus' Parable*, 240–47; cf. 169–73. Wilder refers to Jesus' parable "of the wisdom tradition" and identifies wisdom and prophecy as two dominant influences in Jesus' parables (*Early Christian Rhetoric*, 78).

In the Greek Bible (Septuagint), the term *parabolē* appears more frequently in wisdom texts than in any other type of literature. Seventeen of the forty-five uses of *parabolē* in the Septuagint occur in texts commonly assigned to the wisdom corpus (Psalms, Proverbs, Qoheleth, Ben Sira, and Wisdom). The term *parabolē* is associ-ated with other sapiential terms: a wise person (*sophos*) can understand a *parabolē* (Prov 1:5-6); Qoheleth associates *parabolai* with wisdom (*sophia*), knowledge (*gnō-sis*), and understanding (*epistēmē*) (1:17; cf. 12:9); Ben Sira links *parabolai* both with wisdom (*sophia*) and the sagacious (*sunetos*) person (1:25; 3:29). The term is also associated with Solomon, who is said to have written three thousand *parabolai* (1 Kgs 5:12 LXX). For these and other reasons, Maurice Gilbert classifies "parable" as one of four types of wisdom literature (*Les cinq livres des Sages: Les Proverbes de Salomon, Le livre de Job, Qohélet ou l'Écclésiaste, Le livre de ben Sira, La Sagesse de Salomon* [Paris: Cerf, 2003]). Hultgren recognizes the "Jewish wisdom tradition" as a key component of Jesus' parables (*Parables of Jesus*, 10–11; cf. Scott, *Hear Then the Parable*, 68).

59   Origen, *Commentary on John* 1.109–24. Origen cites other titles for Jesus (e.g., Word, Life, Truth), but he favors Wisdom. James G. Williams calls Jesus a "teacher of aphoristic wisdom" (*Those Who Ponder Proverbs: Aphoristic Thinking and Biblical*

Literature [Bible and Literature Series 2; Sheffield: Almond, 1981], 16); cf. Burton L. Mack, *A Myth of Innocence: Mark and Christian Origins* (Philadelphia: Fortress, 1988).

60   James C. VanderKam defines wisdom literature as texts that "grapple in a more universal way with the meaning of life, with life's perplexities, and with how to live it properly" (*An Introduction to Early Judaism* [Grand Rapids: Eerdmans, 2001], 115). On the interest that wisdom texts have with living meaningfully, see Walter Brueggemann, "The Epistemological Crisis of Israel's Two Histories (Jer 9:22-23)," in *Israelite Wisdom: Theological and Literary Essays in Honor of Samuel Terrien* (ed. John G. Gammie et al.; New York: Union Theological Seminary, 1978), 85–105, here 86; C. L. Seow, *Ecclesiastes: A New Translation with Introduction and Commentary* (Anchor Bible 18c.; New York: Doubleday, 1997), 67; John G. Gammie, "From Prudentialism to Apocalypticism: The Houses of the Sages amid the Varying Forms of Wisdom," in *The Sage in Israel and the Ancient Near East* (ed. John G. Gammie and Leo G. Perdue; Winona Lake, Ind.: Eisenbrauns, 1990), 479–97, here 482.

61   By "meaning" I refer to the symbolic domain from which people derive, and to which people ascribe, significance. Anthropologist Clifford Geertz claims that the "imposition of meaning on life is the major end and primary condition of human existence" ("Deep Play: Notes on the Balinese Cockfight," in *The Interpretation of Cultures* [New York: Basic Books, 1973], 412–53, here 434). This attentiveness to meaningful living is not unlike Martha Nussbaum's understanding of the goal of Hellenistic philosophy as "human flourishing, or *eudaimonia.*" Nussbaum underscores the emphasis of *eudaimonia* on "completeness of life," and she prefers to translate the term as "human flourishing" (*The Therapy of Desire: Theory and Practice in Hellenistic Ethics* [Princeton: Princeton University Press, 1994], 15).

62   On "alternative wisdom," see Marcus Borg, *Meeting Jesus Again for the First Time: The Historical Jesus and the Heart of Contemporary Faith* (New York: HarperCollins, 1994).

63   See Rindge, *Jesus' Parable,* 242–43.

64   On these terms, see Ricoeur, "Biblical Hermeneutics"; idem, *Conflict of Interpretations* (Evanston, Ill.: Northwestern University, 1974), 369–70. For an application of these terms to the Psalms, see Walter Brueggemann, "Psalms and the Life of Faith: A Suggested Typology of Function," *JSOT* 17 (1980): 5–21.

65   See Rindge, "Luke's Artistic Parables," 408–14; cf. Funk, *Parables and Presence,* 17.

66   Wilder notes, "The hearer not only learns about that reality, he participates in it. He is invaded by it. Here lies the power and fatefulness of art. Jesus' speech had the character not of instruction and ideas but of compelling imagination, of spell, of mythical shock and transformation" (*Early Christian Rhetoric,* 84).

CONCLUSION

1   Paul Ricoeur, "Manifestation and Proclamation," in *Figuring the Sacred,* 64.

2   Guillermo del Toro, cited in *Interview Magazine,* March 2007, 100.

3   George Miller, cited in Johnston, *Reel Spirituality,* 28, and Michael Frost, *Eyes Wide Open: Seeing God in the Ordinary* (Sutherland, NSW, Australia: Albatross Books, 1998), 100.

4 Wilder notes, "The Gospel did, indeed, combat the myth of the time, but it also was a myth-making movement" (*Early Christian Rhetoric*, 123).

5 Freud notes, "We may . . . consider the interesting case in which happiness in life is predominantly sought in the enjoyment of beauty . . . This aesthetic attitude to the goal of life offers little protection against the threat of suffering, but it can compensate for a great deal. The enjoyment of beauty has a peculiar, mildly intoxicating quality of feeling. Beauty has no obvious use; nor is there any clear cultural necessity for it. Yet civilization could not do without it" (*Civilization and Its Discontents*, 29).

6 "People who are receptive to the influence of art cannot set too high a value on it as a source of pleasure and consolation in life. Nevertheless the mild narcosis induced in us by art can do no more than bring about a transient withdrawal from the pressure of vital needs, and it is not strong enough to make us forget real misery" (Freud, *Civilization and Its Discontents*, 28).

7 This argument has been made with other films. Jean Douchet argues, e.g., that *Rear Window* (d. Hitchcock, 1954) is a metaphor for cinema, and especially film viewing, in general ("Hitch and His Public," trans. Verena Andermatt Conley, in *A Hitchcock Reader* [eds. Marshall Deutelbaum and Leland Poague; Oxford: Wiley-Blackwell, 2009], 17–24).

8 In 1999 the S&P 500 (a measure of the 500 largest U.S. companies) reached an apex. The following chart shows the annualized gains of the S&P 500 over a fourteen-year period:

2002	-23.4%	1995	34.1%
2001	-13.0%	1994	-1.5%
2000	-10.1%	1993	7.1%
1999	19.5%	1992	4.5%
1998	26.7%	1991	26.3%
1997	31.0%	1990	-6.6%
1996	20.3%	1989	27.3%

From 1995–1999 the S&P experienced its highest five-year gain (131.6%) since 1970. The highest five-year *annualized* return since 1970 was also in 1999 (28.56%). The second-highest five-year annualized return was in 1998 (24.06%). 1998–1999 also witnessed the highest 10-year annualized returns since 1970 (19.21% in 1998 and 18.21% in 1999). The fifteen-year annualized returns follow the same pattern: 1999 witnessed the highest fifteen-year annualized returns since 1970 (18.93%), and 1998 had the second-highest fifteen-year returns (17.9%). 1997 ranks third-highest for fifteen-year annualized returns (17.52%), and 1996 is fourth highest (16.8%). It is the same story with twenty-year annualized returns: 1999 is at the top (17.88%), followed by 1998 (17.75%), and 1997 is third (16.65%). 1999 also has the highest twenty-five-year annualized returns since 1970 (17.25%), and 1998 is second in this category (14.94%). This data points to 1998–1999 as the pinnacle of U.S. economic growth (as measured by the broad U.S. stock market indices). The most accelerated growth occurred from late 1994–September 2000.

Stock valuations do not of course tell the entire story, economic or otherwise. For a less optimistic view of the economic health in the 1990's, see M. Miringoff and M. L. Miringoff, *The Social Health of the Nation: How America is Really Doing* (New York: Oxford University Press, 1999); J. DeParle, *American Dream: Three Women, Ten Kids, and a Nation's Drive to End Welfare* (New York: Penguin, 2004), 327. Hedrick Smith identifies income inequality as the greatest threat to the ability of most Americans to realize the American Dream (*Who Stole the American Dream?* [New York: Random House, 2012]).

9   Edward Norton, interview with *Yale Herald*, October 8, 2010, cited in the special features of *Fight Club* supplemental DVD.

Image 1.1 by Mike Ritter © 1995 East Valley Tribune. Used with permission. Image 2.1 © 1999 by Fox 2000 Pictures. Image 2.2 © 1999 by Fox 2000 Pictures. Image 2.3 © 1999 by Fox 2000 Pictures. Image 3.1 © 1999 by Dreamworks LLC. Image 3.2 © 1999 by Dreamworks LLC. Image 4.1 © 2002 by New Line Cinema. Image 4.2 © 2002 by New Line Cinema. Image 4.3 © 2002 by New Line Cinema.

BIBLIOGRAPHY

Adams, James Truslow. *The Epic of America*. Boston: Little Brown, 1931.

Aichele, George and Richard Walsh. *Screening Scripture: Intertextual Connections between Scripture and Film*. Harrisburg: Trinity International, 2002.

Ariès, Philippe. "La mort inverse." *Archives europénnes de sociologie* 8 (1967): 169–95.

———. *Western Attitudes toward Death: from the Middle Ages to the Present*. Translated by Patricia M. Ranum. Baltimore: Johns Hopkins University Press, 1974.

Artaud, Antonin. "Sorcery and Cinema." Pages 103–5 in *The Shadow and Its Shadow*. Edited by Paul Hammond. San Francisco: City Lights Books, 2000.

Auden, W. H. *The Age of Anxiety: A Baroque Ecologue*. Princeton: Princeton University Press, 2011. Originally published in 1947.

Bailey, Michael E., and Kristin Lindholm. "Tocqueville and the Rhetoric of Civil Religion in the Presidential Inaugural Addresses." *Christian Scholar's Review* 32, no. 3 (2003): 259–79.

Ball, Alan. *American Beauty Shooting Script*. New York: Newmarket Press, 1999.

Ball, Alan and Alan Poul, eds. *Six Feet Under: Better Living through Death*. New York: Pocket Books, 2003.

Balzac, Honoré de. *The Jealousies of a Country Town*. Philadelphia: Avil Publishing, 1901.

Bandy, Mary Lea, and Antonio Mondo, eds. *The Hidden God: Film and Faith*. New York: Museum of Modern Art, 2003.

Barrientos, Tanya. "La. Bill: Punch a Flag Burner, Pay $25." *The Philadelphia Inquirer*, June 16, 1990. http://articles.philly.com/1990-06-16/news/25913080_1_flag-burners-flag-burner-address-flag-desecration.

Bazin, André. "Le journal d'un Curé de Campagne and the Stylistics of Robert Bresson." Pages 125–43 in *What is Cinema?* Vol. 1. Edited and Translated by Hugh Gray. Berkeley/Los Angeles: University of California Press, 1967. Originally published as "*Le Journal d'un curé de campagne* et le stylistique de Robert Bresson." *Cahiers du Cinéma* 3 (June 1951): 7–21.

Becker, Ernest. *The Denial of Death*. New York: Free Press, 1997. Originally published in 1973.

Begley, Louis. *About Schmidt*. New York: Ballantine Books, 1996.

Bellafonte, Ginia. "In Milan, a 'Fight Club' Mood, But Real Men Suit Up." *New York Times* Review/Fashion, January 11, 2000. http://www.nytimes.com/2000/01/11/style/review-fashion-in-milan-a-fight-club-mood-but-real-men-suit-up.html.

Bellah, Robert N. "Civil Religion in America." Pages 168–89 in *Beyond Belief: Essays on Religion in a Post-Traditional World*. Edited by Robert N. Bellah. University of California Press, 1970. Originally published in 1967.

Birdsall, N., and C. Graham, eds. *New Markets, New Opportunities? Economic and Social Mobility in a Changing World*. Washington, D.C.: Brookings Institute Press, 2000.

Bonhoeffer, Dietrich. *Letters and Papers From Prison*. Translated by Reginald H. Fuller. Edited by Eberhard Bethge. New York: Collier, 1972.

Bordo, Susan. "The Moral Content of Nabokov's Lolita." Pages 125–52 in *Aesthetic Subjects*. Edited by Pamela R. Matthews and David McWhirter. Minneapolis: University of Minnesota Press, 2003.

Borg, Marcus. *Meeting Jesus Again for the First Time: The Historical Jesus and the Heart of Contemporary Faith*. New York: HarperCollins, 1994.

Browning, Elizabeth Barrett. "Aurora Leigh." In *Aurora Leigh and Other Poems*. Edited by John Robert Glorney Bolton and Julia Bolton Holloway. London: Penguin, 1995.

Bruccoli, Matthew J. "Explanatory Notes." Pages 180–204 in *The Great Gatsby*, by F. Scott Fitzgerald. New York: Collier Books, 1992.

———. Preface to *The Great Gatsby* by F. Scott Fitzgerald. New York: Collier Books, 1992.

Brueggemann, Walter. "The Costly Loss of Lament." Pages 98–111 in *The Psalms and the Life of Faith*. Edited by Patrick Miller. Minneapolis: Fortress, 1995.

———. "The Epistemological Crisis of Israel's Two Histories (Jer 9:22-23)." Pages 85–105 in *Israelite Wisdom: Theological and Literary Essays in Honor of Samuel Terrien*. Edited by John G. Gammie et al. New York: Union Theological Seminary, 1978.

———. "Lament as Wake-Up Call (Class Analysis and Historical Possibility)." Pages 221–36 in *Lamentations in Ancient and Contemporary Cultural Contexts*. Edited by Nancy C. Lee and Carleen Mandolfo. Atlanta: Society of Biblical Literature, 2008.

———. *The Message of the Psalms: A Theological Commentary*. Minneapolis: Augsburg, 1984.

———. "Psalms and the Life of Faith: A Suggested Typology of Function." *Journal for the Study of the Old Testament* 17 (1980): 5–21.

Bultmann, Rudolf. *The History of the Synoptic Tradition*. Translated by John Marsh. Oxford: Blackwell, 1963. Originally published in 1921.

Buscombe, Edward. *'Injuns!': Native Americans in the Movies*. Bodmin, Cornwall: Reaktion Books, 2006.

Buttrick, George A. *The Parables of Jesus*. New York: Harper & Brothers, 1928.

Byrd, James P. *Sacred Scripture, Sacred War: The Bible and the American Revolution*. New York: Oxford University Press, 2013.

Calvin, Jean. *Commentary on a Harmony of the Evangelists, Matthew, Mark, and Luke*. 3 vols. Translated by William Pringle. Grand Rapids: Eerdmans, 1949.

Chrysostom, John. *St. John Chrysostom: On Wealth and Poverty*. Translated by Catharine P. Roth. Crestwood, N.Y.: St. Vladimir's Seminary, 1984.

Christianson, Eric S., Peter Francis, and William R. Telford. *Cinéma Divinité: Religion, Theology, and the Bible in Film*. London: SCM Press, 2005.

Chumo II, Peter N. "*American Beauty*: An Interview with Alan Ball." *Creative Screenwriting* 71 (January–February 2000): 26–35.

Cone, James H. *Martin & Malcolm & America: A Dream or a Nightmare*. Maryknoll, N.Y.: Orbis, 1991.

Crenshaw, James. *Old Testament Wisdom: An Introduction*. 3rd ed. Louisville, Ky.: Westminster John Knox, 2010.

Crossan, John Dominic. *The Dark Interval: Towards a Theology of Story*. Niles, Ill.: Argus Communications, 1975.

———. *In Parables: The Challenge of the Historical Jesus*. New York: Harper & Row, 1973.

———. "Parable and Example in the Teaching of Jesus." *Semeia* 1 (1974): 63–104.

———. "Structuralist Analysis and the Parables of Jesus: A Reply to D. O. Via Jr., 'Parable and Example Story: A Literary-Structuralist Approach.'" *Semeia* 1 (1974): 192–221.

Cullen, Jim. *The American Dream: A Short History of an Idea that Shaped a Nation.* Oxford/New York: Oxford University Press, 2003.

Cummings, Denise K. "'Accessible Poetry'? Cultural Intersection and Exchange in Contemporary American Indian and American Independent Film." *Studies in American Indian Literatures* 2, no. 13 (2001): 57–80.

Deacy, Christopher. "Integration and Rebirth through Confrontation: *Fight Club* and *American Beauty* as Contemporary Religious Parables." *Journal of Contemporary Religion* 17, no. 1 (2002): 61–73.

Deacy, Christopher, and Gaye Williams Ortiz. *Theology and Film: Challenging the Sacred/Secular Divide.* Malden, Mass.: Blackwell, 2008.

DeParle, J. *American Dream: Three Women, Ten Kids, and a Nation's Drive to End Welfare.* New York: Penguin, 2004.

Derrett, J. D. M. "Fresh Light on St. Luke XVI. I. The Parable of the Unjust Steward." *New Testament Studies* 7 (1960–1961): 198–219.

Detweiler, Craig. *Into the Dark: Seeing the Sacred in the Top Films of the 21st Century.* Grand Rapids: Baker Academic, 2008.

Dodd, C. H. *The Parables of the Kingdom.* Revised edition. New York: Scribners, 1961. Originally published in 1935.

Donahue, John. *The Gospel in Parable: Metaphor, Narrative and Theology in the Synoptic Gospels.* Philadelphia: Fortress, 1988.

Douchet, Jean. "Hitch and His Public." Translated by Verena Andermatt Conley. Pages 17–24 in *A Hitchcock Reader.* Edited by Marshall Deutelbaum and Leland Poague. Oxford: Wiley-Blackwell, 2009.

Douglass, Frederick. "What to the Slave is the 4th of July?" Speech given at Rochester, N.Y., July 5, 1852. Pages 188–206 in *Frederick Douglass: Selected Speeches and Writings.* Edited by Philip S. Foner. Chicago: Lawrence Hill, 1999.

Duncan, Glen. *The Last Werewolf.* New York: Alfred A. Knopf, 2011.

Durkheim, Émile. *Le Suicide.* Paris: Felix Alcan, 1897.

Ebeling, Gerhard. "Hauptprobleme der protestantischen Theologie in der Gegenwart." *Zeitschrift für Theologie und Kirke* 58 (1961): 123–36.

———. *Word and Faith.* Translated by J. W. Leitch. Philadelphia: Fortress, 1967.

Ebert, Roger. "American Beauty." *Chicago Sun-Times,* September 24, 1999. http://rogerebert.suntimes.com/apps/pbcs.dll/article?AID=/19990924/REVIEWS/909240301/1023.

———. "Fight Club." *Chicago Sun-Times,* October 15, 1999. http://rogerebert.suntimes.com/apps/pbcs.dll/article?AID=/19991015/REVIEWS/910150302.

Endo, Shusaku. *Silence.* Translated by William Johnston. New York: Taplinger, 1980. Originally published in 1969 as *Chinmoku.*

Epstein, Jean. "De quelques conditions de la photogénie." *Cinéa-Ciné-pour-tous* 19 (1924): 6–8. Translation by Tom Milne in *Afterimage* 10 (1981): 20–23.

Erasmus. *Paraphrase on Luke 11–24.* Edited and translated by Jane E. Phillips. Vol. 48 of *Collected Works of Erasmus.* Toronto: University of Toronto Press, 2003.

Feifel, Herman, ed. *The Meaning of Death.* New York: McGraw-Hill, 1959.

Fisher, W. R. "Reaffirmation and Subversion of the American Dream." *Quarterly Journal of Speech* 59 (1973): 160–67.

Fisher, W. R., and R. A. Fillory. "Argument in Drama and Literature: An Exploration." Pages 343–62 in *Advances in Argumentation Theory and Research.* Edited by R. Cox and C. A. Willard. Carbondale: Southern Illinois Press, 1982.

Fitzgerald, F. Scott. *The Great Gatsby.* New York: Collier Books, 1992.

Flesher, Paul V. M., and Robert Torry. *Film and Religion: An Introduction.* Nashville: Abingdon, 2007.

Foreman, Jon. "Learning How to Die." From the album *Limbs and Branches.* Lowercase People Records, 2008.

Foucault, Michel. *The History of Sexuality Volume 1: An Introduction.* New York: Vintage Books, 1990.

———. *Surveiller et punir: Naissance de la Prison.* Paris: Gallimard, 1975.

Fowler, James W. *Stages of Faith: The Psychology of Human Development and the Quest for Meaning.* San Francisco: Harper & Row, 1982.

Fowler, James W., and Sam Keen. *LifeMaps: Conversations on the Journey of Faith.* Edited by Jerome Berryman. Waco, Tex: Word Books, 1978.

Frankl, Viktor. *Man's Search for Meaning.* New York: Washington Square Press, 1985. Originally published in 1946 as *Ein Psycholog erlebt das Konzentrationslager.*

Freese, Peter. *"America": Dream or Nightmare? Reflections on a Composite Image.* 3rd and revised edition. Arbeiten zur Amerikanistik. Essen: Verlag Die Blaue Eule, 1994.

Freud, Sigmund. *Civilization and Its Discontents.* Translated by James Strachey. New York: W. W. Norton, 1962. Originally published in 1930.

———. "Thoughts for the Times on War and Death." Pages 316–17 in *Collected Papers* 4. New York: Basic Books, 1959. Originally published in 1915.

Friedman, Greg. "Parables on Screen: John Sayles and *Men with Guns.*" Pages 57–70 in *Through a Catholic Lens: Religious Perspectives of Nineteen Film Directors from around the World.* Edited by Peter Malone. Lanham, Md.: Rowman & Littlefield, 2007.

Fromm, Erich. *The Art of Loving.* New York: Harper Perennial, 1989.

———. *The Sane Society.* Greenwich, Conn.: Fawcett Premier, 1955.

Frost, Michael. *Eyes Wide Open: Seeing God in the Ordinary*. Sutherland, NSW, Australia: Albatross Books, 1998.

Fuchs, Ernst. "Das Neue Testament und das hermeneutische Problem." *Zeitschrift für Theologie und Kirke* 58 (1961): 198–226.

Funk, Robert W. "The Good Samaritan as Metaphor." *Semeia* 2 (1974): 74–81.

———. "How Do You Read (Luke 10:25-37)." *Interpretation* 18 (1964): 56–61.

———. *Language, Hermeneutic, and Word of God*. New York: Harper & Row, 1966.

———. "The Old Testament in Parable: A Study of Luke 10:25-37." *Encounter* 26 (1965): 251–67.

———. *Parables and Presence: Forms of the New Testament Tradition*. Philadelphia: Fortress, 1982.

Gammie, John G. "From Prudentialism to Apocalypticism: The Houses of the Sages amid the Varying Forms of Wisdom." Pages 479–97 in *The Sage in Israel and the Ancient Near East*. Edited by John G. Gammie and Leo G. Perdue. Winona Lake, Ind.: Eisenbrauns, 1990.

Gardavský, Vítězslav. *God Is Not Yet Dead*. Translated by Vivienne Menkes. Harmondsworth, UK: Penguin, 1973.

Gardella, Peter. *American Civil Religion: What Americans Hold Sacred*. New York: Oxford University Press, 2014.

Geertz, Clifford. "Deep Play: Notes on the Balinese Cockfight." Pages 412–53 in *The Interpretation of Cultures*. New York: Basic Books, 1973.

Gilbert, Maurice. *Les cinq livres des Sages: Les Proverbes de Salomon, Le livre de Job, Qohélet ou l'Écclésiaste, Le livre de ben Sira, La Sagesse de Salomon*. Paris: Cerf, 2003.

Gressmann, Hugo. *Vom reichen Mann und armen Lazarus: eine literargeschichtliche Studie*. Abhandlungen der Königlich Preussischen Akademie der Wissenschaften: Philosophisch-Historische Klasse 7. Berlin: Verlag der Königlich Akademie der Wissenschaften, 1918.

Haberski, Raymond Jr. *God and War: American Civil Religion Since 1945*. New Brunswick, N.J.: Rutgers University Press, 2012.

Havrilesky, Heather. "An Alan Ball Postmortem." *Salon*, August 20, 2005. http://www.salon.com/2005/08/20/alan_ball/.

Hirschman, E. C. *Heroes, Monsters, & Messiahs: Movies and Television Shows as the Mythology of American Culture*. Kansas City, Mo.: Andrews McMeel Publishing, 2000.

Hoberman, J. "Boomer Bust." *The Village Voice*, September 14, 1999. http://www.villagevoice.com/1999-09-14/film/boomer-bust/.

Hogan, James. *Reel Parables: Life Lessons from Popular Films*. Mahwah, N.J.: Paulist Press, 2008.

Hughes, Langston. *The Collected Poems of Langston Hughes.* Edited by Arnold Rampersad and David Roessel. New York: Vintage Books, 1994.

Hugo, Victor. *La Préface de Cromwell.* Paris: Ambroise Dupont, 1827.

Hultgren, Arland J. *The Parables of Jesus: A Commentary.* Grand Rapids: Eerdmans, 2000.

Irwin, Alexander. *Saints of the Impossible: Bataille, Weil, and the Politics of the Sacred.* Minneapolis: University of Minnesota Press, 2002.

Jacques, Eliot. "Death and the Mid-Life Crisis." *International Journal of Psychoanalysis* 46 (1965): 502–14.

Jeremias, Joachim. *The Parables of Jesus.* 2nd ed. Translated by S. H. Hooke. Upper Saddle River, N.J.: Prentice Hall, 1972.

Jewett, Robert. *Saint Paul at the Movies: The Apostle's Dialogue with American Culture.* Louisville, Ky.: Westminster John Knox, 1993.

———. *Saint Paul Returns to the Movies: Triumph over Shame.* Grand Rapids: Eerdmans, 1999.

Johnston, Robert K. "Film as 'Parable': What Might This Mean?" Pages 19–32 in *Doing Theology for the Church: Essays in Honor of Klyne Snodgrass.* Edited by Rebekah A. Eklund and John E. Phelan Jr. Eugene, Ore.: Wipf & Stock; Chicago: Covenant Press, 2014.

———. *Reel Spirituality: Theology and Film in Dialogue.* Updated version. Grand Rapids: Baker Academic, 2006.

———, ed. *Reframing Theology and Film.* Grand Rapids: Baker Academic, 2007.

———. *Useless Beauty: Ecclesiastes through the Lens of Contemporary Film.* Grand Rapids: Baker Academic, 2004.

Johnston, Robert M., and Harvey K. McArthur. *They Also Taught in Parables: Rabbinic Parables from the First Centuries of the Christian Era.* Grand Rapids: Zondervan, 1990. Repr., Eugene, Ore.: Wipf & Stock, 2014.

Jones, G. V. *The Art and Truth of the Parables: A Study in Their Literary Form and Modern Interpretation.* London: SPCK, 1964.

Jülicher, Adolf. *Die Gleichnisreden Jesu.* 2 vols. Tübingen: Mohr Siebeck, 1888–1899. Repr., 1910.

Jump, Hebert. "The Religious Possibilities of the Motion Picture." New Britain, Conn.: South Congregational Church, 1911.

Jung, Carl. *Modern Man in Search of a Soul.* Translated by W. S. Dell and Cary F. Baynes. San Diego: Harvest/HBJ, 1933.

Karlyn, Kathleen Rowe. "Too Close for Comfort: *American Beauty* and the Incest Motif." *Cinema Journal* 44 (2004): 69–93.

Kelley, Shawn. *Racializing Jesus: Race, Ideology and the Formation of Modern Biblical Scholarship.* New York: Routledge, 2002.

Kermode, Frank. *The Sense of an Ending.* New York: Oxford University Press, 1967.

Kilpatrick, Jacquelyn. *Celluloid Indians: Native Americans and Film.* Lincoln: University of Nebraska Press, 1999.

King, Martin Luther Jr. "The American Dream." Speech given at Drew University, Madison, N.J., February 5, 1964. http://depts.drew.edu/lib/archives/online _exhibits/King/speech/TheAmericanDream.pdf.

―――. *A Call to Conscience: The Landmark Speeches of Dr. Martin Luther King, Jr.* Edited by Clayborne Carson and Kris Shepard. New York: IPM, 2001.

―――. "Why I Am Opposed to the War in Vietnam." Sermon given at Riverside Baptist Church, New York, April 30, 1967. http://www.lib.berkeley .edu/MRC/pacificaviet/riversidetranscript.html.

Kleinhans, C. "Working Class Film Heroes: Junior Johnson, Evel Knievel, and the Film Audience." Pages 64–82 in *Jump Cut: Hollywood, Politics and Counter-Cinema.* Edited by Peter Steven. Toronto: Between the Lines, 1985.

Kreitzer, Larry J. *Gospel Images in Fiction and Film: On Reversing the Hermeneutical Flow.* The Biblical Seminar 84. London: Sheffield Academic, 2002.

Lacey, Marc. "Via Hollywood, a Glimpse of African Poverty." *New York Times,* December 21, 2002. http://www.nytimes.com/2002/12/21/movies/via -hollywood-a-glimpse-of-african-poverty.html.

Laderman, Gary. *American Civil Religion.* Minneapolis: Augsburg Fortress, 2012.

―――. *Rest in Peace: A Cultural History of Death and the Funeral Home in Twentieth-Century America.* New York: Oxford University Press, 2003.

―――. *Sacred Matters: Celebrity Worship, Sexual Ecstasies, The Living Dead, and Other Signs of Religious Life in the United States.* New York: The New Press, 2009.

―――. *The Sacred Remains: American Attitudes Toward Death, 1799–1883.* New Haven: Yale University Press, 1996.

Lee, Nancy C. *Lyrics of Lament: From Tragedy to Transformation.* Minneapolis: Augsburg Fortress, 2010.

Lemaster, Tracy. "The Nymphet as Consequence in Vladimir Nabokov's *Lolita* and Sam Mendes' *American Beauty.*" *Trans. Internet-Zeitschrift für Kulturwissenschaften* 16 (2006). http://www.inst.at/trans/16Nr/02_2/wendt -lemaster16.htm.

Lévi-Strauss, Claude. "The Structural Study of Myth." Pages 202–28 in *Structural Anthropology.* Edited by Claude Lévi-Strauss. Garden City, N.Y.: Doubleday, 1967.

Lichtheim, Miriam. *Ancient Egyptian Literature: A Book of Readings.* 3 vols. Berkeley: University of California Press, 1973–1980.

Lim, Dennis. "'Fight Club' Fight Goes On." *New York Times,* November 6, 2009. http://www.nytimes.com/2009/11/08/movies/homevideo/08lim .html?_r=0.

Loewen, James W. *Lies My Teacher Told Me: Everything Your American History Textbook Got Wrong.* New York: The New Press, 2007.

Lucian. Translated by A. M. Harmon et al. 8 vols. Loeb Classical Library. Cambridge, Mass.: Harvard University Press, 1915–1967.

Luther, Martin. *Sermons on Gospel Texts for the 1st to 12th Sundays After Trinity.* Volume 4 of *Sermons of Martin Luther.* Edited and translated by John Nicholas Lenker et al. Grand Rapids: Baker, 1983.

Lyden, John. *Film as Religion: Myths, Morals, and Rituals.* New York: New York University Press, 2003.

Lynch, Thomas. "Grave Affairs: HBO's 'Six Feet Under.'" *Christian Century* 121, no. 22 (November 2, 2004): 18–22.

Mack, Burton L. *A Myth of Innocence: Mark and Christian Origins.* Philadelphia: Fortress, 1988.

Maier, Pauline. *American Scripture: Making the Declaration of Independence.* New York: Alfred A. Knopf, 1997.

Marable, Manning. *Malcolm X: A Life of Reinvention.* New York: Viking, 2011.

Marsh, Clive, and Gaye Ortiz, eds. *Explorations in Theology and Film.* Oxford: Wiley-Blackwell, 1997.

Martin, Joel W., and Conrad E. Ostwalt Jr., eds. *Screening the Sacred: Religion, Myth, and Ideology in Popular American Film.* Boulder, Colo.: Westview Press, 1995.

Marty, Martin E. "Addressing the Nation." *Sightings,* July 26, 2004. http://divinity.uchicago.edu/sightings/addressing-nation-%E2%80%94-martin-e-marty.

Maslow, Abraham H. "A Theory of Human Motivation." *Psychological Review* 50, no. 4 (1943): 370–96.

———. *Motivation and Personality.* New York: Harper, 1954.

———. *Religions, Values, and Peak-Experiences.* New York: Viking Press, 1970.

May, John R. "Visual Story and the Religious Interpretation of Film." Pages 23–43 in *Religion and Film.* Edited by John R. May and Michael Bird. Knoxville: University of Tennessee Press, 1982.

McCaffrey, Donald W. *Assault on Society: Satirical Literature to Film.* Lanham, Md.: Scarecrow, 1992.

McCarthy, Michael. "Illegal, Violent Teen Fight Clubs Face Police Crackdown." *USA Today,* July 31, 2006. http://usatoday30.usatoday.com/life/2006–07-31-violent-fight-clubs_x.htm.

McKittrick, Casey. "'I Laughed and Cringed at the Same Time . . .': Shaping Pedophilic Discourse Around *American Beauty* and *Happiness.*" *The Velvet Light Trap* 47 (2001).

McMullen, W. J. "Gender and the American Dream in *Kramer vs. Kramer.*" *Women's Studies in Communication* 19 (1996): 29–54.

McNulty, Edward N. *Faith and Film: A Guidebook for Leaders.* Louisville, Ky.: Westminster John Knox, 2007.

Michaelis, Wilhelm. *Die Gleichnisse Jesu: eine Einführung.* 3rd edition. UCB 32. Hamburg: Furche-Verlag, 1956.

Miles, Margaret. *Seeing and Believing: Religion and Values in the Movies.* Boston: Beacon Press, 1996.

Miller, Arthur. *Death of a Salesman.* New York: Viking Press, 1973.

Miller, Patrick. *Interpreting the Psalms.* Philadelphia: Fortress, 1986.

Miringoff, M., and M. L. Miringoff. *The Social Health of the Nation: How America Is Really Doing.* New York: Oxford University Press, 1999.

Mitchell, Jolyon, and S. Brent Plate. *The Religion and Film Reader.* New York: Routledge, 2007.

Mitford, Jessica. *The American Way of Death Revisited.* New York: Alfred A. Knopf, 1998.

Nabokov, Vladimir. *Lolita.* New York: Vintage International, 1997. Originally published in 1955 by Olympia Press.

Nathanson, Paul. "Between Time and Eternity: Theological Notes on *Shadows and Fog.*" Pages 284–98 in *The Films of Woody Allen: Critical Essays.* Edited by Charles L. P. Silet. Lanham, Md.: Scarecrow Press, 2006.

Nickelsburg, George W. E., and James C. VanderKam. *1 Enoch: A New Translation.* Minneapolis: Augsburg Fortress, 2004.

Nohria, Nitin. "Envy and the American Dream." *Harvard Business Review,* January–February 2013.

Nussbaum, Martha C. *The Therapy of Desire: Theory and Practice in Hellenistic Ethics.* Princeton: Princeton University Press, 1994.

O'Hehir, Andrew. "American Beauty." *Salon,* September 15, 1999. http://www.salon.com/1999/09/15/beauty/.

Palahniuk, Chuck. *Damned.* New York: Anchor Books, 2011.

———. *Fight Club.* New York: W. W. Norton, 1996.

———. *Non-Fiction.* London: Vintage, 2005.

———. "This Much I Know." *The Guardian,* November 1, 2014. http://www.theguardian.com/books/2014/nov/01/chuck-palahniuk-this-much-i-know?CMP=fb_gu.

Parker-Pope, Tara. "Suicide Rates Rise Sharply in U.S." *New York Times,* May 2, 2013. http://www.nytimes.com/2013/05/03/health/suicide-rate-rises-sharply-in-us.html?_r=0.

Patel, Raj. *Stuffed and Starved: The Hidden Battle for the World Food System.* Brooklyn: Melville House, 2012.

Peck, M. Scott. *The Different Drum: Community Making and Peace*. New York: Touchstone, 1987.

Plate, S. Brent. *Representing Religion in World Cinema: Filmmaking, Mythmaking, Culture Making*. New York: Palgrave Macmillan, 2003.

Pliny. *Natural History*. Translated by H. Rackham et al. 10 vols. Loeb Classical Library. Cambridge, Mass.: Harvard University Press, 1938–1963.

Postman, Neil. *Amusing Ourselves to Death: Public Discourse in the Age of Show Business*. New York: Penguin, 1986.

Powell, Larson. "Mama, ich lebe: Konrad Wolf's Intermedial Parable of Antifasicsm." Pages 63–75 in *Contested Legacies: Constructions of Cultural Heritage in the GDR*. Edited by Matthew Philpotts and Sabine Rolle. Edinburgh German Yearbook 3. Rochester, N.Y.: Camden House, 2009.

Quenqua, Douglas. "Fight Club Generation." *New York Times*, March 15, 2012. http://www.nytimes.com/2012/03/15/fashion/mixed-martial-arts -catches-on-with-the-internet-generation.html?pagewanted=all.

Rad, Gerhard von. *Old Testament Theology*. Vol. 1, *The Theology of Israel's Historical Traditions*. Translated by D. M. G. Stalker. Louisville, Ky.: Westminster John Knox, 1962.

Reinhartz, Adele, ed. *Bible and Cinema: Fifty Key Films*. New York: Routledge, 2012.

———. *Bible and Cinema: An Introduction*. New York: Routledge, 2013.

———. *Scripture on the Silver Screen*. Louisville, Ky.: Westminster John Knox, 2003.

Ricoeur, Paul. "Biblical Hermeneutics." *Semeia* 4 (1975): 29–148.

———. *Conflict of Interpretations*. Evanston, Ill.: Northwestern University, 1974.

———. *Figuring the Sacred: Religion, Narrative, and Imagination*. Translated by David Pellauer. Edited by Mark I. Wallace. Minneapolis: Augsburg Fortress, 1995.

Rindge, Matthew S. "The 'Good' Samaritan." *Bible Odyssey*. Society of Biblical Literature, July 3, 2014. http://bibleodyssey/passages/main-articles/ good-samaritan.

———. *Jesus' Parable of the Rich Fool: Luke 12:13–34 among Ancient Conversations on Death and Possessions*. Early Christianity and Its Literature 6. Atlanta: Society of Biblical Literature, 2011.

———. "Lament in Film and Film as Lament." Pages 379–90 in vol. 1 of *The Bible in Motion: Biblical Reception in Film*. Edited by Rhonda Burnette-Bletsch. Berlin: De Gruyter, 2016.

———. "Luke's Artistic Parables: Narratives of Subversion, Imagination, and Transformation." *Interpretation* 68, no. 4 (2014): 403–15.

————. "Lusting after Lester's Lolita: Perpetuating and Resisting the Male Gaze in *American Beauty.*" In *Now Showing: Film Theory in Biblical Studies.* Edited by Caroline Vander Stichele and Laura Copier. Semeia Series. Atlanta: Society of Biblical Literature, 2016.

————. "Mortality and Enjoyment: The Interplay of Death and Possessions in Qoheleth." *Catholic Biblical Quarterly* 73 (2011): 265–80.

————. "Reconfiguring the Akedah and Recasting God: Lament and Divine Abandonment in Mark." *Journal of Biblical Literature* 131, no. 4 (2012): 755–74.

————. "Teaching the Bible *and* Film: Pedagogical Promises, Pitfalls, and Proposals." *Teaching Theology and Religion* 13, no. 2 (2010): 140–55.

Rosen, Alison. "Alan Ball: The *Six Feet Under* creator returns to his theatrical roots." *Timeout*, February 1, 2007. http://www.timeout.com/newyork/theater/alan-ball.

Rudd, Niall. *Themes in Roman Satire.* London: Duckworth, 1986.

Russell, Mary Doria. *The Sparrow.* New York: Ballantine, 1996.

Sacks, Sheldon. *Fiction and the Shape of Belief.* Berkeley: University of California Press, 1966.

Schmidt, Francis. *Le Testament grec d' Abraham: Introduction, édition critique des deux recensions grecques, traduction.* Tübingen: J.C.B. Mohr (Paul Siebeck), 1986.

Sconce, Jeffrey. "Irony, Nihilism and the New American Smart Film." *Screen* 43, no. 4 (2002): 349–69.

Scott, Bernard Brendan. *Hear Then the Parable: A Commentary on the Parables of Jesus.* Minneapolis: Augsburg Fortress, 1989.

————. *Hollywood Dreams and Biblical Stories.* Minneapolis: Augsburg Fortress, 1994.

Seneca. *Moral Epistles (Ad Lucilium Epistulae Morales).* Translated by Richard M. Gummere. Loeb Classical Library. 3 vols. Cambridge, Mass.: Harvard University Press, 1917–1925.

Seow, C. L. *Ecclesiastes: A New Translation with Introduction and Commentary.* Anchor Bible 18c. New York: Doubleday, 1997.

Sinclair, Marianne. *Hollywood Lolita.* London: Plexus, 1988.

Smith, Hedrick. *Who Stole the American Dream?* New York: Random House, 2012.

Staley, Jeffrey L., and Richard Walsh. *Jesus, the Gospels, and Cinematic Imagination: A Handbook to Jesus on DVD.* Louisville, Ky.: Westminster John Knox, 2007.

Stein, Robert H. *An Introduction to the Parables of Jesus.* Philadelphia: Westminster Press, 1981.

Steinbeck, Elaine and Robert Wallstern, eds. *Steinbeck: A Life in Letters.* New York: Viking Press, 1975.

Stroker, William D. "Extracanonical Parables and the Historical Jesus." Pages 186–209 in vol. 4 of *The Historical Jesus: Critical Concepts in Religious Studies*. Edited by Craig A. Evans. London: Routledge, 2004.

Tillich, Paul. *Theology of Culture*. Oxford: Oxford University Press, 1959.

Travers, Peter. "Fight Club." *Rolling Stone*, October 15, 1999. http://www.rolling stone.com/movies/reviews/fight-club-19991015.

Turan, Kenneth. "The Roundhouse Miss." *Los Angeles Times*, October 15, 1999. http://articles.latimes.com/1999/oct/15/entertainment/ca-22382.

Uhls, Jim. *Fight Club: The Original Screenplay*. ScreenPress, 2000.

VanderKam, James C. *An Introduction to Early Judaism*. Grand Rapids: Eerdmans, 2001.

Via, Dan O. "A Response to Crossan, Funk, and Petersen." *Semeia* 1 (1974): 222–35.

———. *The Parables: Their Literary and Existential Dimension*. Philadelphia: Fortress, 1967.

Walsh, Richard. *Mapping Myths of Biblical Interpretation*. Playing the Texts 4. Sheffield: Sheffield Academic, 2001.

———. *Reading the Gospels in the Dark: Portrayals of Jesus in Film*. Harrisburg: Trinity International, 2003.

Warner, W. Lloyd. *American Life*. Chicago: University of Chicago Press, 1962.

Welch, Michael, and Jennifer L. Bryan. "Reactions to Flag Desecration in American Society: Exploring the Contours of Formal and Informal Social Control." *American Journal of Criminal Justice* 22, no. 2 (1998): 151–68.

Westermann, Claus. *Praise and Lament in the Psalms*. Translated by Keith R. Crim and Richard N. Soulen. Atlanta: John Knox, 1981.

Wilde, Oscar. "The Soul of Man under Socialism." Pages 133–34 in vol. 8 of *The Works of Oscar Wilde*. New York: Lamb Publishing, 1909. Originally published in 1891.

Wilder, Amos. *Early Christian Rhetoric: The Language of the Gospel*. Cambridge, Mass.: Harvard University Press, 1971.

Williams, James G. *Those Who Ponder Proverbs: Aphoristic Thinking and Biblical Literature*. Bible and Literature Series 2. Sheffield: Almond, 1981.

Williams, William Carlos. "An Approach to the Poem." *English Institute Essays 1947*. New York: Columbia University Press, 1948.

Willis, Louis-Paul. "From Jocasta to Lolita: The Oedipal Fantasy Inverted." *International Journal of Žižek Studies* 6, no. 2 (2012): 1–19. http://zizekstudies .org/index.php/ijzs/article/view/375/435.

Winn, J. Emmett. *The American Dream and Contemporary Hollywood Cinema*. New York: Continuum, 2007.

Wright, Melanie J. *Religion and Film: An Introduction*. London: I.B. Tauris, 2007.

X, Malcolm. *Malcolm X Speaks.* Edited by George Breitman. New York: Grove
    Press, 1966.

X, Malcolm, and Alex Haley. *The Autobiography of Malcolm X.* New York: Ballan-
    tine Books, 1973. Originally published in 1965.

Zabell, Martin. "Flag-burning Retaliation May Come Cheap." *Chicago Tribune,*
    June 22, 1990. http://articles.chicagotribune.com/1990–06–22/news/
    9002200728_1_flag-burner-assaulting-resolution.

Zilboorg, Gregory. "Fear of Death." *Pschoanalytic Quarterly* 12 (1943): 465–75.

FILMOGRAPHY

About Schmidt (d. Payne, 2002)
American Beauty (d. Mendes, 1999)
The Apartment (d. Wilder, 1960)
As Good as it Gets (d. Brooks, 1997)
Avatar (d. Cameron, 2009)
Badlands (d. Malick, 1973)
Batman (d. Burton, 1989)
Being John Malkovich (d. Jonze, 1999)
Born on the Fourth of July (d. Stone, 1989)
Breaking Away (d. Yates, 1979)
Chinatown (d. Polanski, 1974)
Citizen Kane (d. Welles, 1941)
Citizen Ruth (d. Payne, 1996)
Cidade de Deus (d. Meirelles and Lund, 2002)
The Constant Gardener (d. Meirelles, 2005)
Dances with Wolves (d. Costner, 1990)
Dogville (d. von Trier, 2003)
The Descendants (d. Payne, 2011)
Donnie Darko (d. Kelly, 2001)
A Few Good Men (d. Reiner, 1992)
Easy Rider (d. Hopper, 1969)

Election (d. Payne, 1999)

Eyes Wide Shut (d. Kubrick, 1999)

Fight Club (d. Fincher, 1999)

The Firm (d. Pollack, 1993)

The Fisher King (d. Gilliam, 1991)

Five Easy Pieces (d. Rafelson, 1970)

The Flamingo Kid (d. Marshall, 1984)

Flashdance (d. Lyne, 1983)

Ghost World (d. Zwigoff, 2001)

The Girl in the Café (d. Yates, 2005)

Glengarry Glen Ross (d. Foley, 1992)

The Godfather I, II, III (d. Coppola, 1972, 1974, 1990)

Good Will Hunting (d. Van Sant, 1997)

Hoffa (d. DeVito, 1992)

Horrible Bosses (d. Gordon, 2011)

The Insider (d. Mann, 1999)

It's a Wonderful Life (d. Capra, 1946)

Jerry Maguire (d. Crowe, 1996)

Kramer vs. Kramer (d. Benton, 1979)

Little Miss Sunshine (d. Dayton and Faris, 2006)

Lolita (d. Kubrick, 1962)

Lolita (d. Lyne, 1997)

Maid in Manhattan (d. Wang, 2002)

Marathon Man (d. Schlesigner, 1976)

The Matrix (d. Wachowskis, 1999)

Midnight in Paris (d. Allen, 2011)

Mrs. Winterbourne (d. Benjamin, 1996)

Nebraska (d. Payne, 2013)

No Country for Old Men (d. Joel and Ethan Coen, 2007)

Office Space (d. Judge, 1999)

An Officer and a Gentleman (d. Hackford, 1982)

One Flew over the Cuckoo's Nest (d. Forman, 1975)

Ordinary People (d. Redford, 1980)

Passion Fish (d. Sayles, 1992)

Pocahontas (d. Gabriel and Goldberg, 1995)

Pretty Woman (d. Marshall, 1990)

The Pursuit of Happyness (d. Muccino, 2006)

A Raisin in the Sun (d. Petrie, 1961)

Rear Window (d. Hitchcock, 1954)

Revolutionary Road (d. Mendes, 2008)

Rocky (d. Avildsen, 1976)
Saturday Night Fever (d. Badham, 1977)
The Searchers (d. Ford, 1956)
The Shining (d. Kubrick, 1980)
Shut Up & Sing (d. Kopple and Peck, 2006)
Sideways (d. Payne, 2004)
Smoke Signals (d. Eyre, 1998)
Someone to Watch over Me (d. Scott, 1987)
Sunset Blvd. (d. Wilder, 1950)
Stagecoach (d. Ford, 1939)
There Will Be Blood (d. Anderson, 2007)
Titanic (d. Cameron, 1997)
To the Wonder (d. Malick, 2012)
Top Gun (d. Scott, 1986)
Towelhead (d. Ball, 2007)
The Tree of Life (d. Malick, 2011)
Wall Street (d. Stone, 1987)
White Palace (d. Mandoki, 1990)
Witness (d. Weir, 1985)
Working Girl (d. Nichols, 1988)

TELEVISION

Breaking Bad (c. Gilligan, 2008–2013)
Enlightened (c. White and Dern, 2011–2013)
House of Cards (w. Willimon; d. Foley, 2013–)
Side by Side: The Science, Art, and Impact of Digital Cinema (d. Kenneally, 2012)
Six Feet Under (c. Ball, 2001–2005)
The West Wing (w. Sorkin, 1999–2006)

INDEX

CPSIA information can be obtained
at www.ICGtesting.com
Printed in the USA
LVHW111735131119
637254LV00003B/114/P

9 781602 589940